A Wider Type of Freedom

The publisher and the University of California Press Foundation gratefully acknowledge the generous support of the Anne G. Lipow Endowment Fund in Social Justice and Human Rights.

A Wider Type of Freedom

HOW STRUGGLES FOR RACIAL JUSTICE
LIBERATE EVERYONE

Daniel Martinez HoSang

UNIVERSITY OF CALIFORNIA PRESS

University of California Press
Oakland, California

© 2021 by Daniel Martinez HoSang

First Paperback Printing 2023

Library of Congress Cataloging-in-Publication Data

Names: HoSang, Daniel, author.
Title: A wider type of freedom : how struggles for racial justice liberate everyone / Daniel Martinez HoSang.
Description: Oakland, California : University of California Press, [2021] | Includes bibliographical references and index.
Identifiers: LCCN 2021012050 (print) | LCCN 2021012051 (ebook) | ISBN 9780520321427 (cloth) | 9780520395602 (pb) | 9780520974197 (ebook)
Subjects: LCSH: Race discrimination—United States—History. | Racial justice—United States—History.
Classification: LCC E184.A1 H659 2021 (print) | LCC E184.A1 (ebook) | DDC 305.800973—dc23
LC record available at https://lccn.loc.gov/2021012050
LC ebook record available at https://lccn.loc.gov/2021012051

Manufactured in the United States of America

30 29 28 27 26 25 24 23
10 9 8 7 6 5 4 3 2 1

For Gary and George, with gratitude

Contents

Figures

Preface

Freedom is a contested ideal. Many political visions in the United States and across the world have been pursued in its name. But what kind of freedom, and for whom? Partial, proprietary, and market-based models of freedom have shaped, and continue to shape, conditions of unfreedom and inequality in this country. Other possibilities exist. They have emerged within movements for racial justice and are predicated on a wider type of freedom—one that would transform whole societies, not just particular circumstances, and end subordination, rather than simply shifting its terms.

In one of the most iconic photos of the civil rights era, George Wallace, the segregationist governor of Alabama, stands on the steps of the University of Alabama's Foster Auditorium in Tuscaloosa. He is staring down US deputy attorney general Nicholas Katzenbach, while a gaggle of national reporters looks on. Outside the frame on that June morning in 1963 were Vivian Malone and James Hood, two Black students whose enrollment Wallace had sought to prevent, in defiance of a desegregation order from a federal judge. When after several hours Wallace abandoned his stand "at the schoolhouse door," and Malone and Hood completed

George Wallace stares down US deputy attorney general Nicholas Katzenbach at the University of Alabama, June 11, 1963. Credit: Warren K. Leffler/Library of Congress, Prints and Photographs Division, U.S. News & World Report Magazine Photograph Collection [LC-DIG-ppmsca-04294].

their enrollment, the episode was woven into a story about national progress against the moral wrongs of racism. That same evening, John F. Kennedy took to the airwaves promising new legislation to combat discrimination and end segregation in public education.[1]

The story that Kennedy told pitted Wallace's racist image of freedom, in which the liberties of white people depend on the subordination of others, against a state-sanctioned anti-racism defined in terms of liberal values and full inclusion in the US market economy. Two points stand out. First, Malone and Hood are themselves erased from the picture, leaving two (white male) representatives of the state, Wallace and Katzenbach, center stage, and a third, Kennedy, as narrator. Second, the model of freedom that Kennedy celebrated was ambivalent at best. The abstract values of US liberalism—fairness, opportunity, equality—can expose people to, rather than shelter them from, violence, dispossession, and early death. And full incorporation into the market, as consumers, workers, citizens, and soldiers, can extract more than it provides.

The gains represented over the last half-century by a growing middle class of color, the opening of US immigration policy, resurgent demands for tribal recognition and sovereignty of Indigenous peoples, and claims for recognition by women and queer people of color are real and substantial. But liberal anti-racism based on individual rights and market opportunities alone also carries with it serious jeopardy. Once granted the freedom of opportunity, individuals become more, rather than less, responsible for their fate in the world. If that fate is hunger or unemployment, addiction or prison, we know who is at fault. This form of "moral entrapment" has a long history, unfolding through liberal policies that conferred freedom upon Black and other minoritized subjects who were looked on as inherently degraded. Communities and individuals "freed" by emancipation from bondage or the bestowal of citizenship, civil rights or other grants of opportunity, find themselves unable to refuse the culpability that shadows them.[2]

Liberal rights and freedom, of the kind celebrated by Kennedy, can take as much as they give. They are fully compatible with industrialized forms of punishment and incarceration. They can serve to negate collective identities and historical perspectives, demanding that efforts to address disadvantage be channeled through individuals, not groups, and that past injustices play no part in present claims. In the context of the Cold War, they also played a crucial role in state-sponsored narratives justifying US militarism and global domination.[3]

Malone's and Hood's admission to the University of Alabama, and other stories like theirs, thus were simultaneously an affirmation of rights and a conscription into existing structures of power. As a form of redress they required the renunciation of many strategies that might actually dismantle prevailing structures of inequality—material redistribution, historical reparation, or the recognition of collective demands. Dreams of emancipation can end with incorporation in the status quo.

But there have also been collectives who believed that the everyday functions of liberal democracy—its models of governance, hierarchy, violence, and power—were the source of their subordination, rather than their redemption. They have turned their intention instead to the abolition of militarism, state violence, and the appropriation of land and labor, to imagine the world anew.

At about the same time that Vivian Malone was finishing her first year of classes in Tuscaloosa, the organizer and social movement trainer Ella Baker gave a short talk to volunteers organized by the Student Nonviolent Coordinating Committee (SNCC), who had come to register voters in Hattiesburg, Mississippi. Baker, who guided so many episodes of the Black Freedom movement, explained the stakes of their collective work: "Even if segregation is gone," she told the group, "we will still need to be free; we will still have to see that everyone has a job. Even if we can all vote, if people are still hungry, we will not be free . . . Remember, we are not fighting for the freedom of the Negro alone, but for the freedom of the human spirit, a larger freedom that encompasses all mankind."[4]

Baker recognized that rights in the abstract could not secure justice in the concrete. History mattered. Structure and context mattered. Jobs and food mattered. A government that for centuries had forcefully defended and facilitated the theft of lands and the dispossession of bodies could not suddenly become an impartial referee. What had been done had to be undone.

Baker's understanding of freedom, however, could not be found in the realization of comparable rates of Black and white unemployment, infant mortality, or poverty. She was not interested in the equitable distribution of misery, nor did she imagine that the incorporation of a people within the same institutions that had long subjugated them could serve as a horizon for justice. The "freedom of the human spirit" that she asked those gathered outside the Hattiesburg Freedom House to imagine could not be realized without a broader transformation, "a larger freedom that incorporates all mankind."

This book is about the larger freedom that Baker insisted was at stake in the struggle for voting rights in Mississippi. It considers how demands for justice advanced by racially subordinated groups have included ideas of liberation, interdependence, and anti-subordination never envisioned in the nation's dominant political framework. These are freedoms called forth in places such as Hawaii and Puerto Rico to end the hegemony of the US military there and to sow the seeds for an economy and society no longer rooted in militarism. They can be witnessed in the experiments in democracy fashioned by radical abolitionists in the nineteenth century, and those forged by Indigenous nations contending with the twinned forces of expulsion and incorporation imposed by white settlers. They have been expressed in the labor organizing of migrant women who imagined approaches to labor rights and bodily autonomy rooted in solidarity across forms of difference.

These wider types of freedom have encompassed a broad social totality, one that stretches across centuries and oceans. They take aim at the fundamental ways we think about human capacity and difference, and address the material relations of power that naturalize and reproduce such impoverished ideas of human possibility. Disparate and wide-ranging struggles against racial domination have been linked by the view that suffering, exploitation, and domination are not natural, but are the consequence of historically specific relations of power. And these struggles have sought to transform dominant assumptions about power, violence, the body, labor, ownership, democracy, culture, and autonomy that have long structured and conditioned the nation's political culture.

The traditions, practices, and ways of thinking examined in this book do not fall neatly into a single genealogy. They do not constitute a unified approach marked by a shared vocabulary of analysis. Their insights do not yield a fully formed theory of social transformation or revolution, or even a straightforward list of anti-racist strategies and principles. They are instead heterogeneous, episodic, and often disconnected. And yet they all make visible the existence and potential of an anti-racism that has sought to transform material conditions, rather than simply accepting the norms of US liberalism and market freedoms. That is, they have been aware of the violence and danger imposed by George Wallace *and* John F. Kennedy—and have sought alternatives beyond the remedies counseled by both.

These struggles, moreover, have sought to transform a broad range of intersecting social, political, and economic structures, not merely those presumed to be racist. In this analysis, race does not define discrete populations on the basis of ancestry, culture, national identity, or phenotype. If this were the case, then racial justice would become a limited kind of parity defined by the equitable allocation of social benefits and harms. Anti-racism would be reduced to the pursuit of "racial interests" rooted in a market model of competition for scarce goods. Instead, movements to confront and abolish particular forms of racial domination have yielded universal articulations of freedom.

Dr. Martin Luther King Jr. came to this very conclusion in the final years of his life. In his last address to the Southern Christian Leadership Conference in 1967, less than a year before his death, Dr. King insisted that securing "civil rights" alone would not illuminate "the sunlit path to racial justice." He contended that "the movement must address itself to the question of restructuring the whole of American society." Dr. King rejected the dominant view that compared racism to a kind of tumor that could be excised from an otherwise healthy body. Instead, he argued that the "whole structure must be changed" because racism underlay the foundations of the nation itself: "A nation that will keep people in slavery for 244 years will 'thingify' them and make them things. And therefore, they will exploit them and poor people generally economically. And a nation that will exploit economically will have to have foreign investments and everything else, and it will have to use its military might to protect them. All of these problems are tied together."[5]

A broad array of social movements, cultural forces, and political visions have sought to transform what Dr. King described as a "philosophy based on a contempt for life" into its antithesis: *an anti-subordination ideology and practice that comprehends difference, vulnerability, and interdependence as central and productive facets of human experience.* The stories of the social movements, activist intellectuals, artists, and cultural formations that have similarly shared a transformative vision can, in our own time, allow us to reimagine racial justice as a wider type of freedom, one capable of speaking to the many crises of our world.

Introduction

"A NEW HUMANITY"

The African bruises and breaks himself against his bars
in the interest of freedoms wider than his own.

C. L. R. James, *A History of Pan-African Revolt*

The social movements, activist intellectuals, and cultural formations described in this book have produced conceptions of freedom, interdependence, and anti-subordination never envisioned in the nation's dominant political framework. Together, these stories recast the long struggle to abolish racial subordination as a movement of broad-based social transformation. Their vision of racial justice goes beyond asserting the rights of subordinated people within present structures, or inclusion into the nation on its existing terms. They have insisted instead that the abolition of particular forms of racial domination can yield universal horizons of freedom.

To understand the contours of this assertion, we can turn to one of its most astute chroniclers, the Trinidadian-born writer and political critic C. L. R. James. James stands in a long tradition of Black radical intellectuals, including Ella Baker, Ida B. Wells, Fannie Lou Hamer, Anna Julia Cooper, and W. E. B. Du Bois, who have advanced this analysis.[1] His insights remain as relevant today as when they were written more than 75 years ago.

In 1938, as the tremors of war began pulsating across Europe, the 37-year-old James penned a series of pamphlets from his London flat. Like many of his contemporaries on the left, James sought to make sense of the broad forces that produced continual crisis and upheaval in the modern world. What political traditions and optics on life might prove capable of liberating humanity before it destroyed itself?[2]

James turned his attention to what he described as a "revolutionary history" that was "rich, inspiring, and unknown." A particular tradition of Black revolt and struggle, he argued, represented the repudiation of the West's most corrupting tendencies: slavery and labor exploitation; land appropriation and control; authoritarian governance and genocide. Published together as *A History of Negro Revolt* (and 31 years later, with a new epilogue under the title *A History of Pan-African Revolt*), the short essays took aim at a prevailing historical record that depicted Black people as passive objects of history, destined to realize a painful but inevitable fate of servitude. James subverted this narrative, describing instead a people in constant revolt: striking for better wages in the mines of West Africa; leading uprisings on the plantations of Haiti and Jamaica; acting decisively to win their liberation during the Civil War; building new churches, schools, and associations in the aftermath to secure their freedom. As he explained in an essay published a year later, "The only place where Negroes did not revolt is in the pages of capitalist historians."[3]

James argued that these particular struggles for Black liberation had universal implications; they were responsible for nothing less than the "transformation of western civilization." This was not because of a mystical predisposition within Black social formations toward revolt, though James did note the cultural practices, memories, and traditions that nourished these efforts. It was a quality instead of the particular forms of political consciousness and practice produced in response to the domination they endured. In Haiti, for example, James described the way in which enslaved people who lacked formal education and who suffered the degradations of bondage achieved "a liberality in social aspiration and an elevation of political thought equivalent to anything similar that took place in France."[4] Similarly, after the Civil War, the forms of schooling and governance enacted by free women and men in the South reflected "the policy of a people poor and backward seeking to establish a community where all, black and white, could live in amity and freedom." In the crucible of their despair, new understandings of freedom and human possibility emerged, ideas that could never be imagined by polities premised on the buying and selling of human flesh.

James urged others on the left to pay attention to these traditions, stories, and histories, insisting they held invaluable lessons for a world in continual crisis. James concluded the last essay of *The History of Negro Revolt* in this way: "The African bruises and breaks himself against his bars in the interest of freedoms wider than his own."

On first blush, James's assertion might seem puzzling. Political struggles led by a particular group appear by definition to be parochial, applicable only to the specific conditions and experiences of those group members. Within market- or interest-based frameworks of understanding political conflict and power, one group's gain is interpreted to be another group's loss. This contention forms a cornerstone of white supremacist political logic, in which assertions of life and sovereignty among nonwhite people are marked as inherently threatening those who identify as white. From this perspective, struggles authored in the interests of Black people are at best relevant only to other Black people. At worst, they may challenge the interests of those who are not Black.

James thought and wrote from a much different perspective. He understood that prevailing capitalist economies and governance structures required the social production of difference and hierarchy for their legitimacy. Elite power depends on putting people who are denied assurances to life and land and kin into competition with one another. The modern formations of race and nation are indispensable to producing these relationships of estrangement and rivalry.

Black revolts against elite power and domination challenged the fundamental contention that hierarchies are inevitable and that human solidarity is folly. They enacted new forms of social relations that rejected the unequal ordering of humanity that constituted the modern world. These uprisings and rebellions illustrated possibilities for social and political life in opposition to the edicts of nationalism and hereditarianism ascendant across the US and much of Europe. Thus, the specific struggles James recounted—the abolition of slavery in the French colonies; the end of lynching in Alabama; the demand for fair wages in the Congo—produced wider interrogations of power. At stake in these particular Black-led collective movements were universal possibilities for liberation.

In a 1948 essay James noted that Black resistance in the United States had a "vitality and validity of its own" and "an organic political perspective" that was not simply derived from the broader labor movement or the dominant framework of rights-based liberalism. This perspective included a deep skepticism of "imperialist war[s]" that were never meant to secure the "freedom of the persecuted peoples by the American bourgeois." These insights consistently led to forms of self-organization and mass action, as Black people in the South in particular understood that ordinary structures of representative government, including voting, the two-party system, and other routine forms of political participation (what James derided as "telegrams to Congress") were incapable of addressing their grievances. As a result, Black movements have been able "to intervene with terrific force upon the general and social and political life of the nation."[5]

In rebelling against the terms of their own subordination, these movements also confronted the broad foundations of exploitation and despotism that defined so much of the development of the West. At particular moments in the history of the United States, James later explained, these rebellions "formed a force which initiated and stimulated" other sections of the population, acting "as a ferment" for much broader opposition.[6] They demanded structural changes including the redistribution of land and resources, and the reorganization of social and political life. Thus, James argued, Black people had long toiled "in the interest of freedom wider than [their] own."

RELATIONAL ANTI-RACISMS

Many of the examples in this book extend from the legacies and practices of Black-led social movements described by James, and the capacious alternatives they have developed to a society suffused in domination.[7] These practices have an expansive genealogy. For example, across time and place Indigenous people have revolted against the appropriation, commodification, and desecration of their lands and attempts to abolish their political and cultural sovereignty. Such practices are evident in the complex ways that Indigenous nations and societies have survived the twinned modes of elimination and incorporation they have faced since first contact with European settlers. These struggles to preserve life and ways of being have been rooted in practices of relationality to land and human and nonhuman life that have exceeded the profoundly limiting version of citizenship and rights that has prevailed in the United States.

The particular demands of such resistance are well documented across a rich archive, foregrounding issues of sovereignty, genocide, land theft, and the destruction of tribal practices. The specific resistance over these issues has directly confronted the same regimes of private property and state violence that undergird the United States economy as a whole. Thus, Indigenous-led action against uranium mining on Diné (Navajo) lands in the Southwest, and the generations-long resistance against treaty violations and extractive capitalism evident in recent organizing against the Dakota Access Pipeline at Standing Rock, have universal implications. The Lakota Sioux scholar and organizer Nick Estes explains that these practices assert a common social vision of "caretaking and creating just relations between human and nonhuman worlds on a planet thoroughly devastated by capitalism."[8] They too are bruising and breaking themselves against their bars in the interest of freedoms wider than their own.[9]

Consider also migrants who have come to the United States since the late nineteenth century, particularly from outside of western Europe. A continuous series of racist immigration laws and state-sponsored and extralegal violence has barred many from entrance or civic rights and recognition. The alternative to such a fate has been incorporation and naturalization, with its obligations of national patriotism and allegiance to US militarism, economy, and state. What can we learn then from those who have refused both offers, who have demanded entry into the nation while still inhabiting and constructing lifeworlds that exceed the narrow terms of national incorporation? These "migrant imaginaries" have rejected the inevitability of militarism, colonialism, and US exceptionalism and have been premised on forms of connection and kinship rooted in neither blood nor soil.[10]

Particular traditions of collective resistance emanating from Chicanx, Puerto Rican, and other Latinx communities have challenged wide-ranging forms of power. For example, as explored in chapter 1, in the 1970s in New York and Los Angeles, Latinas mobilized to end practices of coercive and involuntary sterilizations performed on thousands of women deemed unfit to make their own decisions about bearing children. Latina-led organizations such as the Committee to Stop Forced Sterilizations centered their organizing on the women most directly affected by abusive sterilization practices. But they explained that the stakes were much wider. Public discourse diverted anger about high taxes toward Black and brown families by claiming they were having too many children, blaming these families for their own poverty while shielding the government and wealthy corporations from responsibility.[11] The Committee to Stop Forced Sterilizations linked their demand to eradicate compulsory sterilizations to a wider vision of economic justice and redistribution that would no longer view poor women of color as failed objects of social policy.

Likewise, groups such as the New York-based DRUM–South Asian Organizing Center (formerly Desis Rising Up and Moving), which organized against the profiling and detention of Muslim and South Asian Americans after 9/11, represent the latest chapter of a much longer history of Asian American resistance against militarism and racial profiling. The working-class Muslim, Arab, and South Asian communities DRUM organizes challenge both the particular surveillance and detention programs that wreak havoc on their lives and other interconnected forms of state violence, from the militarization of the US border with Mexico to drone strikes in Pakistan. DRUM has consistently opposed reforms to immigration laws that might benefit some undocumented immigrants, including many South Asians, because they would inevitably criminalize and exclude other groups. As DRUM founder Monami Maulik writes, "We never framed our analysis nor centered our campaigns on bias crimes against Muslims or South Asians alone. Instead, we worked proactively to model Muslim and other youth of color organizing together to end over-policing and for dignity in their schools."[12] DRUM advocates a "transformational solidarity" in which "masses of oppressed communities choose to forgo something that would benefit them, and do not take it because it comes at the expense of other oppressed communities."[13] The organization took its name from the Dodge Revolutionary Union Movement, a collective of Black workers in the late 1960s that linked the racist hierarchies within auto factories in Detroit to US imperial wars in Southeast Asia (see chapter 4). In both iterations, DRUM rejected measures that simply shifted the terms of subordination onto other groups.

There are important specificities within each of these traditions; they cannot be collapsed together or imagined as interchangeable.[14] The histories of Black insurgency described by James emerged within the particular context of the transatlantic slave trade, the revolts of the enslaved that produced abolition, and the building of new lifeworlds that followed. In the same way, Indigenous experiences of land appropriation, resistance, tribal recognition, treaty violation, and assertions of sovereignty are undergirded by specific relations to the land and particular bodies of federal law and jurisprudence. The contemporary racial formations of Latinx and Asian Americans were similarly produced through diverse yet distinct histories of US imperialism, migrations, nativism, demands for labor, and the forging of diasporic communities and social relations. These specificities demand attention.

But there is also a danger of reproducing a core logic of white supremacy that imagines these racial formations and histories as unrelated and discrete, rather than interdependent and coproduced.[15] Treating histories of contestation and freedom in the same way—as isolated, discrete, and unconnected—only reproduces this diminished understanding of humanity. Imperialism and white supremacy are always relational—producing groups as differentiated and ranked within a broader hierarchy of human value. Rebellions against such hierarchies have long recognized these connections. As Audre Lorde explained, "There is no such thing as a single-issue struggle because we do not live single-issue lives ... Our struggles are particular, but we are not alone." The work to forge such collectivities was critical precisely because "we share a common interest, survival, and it cannot be pursued in isolation from others simply because their differences make us uncomfortable."[16]

Thus, the "revolutionary history" described by C. L. R. James more than 80 years ago as "rich, inspiring, and unknown" extends across many sites and traditions of resistance. Black Freedom movements, Indigenous sovereignty struggles, and revolts led by migrants and the minoritized have sought transformations in our material and social relations that could produce universal possibilities for emancipation. Rejecting a market framework of politics rooted in a zero-sum understanding of interests and power, these episodes demonstrate the ways that particular anti-racist struggles are capable of a broad interrogation and transformation of power. They do not seek integration into dominant systems of power or to desegregate the ranks of those who wreak violence on the world. Their demands are not for a diversification of the elite.[17]

These movements have also refused to make whiteness, or white racial consciousness and attitudes, the center of their political energies. Take the example of Ella Baker and the many legions of voting rights organizers she mentored with the Student Nonviolent Coordinating Committee (SNCC) in rural Mississippi in the early 1960s. As discussed in chapter 2, their efforts were often opposed by racist county voting officials through the use of discriminatory literacy tests and other measures. But Baker and SNCC leaders and organizers were uninterested in the diminished framework of governance and democracy those officials embraced, considering it, in the words of W. E. B. Du Bois, "unworthy of grown folk."[18] They focused their labor instead on the tens of thousands of Black Mississippians who were eager to collectively govern their lives. They opened Freedom Schools committed to developing these capacities, and engaged in direct actions to assert and demand new institutions that would meet their needs.

Toni Morrison explains that the "monumental fraud" of racism was continually hidden in plain sight. For the white supremacists who engineered and celebrated slavery, land theft, imperialism, and national expansion, their demand was "always jobs, land, or money." Morrison saw no salvation or promise in addressing one's powers toward changing the consciousness of those who profess such beliefs. To do so required one to "define Black people as reactions to White presence" and to focus one's attentions on responding to allegations of inferiority rather than ending the practices of domination. "Where the mind dwells on changing the minds of racists is a very dank place." For Morrison, Baker, and all of the other movements chronicled in this book, the challenge instead was to build the capacity of everyday people to transform structures of domination into conditions of collective liberation.

DEPOLITICIZED ANTI-RACISM: INTEGRATING INTO A BURNING HOUSE

Despite this long tradition, anti-racism cannot be said to have a single meaning in economic, political, or ethical terms. Different modes of anti-racism propose different models of freedom and equality, and varying relationships with existing structures of power.

This point was made forcefully by Dr. Martin Luther King Jr. in a startling 1967 confession he made to the actor Harry Belafonte, a close friend and key figure in the Civil Rights movement. King told Belafonte, "I fear I am integrating my people into a burning house."[19] Just a few years after the passage of new federal laws outlawing discrimination in many realms of public life, Dr. King had come to believe that the institutions into which Black people were demanding integration were in deep crisis. Dr. King's alarm cuts against the dominant story told about the Civil Rights movement and the 1960s as one of triumph and inclusion into the nation that promised to secure the freedom that Black people and other minoritized groups had long demanded. Yet for Dr. King, these incorporations promised harm rather than safety, suffering rather than emancipation. To understand why is to grasp the difference between the movements described in this book, and a liberal, state-sanctioned form of inclusion that leaves existing structures of power and inequality intact.

In Alabama, for example, where Vivian Malone and James Hood became the first Black students to enter the state's public university in 1963, advances in civil rights have gone hand in hand with soaring rates of incarceration. In 1963 Alabama's prisons and jails counted fewer than 2,000 inmates, an incarceration rate of about 50 per 100,000. In 2018, more than 49,000 people were held captive in this way. Alabama that year had an incarceration rate of 946 per 100,000, placing it fifth in a nation that claims the world's highest rate of incarceration. African Americans in Alabama are locked up at more than three times the rate of white Alabamans. And even still, the white incarceration rate of 535 per 100,000 is also higher than the rate in all but four other nations in the world. Welcome to the burning house.[20]

All of these people have been arrested, charged, and sentenced through the operations of a criminal justice system undergirded by the state and federal Constitution—formally protected by a long host of procedural rights and protections that were central to the promises of state-sponsored anti-racism. Most of the people incarcerated are poor. Across a wide swath of the state's Black Belt, upward of 40 percent of the households live in poverty; nearly one in four children statewide regularly go hungry. They have no claim on the large fortunes amassed in cotton, mining, timber, and other industries by a small number of families in the state, a concentration of wealth that has accelerated rapidly in the last 50 years. Their rise has corresponded almost precisely with the decline of Alabama's labor movement, once a relative stronghold in the South.[21]

For Indigenous people also, the promises inherent in racial liberalism have yielded little. The name "Alabama" is derived from the language of the Muskogee (Creek) people, one of eight Indigenous groups whose ancestral territories lie within the current geographic boundaries of the state. These lands, all "ceded" through treaties negotiated with the democratically elected government of the United States in the early nineteenth century, have never been returned. The promises of "life, liberty, and the pursuit of happiness" give the Muskogee and other Indigenous people no title to the places claimed by settlers after their forced removal. The rights-bearing citizens of Alabama have no intention of returning this land. Today, the Poarch Band of Creek Indians stands as the sole federally recognized tribe in Alabama, exercising sovereign control over a small parcel of land in the southwestern corner of the state.[22]

The US military, by contrast, maintains five active bases within Alabama, collectively covering more than 1,000 square miles. In the early 1940s, to make room for one of the largest of chemical weapons plants in the world, the army evicted hundreds of tenant and sharecropper families near Huntsville. In 1965, the US Army's Missile and Munitions Center and School opened near that base to train American soldiers in the fine arts of using their guns, tanks, and bombers to advance what President Kennedy described as "a worldwide struggle to promote and protect the rights of all who wish to be free."[23]

Alabama, as Wallace instructed us more than 50 years ago, is of the nation, not apart from it. The same patterns of separation, extraction, and fatality witnessed in the Heart of Dixie—segregated and underfunded schools, yawning gaps in wealth and wages, mass banishments from participating in governance—exist in every part of the country. It is not just opportunity that is unevenly distributed, but life itself.

These modes of domination clearly work through race—they map on to histories of land theft, bondage, and apartheid. But many white Alabamans today are not spared from contending with the increasing prospects of early death. The state's opioid-related overdose deaths increased six-fold from 1999 to 2016. A large majority of the dead are people whom Wallace counted as fellow members of a "race of honor." The state's suicide rate has doubled since 1970. The badge and virtues of whiteness do not prevent many hundreds of people each year from ending their lives prematurely.[24]

These widespread experiences of impoverishment, incarceration, and early death were not among the vaunted "privileges of being American" promised by Kennedy in his 1963 civil rights address. But the president concluded his speech with a telling reminder: "We have a right to expect that the Negro community will be responsible, will uphold the law, but they have a right to expect the law will be fair, that the Constitution will be colorblind."[25] The "we" used here is unmistakably a racial referent; a statement on behalf of white America about the culpability of Black people in their own destiny.

Culpability is key. For racially stigmatized groups, once "freed" by emancipation from bondage or the bestowal of citizenship, civil rights, or other grants of opportunity, culpability and blameworthiness cannot be refused. This regime of blameworthiness makes the very regime of liberal anti-racism productive of "demons"—immoral subjects and market failures who threaten to burden us all. Thus, liberal rights and freedom then are fully compatible with industrialized forms of punishment and incarceration. Liberal incorporation does not promise universal emancipation, or even guarantees to life. It only offers a chance to distinguish and offer oneself as a "good" moral subject, worthy of the select rights that might be bestowed by the state.[26]

The legacies of Kennedy's liberal anti-racism are evident everywhere today. The promise of inclusion into US nationalism, markets, and militarization often seems to provide the sole framework to address racial subordination. As a result, institutions and structures that produce insecurity and suffering continually invite incorporation into their ranks. Corporations like Amazon, Citibank, Nike, and Goldman Sachs, whose everyday activities reap huge sums for their investors and executives and accelerate global inequality, announce their support for Black Lives Matter and new diversity hiring plans.[27] In this way, collective movements that demand the end of state violence and economic predation become transfigured into diversity initiatives for the elite. Militarism and policing are celebrated as vehicles for racial equity and inclusion, evident in the massive diversity recruitment and public relations budgets of the military branches and law enforcement agencies.[28] Elite colleges and universities sustain thinly funded offices for equity and inclusion, even as the institutions as a whole reproduce profound race and class hierarchies in education. All of these dominant efforts promote modest incorporation into their ranks without disturbing the underlying relations of power from which they profit.

Dr. Vincent Harding, the influential historian of the Black freedom struggle and an important confidant of Dr. King, suggests that the very struggle against segregation and racism produces the complicity to participate in such a system. As the Civil Rights movement passed its crescendo, and Dr. King's appeal to struggle against the "triple threats" of capitalism, militarism, and racism faded from collective memory, Harding called for a critical self-examination that would "see how much over the past fifteen to twenty years we black folks have decided (consciously or not) to fight racism by seeking 'equal opportunity' or a 'fair share' in the nation's militarism and its materialism. In other words, we have chosen to struggle against one of the 'triple threats' by joining the other two, a destructive choice."[29] Harding warned that in pursuing such a course, "we have imbibed much of the spirit . . . of greed, belligerency, fearful callouses, and individualism, a spirit that makes us anti-poor people, anti-immigrants, that creates injustice, that makes for war."[30]

Writing 40 years after Dr. King's death, Harding cautioned about the risks of such complicity, explaining that it would be "unfaithful to our own best history of struggle and to the hopes of the exploited peoples of the world, if black folk in the U.S.A. were to settle for what is now called 'a piece of the pie'—some proportionate cut of the wealth amassed by this nation's military-industrial empire." Harding argued that Dr. King "understood how fundamentally the structures of military and economic domination are built on the exploitation and deprivation of our own poor people" and that "by definition, . . . the shares of this system could never be fair." Put another way, they were not interested in a simple framework of equity, or a demand for a racially proportionate allocation of harms and goods. Parity in suffering and domination is not justice.[31]

Harding, like King, rejected the belief that racism is a distortion or a perversion of an otherwise neutral market and state. Racism is not an

outside force, like a virus, that infects an otherwise healthy body. It ema-
nates from the body. It is the necessary structuring condition of the corporate economy. It organizes labor markets and shapes the gendered division of labor that is critical to the functioning of the economy. It is the
main precondition of state violence. It undergirds our deeply hierarchical
system of education, rooted in distinctions of status and innate intellectual ability. The abolition of racism requires the fundamental reorganization of all of these structures.[32]

For Harding and Dr. King, the possibilities for articulating what
Harding called "a greater, richer vision of freedom" lay precisely in those
traditions of struggle and solidarity that refused such complicity.[33]
Harding explained that Dr. King "urged us to see ourselves moving forward always, urgently holding ourselves in the vanguard of humanity's
best possibilities," and "asked us to see our freedom as empowering us to
create new values, to envision a new society" that would "break beyond
self-centered goals, to work for a new humanity."[34]

BEYOND THE BURNING HOUSE

Dr. King insisted that rather than running into the burning house, or
"standing by and watching it burn," the charge of a Black-led freedom
movement was "to become the firefighter" and to save the house. Dr. King
was not invoking a vision of sacrifice or martyrdom, in which the lives of
Black people would be subordinated to the interests of others. Instead, he
sought to make clear that Black freedom could not be achieved through
incorporation into prevailing institutions. The conditions necessary for
Black life to flourish would also provide the conditions under which all
people could be free. As the Black feminist organizers who penned the
famed Combahee River Collective Statement in April 1977 explained,
Black women's freedom would "mean that everyone else would have to be
free since our freedom would necessitate the destruction of all the systems
of oppression."[35] Similarly, Judith LeBlanc, a member of the Caddo tribe
and the director of the Native Organizers Alliance, explains that true sovereignty for Indigenous people can never be achieved within the current
economic and political configuration of the United States. The conditions

for native sovereignty and life to thrive would require ending structures of domination and control affecting many people.[36]

In the wake of the twin pandemics of 2020—Covid-19 and the endurance of anti-Black violence by the populace and the state—the caution about integrating into a burning house is more relevant than ever. The limits of seeking "equity and inclusion" within institutions and structures that continue to thrive on disposability and distinctions between good and bad subjects have never been more clear. The use of violence and torture in the name of safety and security has quickened. The nation's prison system has become industrialized and nationalized—engorging itself on more and more bodies. Civil rights legislation has reshaped but not transformed an education system marked by inequality and segregation. The imprint of militarization has stretched into ever more places: the suburban subdivision and the inner city; the border wall and the forward army base. Meaningful work and meaningful wages have declined. Poisoned waters, land, and air continue to wage their slow violence.

Dr. King believed that alternatives were possible, even as they are not easily realized. No simple story of revolt or revolution will lay them bare. They will never be the province of a single protagonist or heroine. Such examples will not be handed down in corporate diversity workshops, from academic offices of equity and inclusion, or by individuals trying to shift their own consciousness and awareness in isolation from one another. But there are important episodes of groups of everyday people, who in fighting against their own subordination, have produced accounts of interdependence, mutuality, and emancipation that can help point the way.

The chapters that follow explore the ways that struggles against racial domination have developed new conceptions of the fundamental categories of social and political life—of work and the economy, of governance and democracy, of the body and care—that summon and implicate all of us. The chapters mine anti-racist social movements, cultural forces, and political visions that sought to transform what Dr. King called a "philosophy based on a contempt for life" into its antithesis, an anti-subordination ideology and practice that comprehends difference, vulnerability, and interdependence as central and productive facets of human experience.

These stories do not cohere into a fully formed and unified manifesto, platform, or normative political vision, and this book makes no attempt to narrate a singular and encompassing history of anti-racism. To do so would be distort the movements described, which take part of their power from being centered within their specific conditions and experiences. Each is complex and fundamentally distinct, yet all are interconnected. They are more productively understood as episodes of rebellion that have yielded an archive of political practices, perceptions, and enactments that offer important lessons for those hoping to reverse the widening gulf in power, life, and freedom that marks contemporary life. Like any good archive, this collection of stories is a shared resource, a site of learning, open to interpretation, and accessible to a broad range of questions and priorities. It elevates salient themes and traces important through lines, linking and aggregating struggles that have always been particular in their form and aspiration, yet universal in their insights. As the writer and organizer Grace Lee Boggs counsels, history "is not the past but the stories we tell about the past. How we tell these stories . . . has a lot to do with whether we cut short or advance our evolution as human beings."[37]

Chapter 1, "The Body: 'A World Where All Human Life Is Valued,'" charts efforts to transform and reconstruct assumptions about the body, including struggles against sexual violence, forced sterilization, and fights for reproductive and sexual health and autonomy. White supremacist theories of racial difference and subordination have taken the body as a preeminent site of power and the production of social meaning. The human sciences that gave rise to these doctrines were embedded in the structures of colonial and imperial militarism, and shaped by hierarchical understandings of bodies and their value. In resisting such regimes, new accounts of the body as collective and interdependent have emerged. The chapter moves from the outskirts of Albuquerque to Ciudad Juárez to a jail in North Carolina to a maternity ward in downtown Los Angeles to examine the ways that women-of-color organizers have conceptualized the body on such terms, rejecting theories of disposability and degradation.

Chapter 2, "Democracy and Governance: 'My Rise Does Not Involve Your Fall,'" foregrounds stories that displace the notion of the self-determining, independent citizen-subject, based on a model of white masculinity, that has been a foundational political and cultural category in US history. These racial justice projects have instead pursued a vision of political, social, and economic interdependence, reciprocity, and interchange.

The Indigenous struggle against settler colonialism has long been animated by an alternative vision over the relationship between humans, food, land, production, and the broader eco-system. The abolition democracy of Reconstruction advanced ideas of governance and representation that rejected hierarchies of autonomy and civility. This lineage of racial justice undermines dominant assumptions that leadership, talent, creativity, intellect, and power inhere in and develop entirely as individual qualities. It demonstrates instead the ways these attributes and capacities are produced socially and relationally, even when they seem to manifest in a single individual.

Collective efforts linking racial justice and liberation within the nation to the end of US militarism and occupation abroad are examined in chapter 3, "Internationalism: 'Sing No More War of War.'" It traces efforts from the editorial pages of the Black press that condemned the US occupation of the Philippines at the end of the nineteenth century to Indigenous formations that have sought to undo the "nuclear economy" that has fueled war-making and environmental degradation since World War II to more recent efforts to close US military bases in Hawaii and Puerto Rico and to build new social relations in their place. All of these struggles have confronted the ways that military service has often been celebrated as a means for racially subordinated groups to achieve social mobility and political inclusion. These groups refuse the logic that to avoid being exploited one must become an exploiter, and that to exercise political agency, one must dominate others.

This collective vision of solidarity has been cultivated within worker movements that have pressed visions of emancipation that extend far beyond the workplace. Chapter 4, "Labor: 'To Enjoy and Create the Values of Humanity,'" surveys efforts to challenge the hierarchy of human value through which capitalism operates, linking the realization of racial justice to fundamental transformations in the political economy. These connections are made plain in the struggles of farm and food production workers in the Southeast, women of color laboring as domestic workers and in other caregiving fields, autoworkers in Detroit, and grocery and restaurant workers in Los Angeles. All have contested the ways that capitalism relies on racial categories that naturalize relationships of ownership, labor, exploitation, markets, consumption, autonomy, and property. In doing so, they have sought to overcome the fragmentation that locks workers into competition with each other in order to envision and practice new forms of solidarity and power.

The concluding chapter, "A New Recipe," considers some of the principles of social change and transformation that connect the racial justice struggles, ideas, and formations discussed in the book. It considers, in the words of Dr. Vincent Harding, the challenge "to search for a new recipe, create a new vision of what needs to be baked, develop a new pie based on compassion and human solidarity rather than on maximum profits."[38] It distills from the episodes of the book a provisional series of practices and principles to provide some of the ingredients for this new recipe, one that might help to realize a wider type of freedom.

One final point bears emphasis. Nearly all of the episodes chronicled within this book focus on the United States and efforts to transform its economy, governance, and social relations. Many of these projects have been attuned to the dangers these structures have posed not just to those within the nation, but to people and places in other parts of the world. And these places—Manilla, Dakar, Chile, Kingston, Okinawa, Palestine, and many others—have produced rich visions of freedom and interdependence that hold the great hopes for humanity and for the planet.[39] Indeed, C. L. R. James rooted only a small part of *A History of Pan-African Revolt* in the United States; it was but one site within a global circuit of rebellion. These movements and solidarities emanating from outside the United States, steeped in traditions of anti-colonialism, trade unionism, and international feminism, require all of our attention. Any possibilities for life, land, bread, and peace within the US rest on the success of these efforts in other parts of the world.

1 The Body

"A WORLD WHERE ALL HUMAN LIFE IS VALUED"

"I feel that I am a prisoner and have been mistreated." So explained Chris Thompson in an interview with renowned trans organizer Sylvia Rivera of Street Transvestite Action Revolutionaries (STAR) and Arthur Bell of the Gay Activist Alliance (GAA) that appeared in November 1970 in *Gay Flames*, a self-described "Bulletin of the Homofire Movement." Rivera and Bell interviewed Thompson in the psychiatric wing at Bellevue Hospital in Manhattan, where he was being involuntarily detained and "kept under control" after coming to the hospital to seek treatment for his asthma. Thompson described the humiliating treatment he received from the medical staff, who forced him to sleep in the hall and to remove his makeup and hair curlers during his detention.[1]

The connection Thompson made between incarceration and biomedical care, between the cage and the hospital ward, was not mere hyperbole. He experienced these overlapping forms of domination in the hospital's assertion of control over his body. Thompson described a continuum of violence carried out by police, medical institutions, and the legal system against trans people of color, a legacy that continues to this day. The interview, part of a broad archive of trans history, politics, and social movements compiled by the writer, organizer and filmmaker Reina Gossett, details the very distinct forms of violence and control experienced by Black trans people, as well as the collective responses and communities of power and care groups like STAR that arose in response.

Rivera later explained that "STAR was for the street gay people, the street homeless people, and anybody that needed help at that time." Rivera visited jails, hospitals, shelters, piers, and street corners to connect with trans youth who had been kicked out or had run away from their homes and were hustling to make their living on the street. It was their lives, safety, and survival that Rivera and cofounder Marsha Johnson always placed at the center of their work. STAR emphasized that survival and freedom meant both meeting people's immediate needs and transforming the regimes—of health care, policing, housing, food, interpersonal violence—that jeopardized their lives. Personal trauma required collective responses. Bodies become particularly vulnerable to violence and control when they are isolated and atomized, divorced from larger collectives of protection and care. As Rivera's visit to Thompson demonstrated, such transformations were rooted in a deep-seated commitment to mutual avowal and interdependence. Much of her political labor forged such ties; she was influenced by Huey P. Newton and the Black Panther Party and became a member of the Young Lords Party, a group of revolutionary Puerto Rican youth based in East Harlem. And she continually challenged the mainstream gay rights movement for its failures to avow, recognize, and claim trans people and other queer subjects who bore the worst impacts of state violence and control.[2]

While these stories and their political genealogy remain very specific to trans as well as queer of color organizing, the insights and demands they produced have wide-ranging resonance and relevance. They can be situated within an expansive history across time and place to produce new social conditions and structures that protect the autonomy and collective value of the body for everyone, and to reject the hierarchies of degradation and control that justified Thompson's detention in the first place.[3]

In this way, Thompson's observations about the violation of his body can be connected to an 1893 speech by the writer, educator, and political activist Anna Julia Cooper at the World's Congress of Representative Women. Cooper described a "heroic struggle, a struggle against fearful and overwhelming odds" against what she described as "colored women's oppression." At the center of this struggle was "the despairing fight, as of an entrapped tigress, to keep hallowed their own persons." For Cooper the body represented a central location of struggle and possibility that had stakes for all people. She described Black women "as toilers for the universal triumph of justice and human rights" who demanded "an entrance not through a gateway for ourselves, our race, our sex, or our sect, but a grand highway for humanity."[4]

Following Cooper and Rivera, this chapter explores a set of episodes across time and place—from the dusty outskirts of Albuquerque to Ciudad Juárez to a small courthouse in rural North Carolina to a maternity ward in Los Angeles—in which particular struggles against the control, violation, and domination of the bodies of women and queer people have invoked expansive and liberatory visions. These stories do not yield a fully coherent or unified conception of the body beyond the regulation of race. They point instead to a series of understandings, practices, and demands generated in response to such regulation. Through vigils, legal campaigns, public art, lawsuits, and other means, women of color have found multiple ways to reject the oppressions that threaten their survival. Their resistance in these cases was provoked by murder, rape, labor exploitation, and coerced sterilization. The fragmentation, mutilation, and destruction of bodies through physical violence are integral to the enforcement of race as a system of power and a hierarchy of human value.

RACE AND DEGRADATION

The ideology of race itself had its origin in bodily fragments. In 1775, as the Second Continental Congress was preparing to assemble in Philadelphia in the name of liberty and Captain James Cook was laying claim to the islands of the South Pacific for the Queen, 23-year-old Johann Friedrich Blumenbach published his doctoral dissertation, "On the Natural Variety of Mankind," at the University of Göttingen. Considered one of the first works of modern anthropology, Blumenbach's research was based on a collection of skulls sent to him by military officers and merchants gathered during expeditions across Europe, Africa, Asia, and the Americas.[5] Violence haunted this work from the beginning; Blumenbach's specimens were heads severed from bodies, acquired by agents of colonial expansion, and divorced entirely from the fabric of relationships that constituted their lives and beings. The research methodology was itself a site of race-making that transformed bodies into things.

Like his contemporaries in the emerging academic fields of zoology, geography, and biology, Blumenbach developed a taxonomy to classify and differentiate the variation he perceived. He carefully measured and described hundreds of skulls—the position of the jaw, forehead, chin, and cheeks—and based on accounts passed to him by others, the color and appearance of the skin, hair, and lips. Over the next twenty years, Blumenbach would refine his classificatory observations, and in 1795 he announced he had identified "the most beautiful race of men," which he identified as the "Caucasian variety." He explained that skin "white in color" was "the primitive color of mankind"—skin color free from any degradation. He described the Caucasian variety as belonging to "the inhabitants of Europe (except the Lapps and the remaining descendants of the Finns) and those of Eastern Asia, as far as the river Obi, the Caspian Sea and the Ganges; and lastly, those of Northern Africa."[6]

From this "most beautiful form of the skull," he described four other types that "diverge by most easy gradations" to inferior forms: the "Mongolian variety," the "Ethiopian variety," the "Malay variety," and the "American variety." While Blumenbach reasoned that all these varieties belonged to the human species (other taxonomies of race would later contest this claim), these other types had gone through various processes of "degeneration" and "divergence" from the Caucasian ideal. Scrutinize the body for enough time, Blumenbach insisted, and the degraded nature of different groups of humanity will be revealed.[7]

To be sure, the division of human life into those worthy of life and those worthy of death long preceded Blumenbach's scholarship. Well before 1775, the ancestors of the people who now call themselves European found many creative ways to enslave, slaughter, and exploit one another. The feudal system itself was premised on the tradition of permanent, naturally ordained human hierarchies. Spanish conquistadors did not need to meditate on gradations of skull sizes before massacring the Arawak people of the Caribbean; the Church and Queen announced that it was their duty. The merchants and investors of Liverpool could calculate the profit to be earned from each child extracted from West Africa without the bright minds of the Enlightenment.[8]

But Blumenbach's classification of the "Caucasian variety" still circulates as a legal, demographic, and commonsense category. Its endurance and penetration into diverse spheres of contemporary life reveals nothing about its scientific accuracy. Blumenbach selected a single skull (likely that of young woman from the Georgia region of the Caucuses enslaved by an invading army) to stand in for a uniform and biologically fixed category of human variation. His "Caucasian variety" is as real as the Easter Bunny, Santa Claus, and the Tooth Fairy. Like those figures, the Caucasian is best understood as an artifact of mythology, a shared cultural story that performs critical social, political, and ideological work.[9]

The myth of the Caucasian has endured across more than two centuries not because of Blumenbach's scientific acumen but because of the ideological labor it performs and the relations of power it legitimizes. The worldview Blumenbach helped narrate and make legible, in which certain signifiers of human difference are understood as expressions of degradation, is an optic on human life itself. Amid the high age of European colonialism, Indigenous genocide, and chattel slavery, the account of humanity divided into various conditions of degradation and value performed essential work. Through this lens, barbarous acts of torture on the plains of the Dakotas were rendered as necessary rites of civilization. Heroes could rape and remain heroes. Civilizations could be extinguished in the name of saving humanity. Workers could toil in garment factories, cotton fields, and kitchens without protection. It was not simply that people who called themselves Caucasian visited atrocities upon those they perceived to be different. Instead, the view of human life proposed by Blumenbach required such violence.[10] It produced a legacy that the writer Ta-Nehisi Coates describes in this way: "In America, it is traditional to destroy the black body—*it is heritage.*"[11]

Race operates here, in the account of the historian Barbara Fields, as an ideology, a worldview generative of wide-ranging social meanings, issues, and identities.[12] It is an ideology that is productive of particular conceptions of human hierarchy, vulnerability, and autonomy that are always dependent upon violence and the possibility of elimination to secure and justify their reproduction. For Blumenbach and the many other academics, political elites, writers, artists, and others working within this framework, the body serves as a preeminent site of power and the production of social meaning. Particular forms of physical difference signify the body's place within a broader human order, functioning as the alibi for acts of exploitation, appropriation, and domination. As the Caucasian ideal migrated from the halls of the university into the legislative chambers of the newly independent states and the mainsprings of popular culture, it took on diverse forms and articulations. But at its core, the idea of the Caucasian was premised on the assumption that the body was characterized by natural patterns of degradation. Thus a central task of any modern society was to ensure that the government, economy, and culture were organized in ways that accurately reflected and reproduced these innate differences.

Writing some 130 years after Blumenbach, W. E. B. Du Bois laid bare the grip that the mythology of race held on the dominant political consciousness of the United States. Surveying the two decades following the Civil War, he explained the end of abolition democracy and the South's return to despotism and planter rule as premised on a "phantasmagoria" that "has been built on the most miserable of human fictions." It was a worldview, he explained, that presumed "in addition to manifest differences between men there is a deep, awful and ineradicable cleft which condemns most men to eternal degradation." It is this belief in the inevitability of "eternal degradation" that constitutes race as an ideology, one Du Bois described as "a cheap inheritance of the world's infancy, unworthy of grown folk."[13] With Du Bois, Audre Lorde has famously described the ways in which a "profit economy" necessitates the production of "surplus people" and requires the "destruction" of those differences regarded as subordinate.[14]

Du Bois invoked an alternative political vision in which perceived differences in the body did not become fatally linked to power. Here, the body is not understood as an object or a "thing" that exists to generate profits or consume goods. Du Bois's account is part of a broad assemblage of political movements, intellectual labor, and artistic and cultural formations to transform and reconstruct assumptions about the body and the "fatal coupling" linking power and difference described by Stuart Hall and Ruth Wilson Gilmore.[15] Myriad struggles—against sexual violence, murder, or forced sterilization, as well as fights for reproductive and sexual health and autonomy—can all be understood as efforts to contest this fatal coupling and the social and political claims on the body it requires. Taken together, these efforts link the liberation of the body to a wider type of freedom premised on principles of collective autonomy, interdependence, and the value of difference.

INVENTING THE SAVAGE

The invention of the Caucasian by the great minds of the late eighteenth century also required the making of its negation: the savage. The characteristics ascribed to this mythological creation varied by time, place, and circumstance, and were often articulated through gendered ideas. In the cotton fields of Mississippi, the savage was made as a brute figure whose barbarous nature required permanent enslavement and methodical violence, as well as the mammy, a servile character dedicated to the care, comfort, and pleasure of a genteel family of overlords. When US Navy vessels pointed their cannons at the people of the Philippines, Hawaii, and Puerto Rico, the savage was heathen and contaminated, the white man's doomed burden. In the nineteenth- and twentieth-century boarding schools built to remove many thousands of Indigenous youth from their families and societies, the savage was cast as a soul to be rescued from the body through discipline and violation. And for the physicians and hospitals that sterilized Mexican-origin women in Los Angeles in the 1960s and 1970s without their consent, the savage was a rogue reproducer, overpopulating the nation with social undesirables.[16]

While the ways in which the savage was described, contrived, and subordinated varied widely, these figures share an underlying premise. Insisting on the degraded nature of some bodies as natural, permanent, and inevitable became a necessary precondition for a form of governance that otherwise proved incapable of conceptualizing citizenship, freedom, and autonomy as universal qualities. Thus, the body became the crucial evidence of an enhanced or diminished capacity for freedom and citizenship. The alleged degradation of particular bodies is what permits a democracy's soldiers to fire upon sleeping families in the name of freedom or a city's officers of the law to torture its young people without liability. It permits democratically elected representatives to seize land and cage constituents in the name of the people.

Thomas Jefferson, another contemporary of Blumenbach, wrote in *Notes on the State of Virginia* that race was a "difference fixed in nature." His descriptions of the "Negro body" ("They have less hair on the face and body. They secrete less by the kidnies, and more by the glands of the skin ... Their griefs are transient"[17]) demonstrates Frantz Fanon's point that the colonizer always "fabricates" the colonized.[18]

The deprivation of the body has been key to the production of the savage. Gail Small, a Northern Cheyenne and former leader of the Montana-based group Native Action, reviewed the grim histories of torture and violence committed in the name of freedom and civilization: "You learned, I think, very limited in your history books in this country about what we've suffered. The oral stories that we know are much more barbaric, like the Sand Creek massacre," in which women were repeatedly tortured and mutilated. "I don't know how you can ever say it was civilized people who came to create a society here."[19] For Small, the very histories of US national expansion and development depended upon such acts of violence and barbarity. Physical torture was not an exceptional or extralegal action but an essential element of political authority.

By contrast, the Indigenous groups organizing against the forms of sex- and gender-based violence that continue to this day operate with a much different conception of bodily autonomy, interdependence, and collective care.[20] Differences between and among bodies, and the ways they are inhabited to express identities, kinship, traditions, consciousness, and desires, can never be the basis for degradation and violence. Collective practices of mutual avowal and care are the necessary conditions for any body to thrive; the struggle to secure such conditions for everyone is precisely what Anna Julia Cooper described as the "grand highway for humanity."

ALBUQUERQUE AND JUÁREZ: THE INTERDEPENDENT BODY

In early 2009, a woman walking her dog through a dusty stretch of the West Mesa on the outskirts of Albuquerque discovered a large bone settled in the brittle New Mexico soil. The bone was a human femur. A three-month search of a vast expanse of desert followed, yielding the remains of eleven women and a four-month-old fetus—a mass grave site estimated to be five years old. Even before all the bodies were identified, investigators told the public about their bodies. They belonged to addicts. They belonged to prostitutes. They belonged to poor people. They belonged to brown people. An unknown person may have extinguished their lives, but it was the "high-risk lifestyle" they had allegedly chosen that ultimately explained their deaths. No crowded public memorials followed. Politicians do not make a spectacle out of mourning the lives of such bodies. The "most beautiful form of skull" described by Blumenbach more than two hundred years ago was not among the skulls found in this desert.[21]

Indeed, the discovery of their bodies might have remained only a tawdry account of an unsolved crime if not for the efforts of a group of residents led by an organization called Young Women United (YWU), who had the capacity to conceptualize and remember their bodies in a different way. YWU was founded in the mid-1990s by a group of women of color in their teens and early 20s frustrated by the lack of school-based health and sex education programs. Through weekly "Circle of Strength" meetings convened in their small office in the Southeast Heights neighborhood of Albuquerque, YWU's members linked the silence they encountered about young women's sexuality, health, and sex education in school to the broader ways in which the state fails to recognize the lived realities, experiences, and struggles of poor women of color. Women struggling with addiction, abuse, and poverty encounter stigmatization and erasure. Young women who are pregnant face a double bind: they may be denied access to abortion services if they want to end their pregnancy and yet receive few social, economic, and health resources if they decide to parent. The young Chicana and Native women in YWU drew from a rich legacy of collective organizing in Albuquerque and the Southwest that understands the health and well-being of individuals, families, and communities to be interdependent. All bodies are linked in this way.[22]

Thus, when news of the mass grave site began to circulate along with slurs against the women whose lives had been lost, the YWU's leaders recognized themselves in the accounts. The group began organizing monthly vigils to honor the murdered women, soon drawing hundreds of people.

Young Women United rally in Albuquerque, New Mexico, January 2011. Credit: Adriann Barboa.

"Who were these women?" asked a sign held by a YWU member. They were "mothers, daughters, sisters, healers, believers, friends, wives, students, teachers, community members." "These were our women." The group challenged the insistence of local authorities and news media that the victims were "addicts" and "prostitutes" culpable in their own deaths. YWU's Adriann Barboa, a lifelong Albuquerque resident who lived close to the mesa where the bodies were discovered, instead described them as "brave heroes who faced histories of poverty, abuse and trauma with the best tools they could find."[23]

This reclamation of the women's relationships and identities lay at the core of a wider challenge. In shifting the moral meanings of their bodies, YWU also proposed a transformed understanding of the state's responsibilities toward those most vulnerable to violence and abandonment. YWU and their allies certainly called for a sustained investigation into the murders, demanding that the state take the loss of these women's lives seriously. But in their view, the women's struggles and deaths pointed to a wider crisis that required a much broader horizon of justice. At the monthly vigils and other events, YWU leaders pressed policy makers and the public to remember the ways the state itself had abandoned so many poor women of color in Albuquerque, leaving them susceptible to violence, economic crisis, addiction, and incarceration, where they often reexperienced sexual assault. They insisted that issues such as poverty and joblessness could not be separated from concerns about reproductive health and justice and the right to parent or to not parent. They rallied behind legislation that would increase access for mental health services and substance abuse treatment for young women and pregnant women in a state that had one of the highest rates of overdose deaths in the nation. They led campaigns to preserve abortion rights and access in Albuquerque that integrated reproductive rights in a much broader framework of racial and gender power and public guarantees to health care.[24]

They argued for a state that was not premised on a hierarchy of lives, but one that would safeguard the bodies of those most forcefully marked for stigma and abandonment. Barboa described the wider vision for this effort, explaining that if President Obama had come to Albuquerque to remember their lives and mourn their deaths, she would have wanted him to assert "that this could be a country where you can be born without much, but live a life that is safe, and full of promise. Where you can get a good education, a job, a home. Where if you stray from the path, there are nets to catch you. Where you are never found dead, dismembered, and alone on a mesa."[25]

The members and leaders of YWU always made clear the racialized and gendered dimensions of this crisis. Structures of economic discrimination, sexual violence, and state abandonment left these young women's bodies—ten Latinas and one African American—explicitly vulnerable to premature death. But their analysis linked this racialized vulnerability to the ways the state and economy were organized around the production of disposability and degradation, evident in Barboa's reference to bodies "found dead, dismembered, and alone on a mesa." In demanding public resources and protection for women struggling with addiction, for teen parents, and for women living in poverty, they challenged the state to forsake the racialized worldview that allowed these murders to seem inevitable. Instead, YWU demanded the conditions that would give women autonomy over their bodies while affirming their interconnections with family and community. Their vision of justice required that the bodies scattered across the mesa be understood through the many political, cultural, economic, and familial relationships in which they were enmeshed.

Indeed, the analysis and mobilization led by young women of color in Albuquerque bears vital connections to a struggle 300 miles to the south. "Ni una más"—not one more—served as the rallying cry for a movement in Ciudad Juárez in response to the kidnapping and murders of hundreds of women and girls between 1993 and 2008. In this metropolis of 1.5 million people across the international border from El Paso, Texas, the loved ones of those whose tortured bodies had been abandoned in landfills, motels, vacant lots, and bustling city plazas organized to challenge the "fatal indifference" expressed by the state and its corporate allies to this profound loss of life.[26] They framed this "femicide"—the serial extinction of women's lives—within broader and interconnected structures of power: the low-wage, export-oriented factories and sweatshops known as *maquiladoras* that dominated the city's economy and drew displaced rural women to the region; cultural discourses that portrayed the young women as hypersexualized and unmoored from traditional family structures, making them culpable in their own deaths; and gendered and racialized hierarchies that situated the women as already marked for disappearance and fatality. In the same way the mesa was imagined to preternaturally swallow the disappeared women of Albuquerque, in Juárez, for *"las inditas del sur,"* or the little Indian girls from the south of Mexico, the women's dark skin, indigenous roots, and impoverished conditions signified and naturalized their disposability. Though the dominant racial categories and divisions in Mexico differ in important ways from those in the United States, both are rooted in gendered distinctions that are foundational to racial colonialism.

Native studies scholars and Indigenous activists point not only to the long history of sexual violence that has accompanied colonization across the Americas but also to the "history of mutilation of Indian bodies, both living and dead" that makes it clear that Indigenous people "are not entitled to bodily integrity."[27] This analysis links individual acts of violence and bodily harm to the political, historic, and cultural structures that render particular bodies disposable in this way.

In addition, the femicide in Juárez cannot be separated from the conditions of racialized exploitation enforced by US-based companies in the *maquiladora* zone, the area created by the Mexican government in the 1970s to lure multinational manufacturers through the promise of low wages, beneficial tax treatment, and state-sponsored worker training.[28] Multinational corporations including General Electric, General Motors, RCA, Siemens, and many others employ tens of thousands of mostly female workers for impoverished wages in the sprawling factories. Family members, artists, scholars, and human rights activists organizing against the femicide have pointed out that the processes of dehumanization and disposability operating within the *maquila* system, "which revolve around the reproduction of disposable women," also frame the kidnapping and murders of women and girls in Juárez. Geographer Melissa Wright outlines the correspondences between the anti-violence work of organizations such as Casa Amiga, the rape crisis center in Juárez that brought early attention to the femicide, with labor-organizing efforts to challenge exploitative wage and working conditions inside the factories.[29] Both seek to subvert the devaluation of human beings.[30] In this analysis, one form of devaluation (the commodification of labor on the factory floor) cannot be abstracted from another (the femicide). By showing how women's murders are symptomatic of the structural injustices surrounding them, transformative visions of racial justice in Juárez and Albuquerque linked particular bodies with demands for wider freedoms. In both settings, activists rejected official accounts that used sexual slurs to make women culpable in their own deaths. They also challenged attempts to portray the kidnappings and murders as "disaggregated," discrete and unrelated events that were the tragic work of a few deranged individuals and that could be adjudicated through the criminal justice system alone.[31] These holistic modes of analysis make the meanings of violence clear by illuminating its contexts and by attending to connectedness—of bodies within communities, as well as of forms of oppression, abandonment, and devaluation.

This organizing work carries on today in organizing campaigns in the US and Canada such as the New Mexico–based Coalition to Stop Violence against Native Women and its Missing and Murdered Indigenous

Womxn, Girls, and Two Spirit (MMIWG2S) project, which links histories of European and US colonialism to the devastating levels of sex and gender violence faced by Native nations and people today.[32] Projects like MMIWG2S not only demand attention to this violence and its impacts, but also produce new forms of caregiving, accountability, and community-based power that do not reproduce the logic and structure of the US criminal justice system, in which state violence is asserted as the solution to end interpersonal violence.

In 2019, Young Women United changed its name to Bold Futures, emphasizing that its origins as a reproductive justice formation based in Albuquerque had compelled the group to take on an even wider range of conditions that shape the freedom and collective possibilities for women of color in New Mexico. They focus now not only on access to reproductive health care, pregnancy-related care, and birthing justice, but also on transformations in policing and carceral systems, immigration, and economic justice.[33] With statewide groups like Strong Families New Mexico, they conduct research, engage and organize policy makers, focus on sites of cultural formation and public narrative, and organize, develop, and educate residents across the state. Collectively, they have articulated a vision of the body as both autonomous and interdependent; free from threats of violence, coercion, and exploitation, but also intimately dependent on wider systems of care and collective development.

SAN DIEGO AND NORTH CAROLINA:
DEFENDING THE COLLECTIVE BODY

In 1975, a group of Chicana activists affiliated with a Sacramento-based arts collective named the Royal Chicano Air Force (RCAF) painted a mural titled *Women Hold Up Half the Sky* on a pillar beneath the San Diego–Coronado Bridge. It was one of dozens of murals gracing the enormous pylons towering above Chicano Park, a legendary site of Chicanx organizing and cultural production in the Barrio Logan neighborhood of San Diego. The mural includes images of five women at the top of the pylon whose bodies appear to support not only the sky but also the weight of the bridge itself, making the social labor of their bodies visible.[34]

On the side of the pylon adjacent to the main mural, the RCAF incorporated a portrait of Joan Little, a young Black woman who had just been put on trial for the 1974 murder of a guard in the Beaufort County jail in North Carolina. The guard, a 62-year-old white man named Clarence Alligood, was found dead in Little's cell, stabbed repeatedly with an ice pick he had kept in his own desk drawer. Little escaped the jail but quickly surrendered. She soon went on trial facing the gas chamber, confronted with the nearly impossible task of proving to a jury that she had committed the murder in self-defense after being sexually assaulted by Alligood. At stake in the trial was the contention that the body of a Black woman was her own; neither her incarceration nor the jailer's authority required her to forfeit this autonomy. Little had endured the types of struggles experienced by many poor Black women in rural North Carolina—crises in schools, family, and employment—that led her to leave her home as a teenager. As framed by her critics, these were markers of her inferiority and degradation, staining her claims for self-defense as dubious and implausible.[35]

The RCAF mural included a portion of a poem Little had written while in jail titled "But I Am Somebody." The poem directly expressed Little's understanding of the social forces she was confronting: "I am somebody. I may be down today but I am somebody. I may be considered the lowest on earth but I am somebody." She described both the grinding poverty she endured as a child and the public stigma she faced during the trial, yet concluded, "In the end, I will have freedom." Indeed, Little refused several offers to her help her leave the country to escape prosecution; she insisted on testifying in her own defense.[36]

Nearly all of the 50 murals in Chicano Park depict Indigenous and Chicano/a figures across 500 years of resistance to colonial rule. Why did the words of a poor Black woman from North Carolina become incorporated into a creative project representing the struggles of Chicana and Indigenous women 2,600 miles away? Central to this connection is a shared understanding of the ways race structures sex- and gender-based violence, and a vision of the body's freedom, autonomy, and interdependence produced in response.

Little's case became a galvanizing political event nationally because from the outset, her defenders emphasized the political dimensions of her

Mural featuring Joan Little in Chicano Park, San Diego. Credit:
Daniel Martinez HoSang.

assault and her resistance. If the judicial system was attempting to adjudicate a conflict between Little and her jailer, the social movement that arose in response stressed the collective, historic, and structural dimensions of their confrontation. As Angela Davis explained in a 1975 essay in *Ms. Magazine* about the Little case, "When a white man rapes a black woman, the underlying meaning of this crime remains inaccessible if one is blind to the historical dimensions of the act." She linked the case to a long history of "humiliating and violent sexual attacks as an integral feature of [Black women's] daily lives" that can be traced back to slavery and that presumed Black women's bodies to be the sexual property of others. Davis stressed that "although the immediate victim of rape was the black woman—and it was she who endured its pain and anguish—rape served not only to further her oppression, but also as a means of terrorizing the entire black community." In the dominant view, the "bestial notion of the black women" which "branded her as a creature motivated by base, animal-like sexual instincts" and "openly defined as property" justified both the sexual violation of her body and "played and continues to play a significant role in justifying the overexploitation of her labor." Indeed, the prosecution attempted to make full use of these stereotypes, portraying Little as a seductress and Jezebel figure who lured Alligood into her cell to plot her escape. Davis connected "the rape of the black woman and its ideological justification . . . to the portrayal of the black man as a bestial rapist of white women—and, of course, the castration and lynching of black men on the basis of such accusations."[37] Ruth Wilson Gilmore observes that this violence serves to "guarantee the extraction from Black communities of cheap labor (including sex)" because the object of labor exploitation and the object of sexual violence were the same.[38] Davis remarked that the institutionalization of rape during slavery endured "in such vestiges of slavery as domestic work. How many black women working in the homes of white people have not had to confront the 'man of the house' as an actual or potential rapist?" And while rape and sexual violence are always rooted in gender domination and patriarchy, Davis insisted, "whenever a campaign is erected around a black woman who has been raped by a white man . . . the content of the campaign must be explicitly antiracist."[39]

For Davis and many women of color who organized around the case, Little's experience and her right to self-defense could not be separated from the broader system of labor domination and gendered relations of power that structured the lives of many Black women. This vision is evident in a 1975 song about Little penned by the longtime artist, organizer, and scholar Bernice Johnson Reagon and recorded by the famed a capella ensemble Sweet Honey in the Rock. The opening refrain marks the ubiquity of Little's experiences and challenges those who might disavow their relationship to her.

> Joan Little, she's my sister
> Joan Little, she's our mama
> Joan Little, she's your lover
> Joan the woman who's gonna carry your child.

Reagon's lyrics go on to recount not only the circumstances of the case but also the ways in which a politics of respectability ("you gonna be judged by the company you keep")[40] might prevent others from identifying with a poor Black woman accused of murder and sexual deviance. In the song's final refrain, Reagon disrupts this refusal, insisting:

> Cause now Joan is you and Joan is me
> Our prison is the whole society
> Cause we live in a land that'll bring all pressure
> to bear on the head of a woman whose
> position we share
> Tell me who is this Girl—
> and who is she to you?[41]

In an interview with historian Genna Rae McNeil two decades later, Reagon explained, "My position was [that] I wanted to get as close to her as I could so that anything you were saying about her you were saying about me. And I had this feeling that nobody was going to separate me . . . from this woman . . . in jail . . . or turn us into objects."[42] Reagon's lyrics recognize the ways that Little's body had become a site of social stigma and degradation; her violation was authorized by culture and custom; her resistance was not. The state attempted to take Little's life for killing her attacker and thus defying this sanctioned degradation of her body. Little was expected to endure and assent to this degradation, not resist it. In response, Reagon describes the "position we share" with Little, refusing the persistent pressures to disavow Little and the experiences of poor Black women in general. Reagon exhumes the relationships that many others have to Little ("my sister," "our mama," "your lover"), foregrounding the social and collective stakes of her resistance and of her freedom. Little's body was their body too. In claiming her in this way, they invoked a concept of autonomy that was not simply an individualized right to live free of coercion and violence but a collective condition.

By incorporating Little's struggle, words, and experiences in their mural in Chicano Park, the women of the RCAF similarly provoked the connections between the visions of autonomy, freedom, and defiance expressed by Little and the broad currents of political resistance and imagination led by Chicana and Indigenous women. The muralists, all in their early 20s, had been shaped not only by the nascent Chicano movement but also by a rising women-of-color feminism that transgressed and interrogated gender, race, class, and national borders. Rosalinda Palacios, the artist who proposed incorporating Little's image and words into the mural, had just returned from the 1975 World Conference on Women in Mexico City and had also become involved in the Free Angela Davis campaign a few years earlier. All three of the muralists had also recently spent time in Cuba with the Venceremos Brigade, founded in 1969 to promote political solidarity between Cuba and activists in the US.[43] Their capacity to see the connections between Little's struggle and their own and to represent those convergences in a space conceived for Chicano/a cultural autonomy and expression is rooted in the same relational conception of the body expressed by Reagon. Chicana liberation was linked to and dependent upon Little's freedom.

Indeed, the bodies depicted in *Women Hold Up Half the Sky* are expressive of Little's insistence that "in the end, I will have freedom." They are not objects of extraction or commodification. Their bodies and their labor—artistic, familial, social, and productive—are not the objects of violence or ownership. And in invoking and claiming Little, they invoke their capacity to act decisively to defend their bodies. Little explained that her incarceration and trial changed and emboldened her. "When I came out, I was like a bandit. I'm ready to strike back at any time."[44] Her case symbolized resistance against a social and political vision that marked some bodies as inherently degraded and thus available for violation. Through her actions and words Little summoned a different vision, in which the integrity and autonomy of the body must constantly be asserted, not only in the face of individual attacks but also before the public, forcing the state to acknowledge the integrity of Little's body and her capacity for freedom.

Protests inside and outside the North Carolina Correctional Center for Women (NCCW) in Raleigh, where Little had been held, linked Little's trial to broader patterns of state violence, including the degrading conditions inside the prison. Several weeks before the trial, 200 women in the NCCW led a spontaneous sit-in and strike, linking the violence represented by their incarceration to the state's effort to convict Little.[45]

A jury ultimately exonerated Little, in large part because the broad Free Joan Little movement that drew attention to the case and funneled significant resources to her defense unapologetically framed her resistance in collective, historical, and political terms, not just individual ones.

McNeil notes that Little "understood herself as more than her body, but never separate from it . . . She did not act as if she merely had a body; she acted in a manner that confirmed her consciousness of her well-being as inextricably bound not only to the safety and survival of the body, but also to her authority over it." Little articulated "a defense of her body as inseparable from the defense of her dignity as a person and value as an equal human being."[46] Little's decision to turn herself in, testify in court on her own behalf, and speak to a wider public about the integrity of her body and her capacity for freedom must all be understood as acts of self-defense. In public talks, Little linked her trial to the conditions of "all political prisoners."[47] The movement to free Joan Little as well as Little's narration of her right to self-defense was not just a confrontation of her attacker, a morality tale pitting Alligood against Little. It was instead a wider challenge to a set of political arrangements, cultural norms, and forms of authority that legitimated the attack in the first place, and the institutional violence that undergirded the incarceration of all women held at the NCCW.

The Little case invoked a longstanding vision of freedom, autonomy, and interdependence fashioned at the scene of Black women's defense of their bodies. A central component of civil rights and racial justice activism in the South after World War II focused on ending rape and sexual violence against Black women. Activists such as Rosa Parks understood this violence to be central to sustaining expansive regimes of segregation and domination.[48]

Indeed, resistance against sexual violence and reproductive control has been a central feature of Black women's political struggles since slavery. The legal scholar Dorothy Roberts explains, "Black women struggled in numerous ways to resist slave masters' efforts to control their reproductive lives. They escaped from plantations, feigned illness, endured severe punishment, and fought back rather than submit to slave masters' sexual domination."[49] Angela Davis describes the contradictory forces within slavery that situated Black women on the one hand as "equal" to men in the conditions of their servitude (an equally brutal oppression) but "unequal" in the gendered household and caregiving labor they performed away from the plantation. Black women struggled within the terms of this contradiction, recognizing that this domestic labor was one of the only activities that took place outside the direct oversight of planters, and that thus could become a source of resistance. From this position, they fought, sometimes with force (for example, poisoning food, setting fire to the house of the master), to dismantle a political, economic, and social order that used violence to regulate and extract sexual and reproductive labor from the body. Davis explains "without consciously rebellious black women the theme of resistance could not have become so thoroughly intertwined in the fabric of daily existence."[50] Facing "an intricate and savage web of oppression [that] intruded at every moment" during slavery, Black women refused, in endless scenes of individual self-defense and organized resistance, to accept the dominant account that their bodies were the property of others. Black women's struggles against particular forms of race, gender, and class exploitation served as the basis for resistance against the entirety of what Davis describes as the broad struggle against "the dehumanizing exploitation of a wrongly organized society."[51]

Little's trial and exoneration inspired campaigns in support of other women of color who killed their attackers in self-defense, including Inez García in California, Yvonne Wanrow in Washington state, and Dessie Woods in Georgia. At a time when many white middle-class feminist organizations increasingly framed violence against women in terms of gender domination alone, often appealing to the criminal justice system to punish individual offenders, these campaigns shaped the political consciousness of the participants in explicitly intersectional terms, demonstrating the ways that gender and sexual violence relied upon structures of race and class control.[52] Thus, organizations like the DC Rape Crisis Center (RCC) placed their anti-violence work in far more structural and political terms. As Loretta Ross, a one-time director of RCC, told Thuma, "We always intentionally lifted these cases of women of color who lived at the intersection of violence against women and the criminal justice system."[53]

The organizing around these trials, like Joan Little's, helped participants and the wider public understand the relationship between individual acts of violence and domination and broader, institutionalized structures of power. And in framing these acts of self-defense as an assertion of the autonomy and integrity of a collective body, they advanced an analysis that resonates deeply in contemporary movements against state violence and carceral control. For example, recent campaigns such as #SayHerName, led by Kimberlé Williams Crenshaw and the African American Policy Forum, which emphasize the impact of prisons, policing, school discipline practices, and other forms of state violence on Black women and girls, including those who are transgender and gender non-conforming, build directly on these traditions and practices. Their demands, including an end to no-knock warrants, requiring law enforcement to respect gender identity and expression in their interactions with the public, and reallocating police budgets to human and social services, emerge from the specific experiences of Black women and girls, but have implications and benefits that provide greater freedom to many people.[54]

LOS ANGELES: TAKING CONTROL OF THE BODY

In early June 1978, 23-year-old Consuelo Hermosillo boarded a city bus from her modest home in East Los Angeles toward downtown. She left her three young children in the care of her neighbors, telling them she had found a cleaning job in a restaurant. But unbeknownst to her neighbors, her family, and her husband Oscar, Hermosillo was actually traveling to the federal courthouse to testify as one of ten plaintiffs in a class action case known as *Madrigal v. Quilligan*. Hermosillo was one of several hundred women from the late 1960s to the mid-1970s admitted to Los

Angeles County/USC Medical Center (LACMC) to deliver a child who left the hospital sterilized. The physicians at LACMC, one of the busiest public hospitals in the nation, insisted that they had obtained the consent of their patients to perform the procedure, known as a tubal ligation. The lawsuit contended, however, that many of the women—primarily poor and working-class Mexicanas—were either coerced into the procedure or never consented to it; some did not even realize they had been sterilized until months after the procedure. As Hermosillo would testify at the trial, the doctor told her as she was going into emergency labor: "Lady, the limit for cesarean are three by law. So you have to decide whether you want to risk the next one, because I think the next one you can die." Hermosillo asserted that she had no recollection of consenting to the procedure, and only learned she had been sterilized a few days later when she asked the doctor about her options for birth control.[55]

The hundreds of elective hysterectomies and tubal ligations performed at LACMC during the late 1960s and early 1970s unfolded in the context of a rising "population control" movement that invoked a looming plane-tary crisis of overpopulation that could only be prevented by dramatically reducing the birth rate. In practice, restrictions on reproduction focused mostly on poor women and women of color. A medical technician at LACMC testified that Dr. James Quilligan, the head of obstetrics and gynecology at the hospital and one of the defendants in the case, told her privately that "poor minority women in L.A. County were having too many babies; that it was a strain on society; and that it was good to be sterilized." He also told her that a recent federal grant to the hospital would be used to demonstrate, in his words, "how low we can cut the birth rate of the Negro and Mexican populations in Los Angeles County."[56]

Hermosillo never told her husband, family, or friends about her sterili-zation; the shame was too great to bear. Like many women at the time, she was unaware that the procedure had been performed on hundreds of other women at the same hospital, and she felt as though she was respon-sible for what had happened. But when Antonia Hernandez, a young Chicana lawyer working with the Los Angeles Center for Law and Justice, asked her to join a lawsuit against the hospital seeking to end the practices and to institute protections against involuntary sterilization, Hermosillo agreed. Without telling her family, she boarded the bus each day for the federal courthouse downtown during the trial. She did not know any of the other nine co-plaintiffs in the case. While they were also working-class Mexicanas, each of their stories and lives was distinct. Nor did she know any of the hundreds of other women who had been sterilized at LACMC during the last 10 years but who never joined the lawsuit. She had nothing to gain personally by testifying. But Hermosillo did not need to know these women to know that their bodies were not meant to be violated in this way. She explained later in an interview that she decided to testify because she did not want what happened to her to happen to anyone else.[57] If Blumenbach in the eighteenth century operated from the premise that large groups of people whom he had never met were naturally ordained for degradation, Hermosillo worked from the negation of that assumption. In getting on the bus, and speaking for the interests and safety of women she would never meet, she asserted, like Du Bois, that no one should be regarded as eternally degraded.

The decision of Hermosillo and other women to join the suit came amid a rising tide of grassroots organizing in Los Angeles which asserted that the health and safety of Chicana women's bodies was central to a universal realization of social justice. These groups, including the Committee to Stop Forced Sterilization and Comisión Femenil Mexicana Nacional, connected the wave of sterilizations at LACMC to a broad analysis of class, gender, race, and nation.[58] In a widely distributed bilingual pamphlet titled "Stop Forced Sterilization Now!" the Committee explained that "the US population control movement has its roots in racism," noting that the same coercive practices targeting women in East Los Angeles had also been used with Black women in the South, women in Puerto Rico, Native women on reservations, and women in Latin America. They linked the practices not only to the eugenic commitments of individual doctors but also to an upsurge in federal funding for sterilization procedures and millions of dollars in funding for population control initiatives from private foundations, including the Rockefeller Foundation.

They demanded that hospitals institutionalize a broad range of patient protections to end the practice of coercive sterilization, a claim rooted in a wider vision of freedom: "We believe women have the right to decide how many, if any, children we will have . . . We want to live in a world where all human life is valued, and we have real power to control our lives. For

Committee to Stop Forced Sterilization protest in Los Angeles, 1974. Credit: *Los Angeles Times* staff. Copyright 1974. Used with permission.

women to truly be free there must be enough food, proper health care, jobs, good schools, and childcare centers for everyone." Activists and legal advocates observed that the growth in coercive sterilizations targeting women of color unfolded at the same time that many white middle-class women had secured newfound rights to abortion and birth control as a matter of a right to privacy. But as attorney Antonia Hernandez argued, "The right to be free from a physical intrusion into the body is as fundamental a part of the right to privacy as the decision whether or not to beget children."[59] Women-of-color activists viewed reproductive freedom in a much broader form than the dominant (white) women's movement. They noted that exercising individual choice and freedoms was always dependent on the political, economic, and social contexts in which such decisions were made.[60]

Activists argued that winning these freedoms and rights for all women required a direction confrontation with the racism that legitimated coercive sterilizations. The Committee to Stop Forced Sterilizations explained: "The racism of the sterilizations goes further than who is actually sterilized. White workers are told that the reason taxes take so much out of their salaries is because they are supporting all those non-white people and their kids on welfare. Minority people are told that the reason they are poor is not because of job and education discrimination but because they have too many children. This helps direct the anger of these people towards poor people or towards themselves instead of against the corporations and the government of the rich."[61]

Other organizing efforts against sterilization abuse led by women of color similarly linked particular patterns of coercive sterilizations to wider histories, structures, and visions of freedom. For example, the Women of all Red Nations (WARN) estimated that by the 1970s, more than 40 percent of American Indian women of childbearing age had been sterilized by the Indian Health Services.[62] WARN linked these practices to an extensive history of genocidal policies toward Indigenous people. Native activists, like their Chicana counterparts, understood the wave of sterilizations in gendered, racial, and materialist terms, explaining that "the issue is more than one of the denial of women's rights or one of mindless racism. The economic motivations behind the push for sterilization are becoming increasingly clear: they are part of an attempt to secure the world's resources for the already privileged capitalist class."[63]

Black women in the South organized for many years against involuntary or coercive sterilizations and hysterectomies. In a public speech in Washington in 1964, Fannie Lou Hamer, the famed leader of the Mississippi Freedom Democratic Party, explained that she had been the victim of such a procedure three years earlier after being admitted to Sunflower City Hospital to have a small uterine tumor removed. The physician performed a complete hysterectomy without her consent or knowledge; Hammer estimated that 60 percent of the Black women in Sunflower County had been subject to nonconsensual postpartum sterilizations at the hospital, colloquially described as "Mississippi Appendectomies."[64]

Dorothy Roberts situates the many thousands of involuntary sterilizations in the South during this period within a longer history of treating Black reproduction as a form of "degeneracy"—the public regulation and violation of those bodies deemed to have no productive future. Similar allegations of degeneracy haunt other forms of social policy, such as the arrest of women accused of using drugs during pregnancy or the reduction of welfare benefits to women who choose to have more than one child.

She notes that "a persistent objective of American social policy has been to monitor and restrain this corrupting tendency of Black motherhood."[65]

Thus, the contemporary reproductive justice movement, anchored by groups such as the Atlanta-based Sister-Song Reproductive Health Collective, has continuously challenged the individualistic, choice-based framework that dominates much of the liberal discourse around reproductive rights, a framework that abstracts reproductive issues from the material structures of race, gender, sexuality, and economic distribution. For reproductive justice organizers like Loretta Ross, "prisoners' rights, infant mortality rates, sterilization abuse, and other medical abuses all constituted significant issues to address within a feminist reproductive rights politics."[66] Rather than foregrounding abstract rights, they have organized instead for a vision of "reproductive justice" that would be realized "when women and girls have the economic, social and political power and resources to make healthy decisions about our bodies, sexuality and reproduction for ourselves, our families and our communities in all areas of our lives."[67] They advanced a proactive vision of health and bodily autonomy tied to universal conditions of freedom.

The benefits and rights at stake in the *Madrigal* case extended from the particular conditions shaping the lives of women like Consuelo Hermosillo and her co-plaintiffs. But the freedoms they secured protect us all. Rulings that provide for language access for health care, prevent the state from using welfare benefits to coerce patient decisions, stipulate the rights of patients within health-care institutions, and provide additional counseling and resources to people facing reproductive decisions benefit many people. At stake in their struggle is the contention that everyone possesses the authority, wisdom, and judgment to make decisions about their reproductive lives, and that the ability to make those decisions must be premised on access to health care, social services, and other resources that should be democratically managed.

CODA: THE MYTH OF INDEPENDENCE

The fatal coupling of power and difference that constitutes race must be continuously reproduced, and thus bodies must be continually violated.

The logic of eternal degradation has required bodies to be lynched, raped, sterilized, incarcerated, and eliminated. The scheme must always be renewed. But at the scene of these violations—amid the memorials and eulogies, the protests and proclamations, the dissections and stratagems— new accounts of the body have flourished. These dissident imaginaries have stressed the relations of autonomy and interdependence in which all bodies are embedded. They have inventoried the multiple structures of power—within the family and the economy, culture and society—that determine the body's status and possibilities. And in everyday acts, from getting on the bus to honoring the death of a stranger, they have imagined wider types of freedom.

These insights and imaginaries—about care, interdependence, and collective autonomy—have become even more urgent in the wake of the Covid-19 pandemic and the failures it has exposed in a health-care system organized around individual rather than public and collective health and caregiving. These failures are rooted in what the disability justice writer and organizer Mia Mingus describes as the "myth of independence . . . that somehow we can and should be able to do everything on our own without any help from anyone." Everyone is reliant on others, and those who disavow those dependencies also disavow the oppression and exploitation that sustains the fiction of their autonomy. Mingus writes that as a "as a disabled person, I am *dependent* on other people in order to survive in this ableist society; I am *interdependent* in order to shift and queer ableism into something that can be kneaded, molded and added to the many tools we will need to transform the world." The efforts outlined in this chapter share Mingus's rejection of the myth of independence in favor of "community and movements that are collectively interdependent."[68]

2 Democracy and Governance

In 1919, as Europe sought to reconstruct a future after the Great War and colonial polities in Africa, Asia, and the Caribbean began pressing for their independence, W. E. B. Du Bois contemplated a new vision of governance. "Democracy," he wrote, "is a method of doing the impossible. It is the only method yet discovered of making the education and development of all men a matter of all men's desperate desire."[1]

Du Bois was not simply calling for "first class citizenship" for Black people and other colonized groups within prevailing systems of power. He knew that this formulation—that the education and growth of all of humanity was a matter of everyone's *desperate desire*—had never been realized in practice. Indeed, it was the very absence of such methods that turned humans into commodities and led nations into catastrophic acts of war. In the US, from the earliest days of colonial settlement, the dominant traditions of governance have been preoccupied with a different set of questions: Who must be excluded for the republic to flourish? Who lacks the fitness for individual citizenship? What forms of violence and appropriation are necessary to sustain the nation?[2]

The modes of governance and rule produced in answer to these questions were necessarily based on violence, loss, and degradation. To access the rights and bounties of citizenship within this framework required one to be an accomplice to such violence; to renounce obligations to others. And yet in spite of these traditions and legacies, and even in a moment of intense racial domination—Du Bois could still imagine a method of doing "the impossible." As he would write 16 years later in *Black Reconstruction*, "My rise does not involve your fall. No superior has interest in inferiority."[3]

This chapter examines conceptions of governance, episodes of collective leadership, and sites of mutual development that reject such an "interest in inferiority"—what has arguably been a grounding principle of US state-making. Rather than setting out to determine who must be violated for the polity to exist, these efforts pose different questions: What might be possible when we educate and develop the potential of everyone that surrounds us? What richer freedoms might such collective action allow us to imagine? How might the methods and responsibilities of governance be the province of all people?

In these traditions, governance represents far more than the administration of the state or the distribution of authority among the branches of government. It concerns more than the ways popular consent is secured through elections, political parties, and the delegation of leadership and representation to others. It instead encompasses a wide range of social activity and meaning: the forging of relationships through which people become invested in one another's lives; the creation of spaces for deliberation, consciousness, and imagination; the collective abolition of structures premised on disposability and domination; the reconstruction of new modes of authority, accountability, and power.[4]

"CAUCASIAN DEMOCRACY"

The dominant model of liberal anti-racism in the US asserts that the nation has been historically marked by tiers of citizenship and social standing, a political order that one scholar has described as "democratic for the master race but tyrannical for subordinate groups."[5] From this perspective, subordinated groups—African Americans during Jim Crow, Japanese Americans during World War II internment, undocumented immigrants today—primarily seek access to the so-called "first-class citizenship" that they have been denied and which white people enjoy.

This account is helpful in demonstrating that US citizenship and rights are not universal, but are instead wedded to race, class, and gender inequalities. But this framework misses the ways that this mythologized "first-class citizenship" is itself marked by a set of specific features, including a degraded understanding of popular governance, a predisposition toward private wealth accumulation, and a nearly uninterrupted practice of violence and dispossession. Angela Davis cautioned that repressive state institutions can "become strengthened by the admission of those who were previously barred" when their fundamental terms remain unchanged.[6] There is nothing "first class" about such an order, and an important tradition of anti-racist thought and action has insisted that seeking incorporation into its logics and privileges or demanding a "fair share" of its bounties signifies a great danger, for the rights it grants to some are always tethered to a denial of life for others.

Davis was describing a history and mode of governance that can be described as "Caucasian democracy."[7] As explored in chapter 1, the term "Caucasian," introduced by a skull-collecting Austrian anthropologist in the late eighteenth century, does not refer to any established social group. It has no use to describe patterns of human variation by geography, ancestry, or physiology, and neither science nor the law has ever been able to devise an objective definition or criterion to delineate membership within this phantasmic category.[8]

Socially and historically, "Caucasian" only takes meaning through the exercise of social domination. "Caucasian democracy" thus references an approach to governance that takes human hierarchy, the accumulation of profit, and the unequal distribution of life and death as core premises, centered on three pillars.

The first pillar of Caucasian democracy rests on the sanctity and inviolability of private property and accumulation as ordering principles of governance. This is a pillar that is hidden in plain sight, evident in the overwhelming representation of enslavers and land speculators among the Founding Fathers, the property-owning requirements initially attached to voting rights, the predominance of trade, commerce, and property protections within the Constitution, and the historic antagonism toward taxing any accumulation of private wealth (outside of a 40-year window in the mid-twentieth century).[9] In contemporary contexts, it is witnessed in the preeminence of property taxes and "homeowner politics" as the central issues in many local elections, and in the geographic boundaries that separate suburbs from cities and carve out special business districts to sequester tax revenue. The present-day legal recognition of "corporate personhood" and the permeation of money in every realm of electoral politics and governance represents the culmination of this tradition. To be landless and without property in this system of governance is to already be disenfranchised, even with the right to vote.

The second pillar of Caucasian democracy is violence, and its indispensability to the granting of freedom and rights. The United States was founded on a late eighteenth-century governing charter that legal scholars have described as the "savage constitution" because so many of its provisions and principles reflect the exigencies of settler expansion and the legal and political indemnification of slaveholders.[10] The Second Amendment itself, and the rights of settlers to bear arms, cannot be understood outside this context.[11] Many of the late eighteenth- and early nineteenth-century court decisions around federalism and states' rights reflected compromises over these priorities. A host of legal concepts that maintain their authority today, from the principles of the "doctrine of discovery," which justified the appropriation of Indigenous lands, to the 1901 Insular Cases, which circumscribe the autonomy of "unincorporated territories" such as Puerto Rico, legitimate acts of violence as foundational to US governance. The largest and most visible forms of state-building today—the colossal footprint of the armed forces, the unrivaled infrastructure of prisons, jails, and law enforcement units, the militarization of migration regulation—demonstrate the ways that violence and governance are deeply intertwined.[12]

The third pillar of Caucasian democracy is the conviction that capacities for self-government are limited rather than universal, and that a key task of statecraft is to identify and exclude people who are unfit for democracy. This conviction shapes the legal jurisprudence known as Indian Law, which continues to delimit Indigenous people's sovereignty.[13] It is made plain in a long history of immigration politics and law, beginning with the 1790 Immigration and Naturalization Act, which limited naturalization to "free white persons" and inaugurated a 162-year history of centering immigration law on race, gender, and national exclusions. It is evident in an extensive series of restrictions on voting rights, in which the categorical prohibition of large sections of the populace from voting has been framed as a necessary precondition for democratic rule. It is a principle that legitimates the many contemporary restrictions on suffrage today, such as using voter identification requirements and criminal convictions to restrict voter eligibility. These investments in elite governing authority diminish opportunities for self-governance even for those eligible to vote. Voter turnout today is anemic; in many elections, a majority of eligible voters choose not to participate. Indeed, the very notion that democratic self-governance is realized primarily by casting a vote every two to four years represents a deeply cynical understanding of popular sovereignty and a conviction that everyday people do not have a meaningful role to play in governance. As Angela Davis writes, "When democracy is reduced to the simple fact of elections . . . whatever we might consider to be freedom has disappeared."[14]

Thus, an important genealogy of anti-racist struggles and political formations has contended that a full realization of sovereignty, collective freedom, and democratic self-governance cannot be realized within the framework of Caucasian democracy. These traditions have contested the dominant concepts and structures of liberal governance in the US and its most treasured practices—representation, voting, citizenship, individuated rights, and the nation-state itself—not on the grounds that they are not inclusive enough or have been distorted by elite or partisan interests, but that they are part of a system that remains hostile to democratic engagement more broadly. They have failed both for the people excluded from those arrangements and for many included in them as well. Caucasian democracy has also impaired many people who think of themselves as Caucasian.

Rather than seeking inclusion into these prevailing systems of representation and leadership, movements in the tradition of Du Bois have invoked other practices, concepts, and structures of governance. They have foregrounded the complex relationships and interdependences—both human and nonhuman—that undergird every polity. They have embraced the dynamics of migration, mobility, and movement that are central to social life rather than fetishizing stagnant definitions of citizenship and belonging. They have taken up broad-based and dynamic under-

standings of kinship and care rather than seeking to reproducing patriarchal structures of authority and power. They have developed models of
collective and group-centered leadership rooted in an understanding that
capacities for self-governance are widely distributed, and that the private
interests of property and accumulation deserve no sanctified place in the
governing order. Mutual obligation and shared public commitments, they
insist, are far more robust underpinnings of governance than violence,
appropriation, and death.

Among the many theorists and practitioners of Caucasian democracy,
Thomas Jefferson might be the most esteemed. Jefferson, who penned the
magistral phrase "All men are created equal" as he bought, sold, and enslaved
other humans, including his own children. Jefferson, who wrote with schol-
arly detachment about his perceptions of Black inferiority, even as he relied
on Black plantation labor, as well as Black sexual and intimate labor, to
afford him the life of a statesman and patriarch. Jefferson, who made the US
signatory to dozens of treaties with sovereign Native nations while devising
methods to draw Native peoples into debt so that they would cede their
lands to speculators. Jefferson, who endorsed a set of governing arrangements and structures—the Senate, the electoral college, the Supreme
Court—rooted in elite authority and skepticism of popular sovereignty.[15]

The sections that follow chart various reimaginings of the nature and
sources of rights and freedoms—and the creation of different modes of
democratic governance through transformed relationships to wealth,
property, and land; a rejection of violence and exclusion; and models of
participation that seek to develop collective knowledge and abilities.
Rather than being bestowed by the state, or restricted to activities such as
voting, these rights and freedoms are cultivated as ongoing, communal
practices. For exemplars, we must look far from Jefferson's plantation in
Monticello, turning instead to figures rarely mentioned in histories of US
governance and democracy. Figures like Ella Baker.

A FREEDOM OF THE HUMAN SPIRIT

Eight hundred and fifty miles from Jefferson's Virginia estate lies
Hattiesburg, the seat of Forrest County, Mississippi. In 1960, County

Registrar Theron Lynd, a faithful practitioner of Caucasian democracy, insisted that in his jurisdiction, capacities for self-governance were limited. Sixty thousand people lived in the county; one-third were Black. Lynd used a combination of poll taxes, literary tests, and other devices, such as requiring applicants to interpret portions of the 285 sections of the Mississippi state constitution, to prevent nearly every Black person in the county from registering to vote.[16] Even in the face of a federal suit by the US Justice Department, Lynd remained defiant.

In the spring of 1962, organizers with the fledgling Student Nonviolent Coordinating Committee (SNCC) began a slow and methodical practice of outreach, relationship building, and meetings among local Black residents, including many sharecroppers and agricultural workers, summoning a practice of democracy quite distinct from Lynd's. A year later, working with civil rights groups from across Mississippi, they organized a mock election known as the Freedom Ballot, establishing polling sites in churches, stores, and barber shops around the state; nearly 80,000 black Mississippians statewide cast a vote. Lynd refused to relent.

SNCC declared that January 22, 1964, would be Freedom Day in Hattiesburg. Hundreds of local residents would converge on the courthouse to demand they be registered to vote.[17] A much broader and more transformative model of democratic participation emerges from these efforts—reaching far beyond the issue of voting, to fostering practices of education, knowledge-making, and community development that were themselves forms of collective self-governance. The evening before, there was a mass meeting at a Hattiesburg church, "with every seat filled, every aisle packed, the doorways jammed [with] . . . a thousand people, massed tight in blackness."[18] The crowd rose to its feet to sing freedom songs, and eventually, 61-year-old Ella Baker moved to the podium. With more than three decades of organizing and movement building experience, Baker was deeply respected by the throngs of local people, student organizers, and faith and civil rights leaders assembled in the sanctuary.

Baker began by noting that some civil rights leaders had recently claimed that "the final stages of the freedom struggle" had arrived, implying that once the right to vote had been secured and segregation had been outlawed, freedom would be realized. Baker disagreed. She insisted, "Even tomorrow if every vestige of racial discrimination were wiped out, if all of us became

Ella Baker addressing Mississippi Freedom Democratic Party during 1964
Democratic Convention in Atlantic City. Credit: George Ballis/Take Stock/TopFoto.

free enough to go down and to associate with all the people we wanted to
associate, we still are not free." The freedom struggle was "just at the beginning." Her brief speech, derived from the long record of organizing and leadership development, illuminated three principles of democracy and governance that exceed any of the ideals enshrined at the nation's founding.[19]

First, Baker insisted that the freedom at stake in the Hattiesburg voter
registration drive was inseparable from the material conditions necessary
for social life—food, land, work—and their collective and democratic control. Voting rights alone would not address the "millions of people who go
to bed hungry every night." She insisted, "People cannot be free until there
is enough work in the land to give everybody a job."

Baker was not simply describing the right and capacity to be an individual consumer. As she wrote several years earlier, the burgeoning student
movement that led to SNCC's formation was predicated on "something
much bigger than a hamburger or even a giant-sized Coke."[20] Here, Baker

drew on commitments nurtured since her childhood in the early 1900s in North Carolina. As her biographer Barbara Ransby explains, Baker "spoke fondly of a time when mutual obligations and shared resources were the ties that bound small southern black communities together."[21] In the late 1920s, after graduating as valedictorian from Shaw University in North Carolina, Baker moved to New York City, where she immersed herself in a milieu of socialists, labor educators, anarchists, economic cooperatives, and consumer educators that linked material redistribution to governance. She soon cofounded the Young Negroes' Cooperative League (YNCL) to organize consumer buying clubs and cooperatives led by young people. As explained by one writer at the time, these small-scale cooperative buying enterprises sought to "obtain full control of the supply and distribution of the necessities of life, thereby eliminating the profit motive from trade." The ultimate aim of consumer cooperation was "revolutionary" as it sought to "create a better social structure by making unnecessary the present form of government which is operated by and for the privileged class."[22]

Baker's work with the co-ops, domestic workers, consumer education programs, and labor unions convinced her that freedom meant developing these collective and cooperative capacities to govern the material dimensions of one's life. Voting rights, she insisted to the Hattiesburg crowd, could not be separated from these conditions.

Second, Baker asserted a practice of democracy rooted in the opportunity for everyday people to collectively govern their lives. Leadership was not the provenance of exceptional individuals who would secure the consent of the governed, but a group-based practice that developed political consciousness and analysis. Such consciousness provided the intellectual and political conditions necessary for democracy to flourish and take root. Vincent Harding would later explain this notion of governance: "Human beings are meant to be developmental beings; . . . we find our best identity and purpose when we are developing ourselves and helping to develop our surroundings." Harding asserted that this was the very meaning of democracy and of Baker's work, "encouraging the capacities that are in us all. To create living space, breathing space, acting space, growing space, for each other." It was, he explained, about "much more than voting."[23]

Baker's model of group-centered leadership was developed across many decades of training, supporting, and developing thousands of everyday people in the methods and practices of collective governance, analysis, and organization. It stood in stark contrast to the dominant mode of "charismatic leadership" practiced by groups like the Southern Christian Leadership Conference (SCLC), the alliance of ministers that helped launch Dr. King into national prominence in the early 1960s. Though Baker spent several years helping to organize and launch the SCLC, she remained deeply skeptical of models of leadership that tended to locate, in Erica Edwards's explanation, the "authority or the right to rule in one exceptional figure perceived to be gifted with a privileged connection to the divine."[24] In this way, they largely reproduced the dominant model of elite leadership, which distrusted the capacities of everyday people to lead.

In another interview, Baker counseled that it was a "handicap for oppressed peoples to depend so largely upon a leader, because unfortunately to our culture, the charismatic leader usually becomes a leader because he has found a spot in the public limelight." Such leaders also came to believe that they were "the movement" and thus spent far too little time doing the "work of actually organizing people."[25]

By contrast, Baker had spent dozens of years helping to build small organizations across the South, identifying and recruiting local people to identify the issues that shaped their lives. She embraced models such as the "citizenship schools" activated across the South in the 1950s, which held that democratic participation and governance could not be secured through voter registration alone. New voters would have to think, teach, and learn about what governance meant to them and their communities. These popular education programs marshaled the talents and experiences of Black teachers (mostly Black women) to educate and engage adult learners in this context. They implicitly rejected the dominant models of leadership, in which an exceptional person who allegedly bears unique skills and capacities is elevated and empowered to act on behalf of others in the administration of the state. In this way, their conception of governance bore a strong resemblance to the forms of Athenian democracy described by C. L. R. James in a 1956 article aptly titled "Every Cook Can Govern," which emphasized the role everyday people could play in collective governance.[26]

For Baker, mass meetings like the ones held in Hattiesburg were important, and marches and singing freedom songs were necessary, but they were not sufficient. Indeed, there was a danger in believing that the spectacle of the protest stood in for the more arduous work of collective development. "Certainly we must sing, we must have the inspiration of song, the inspiration that comes from songs . . . but we also must have the information that comes from lots and lots of study." Referencing SNCC's plan to open dozens of Freedom Schools across Mississippi that summer founded in a new curriculum that explored politics, art, history, and culture, she explained, "We are going to have to have these freedom schools and we are going to have to learn a lot of things in them. We are going to have to be concerned about the kinds of education our children are getting in school."[27]

As Baker would explain, in this model, "instead of a leader as a person who was supposed to be a magic man, you could develop individuals who were bound together by a concept that benefitted the larger number of individuals and provided an opportunity for them to grow into being responsible for carrying out a program." These were not, as Ransby counseled, "leaderless" formations. They were better understood as "leaderful" groups in which the capacity to facilitate the development of others became most important. Baker held that she "always thought what is needed is the development of people who are interested not in being leaders as much as in developing leadership among other people."[28] As she would later explain, "I just don't see anything to be substituted for having people understand their position and understand their potential power and how to use it. This can only be done, as I see it, through the long route, almost, of actually organizing people in small groups and parlaying those into larger groups."[29]

Finally, Baker made clear that Black people struggling for the right to vote were not simply trying to obtain an exalted freedom already realized by white Americans, but to develop and proliferate methods and practices based on new values, relationships, and possibilities. It was "the cause of humanity" that was at stake on Freedom Day, with a focus on "a larger freedom that encompasses all mankind." Beyond rights to vote, eat, and work, Baker urged her audience to contemplate what she described as "the drive of the human spirit for freedom." She explained: "We aren't free until within us we have that deep sense of freedom from a lot of things that we don't even mention in these meetings." This was a process that had to be done collectively and that existed outside the assignment of rights or recognition by the state. As she told the congregation at Hattiesburg, "The only group that can make you free is yourself . . . we must free ourselves."

She stressed also that white Mississippians, who had long been "fooled" by the "big lie" that their freedom was dependent on the violation of Black life, were not free. The Hattiesburg struggle, which was led by local Black people and guided by their experience, study, and collective analysis, concerned the right for everyone "to grow and to develop to the fullest capacity." For Baker, even the "white brothers in Hattiesburg" could not realize their full capacity as humans, or "the human spirit for freedom," through a system premised on violence and terror. "People cannot be free until they realize that peace . . . is not the absence of war or struggle, but the presence of justice." She charged the crowd to take seriously this historic imperative, concluding this speech in this way: "And so all of us stand guilty at this moment for having waited so long to lend ourselves to a fight for the freedom, not of Negroes, not of the Negroes of Mississippi, but for the freedom of the American spirit, for the freedom of the human spirit."[30]

Radical social visions associated with the 1960s are often linked with largely white groups like Students for a Democratic Society (SDS) or formations led by men of color, such as the Black Panthers and Brown Berets. Yet it was Baker, and other Black women like Septima Clark, Gwen Patton, Rosa Parks, Fannie Lou Hamer, Bernice Johnson Reagon, and Jo Ann Robinson, among many others, who developed a democratic practice committed to what Baker described as the "radical terms" of social change, or "getting down to and understanding the root cause . . . [of] a system that does not lend itself to your needs and devising means by which to change that system."[31]

These models of group-centered leadership, popular consciousness-raising, and direct action engaged by Hammer and others have endured in many formations. In the South, groups like the Highlander Center, Project South, Kentuckians for the Commonwealth, and Southerners on New Ground have trained tens thousands of people in such traditions and practices. Many of these traditions have evolved from specific Black political formations and conditions, and what the theorist Cedric Robinson has termed the "Black radical tradition." But Baker and many others also made clear that these practices and theories of democratic governance were far more universal in their application and bearing. Black people did not deserve Caucasian democracy, but neither did anyone else, including those who imagined themselves to be Caucasian.[32]

Their work compels us to reimagine democratic governance as not simply seeking a seat at the table or securing rights of participation, but of enacting methods of making every person's development a matter of every person's desperate desire. Concerns of mutual care and development, and the production of knowledge in service of these goals, are not limited to social relationships, however. They extend directly into the realm of human interactions with the nonhuman world with equally transformative potential, as the following section shows.

MNI WIZIPAN WAKAN

On a spring morning in 2019, on the treaty lands of the Yankton Sioux tribe in southeastern South Dakota, tribal members walked to the bank of the Missouri River to collect water samples and survey the basin for medicinal plants. They too were practicing a form of governance, one that integrated Indigenous spiritual practices, Western science, and longstanding relations with the land and the water, through a project titled Mni Wizipan Wakan ("sacred bundle"). They are part of a broad resurgence across the country among diverse Indigenous nations that has set out to repair and regenerate webs of kinship, relationally, and cogovernance between humans, nonhuman animals, water, air, and land. These practices stand in sharp contrast to the ways that "the environment" is conceptualized within Caucasian democracy as an entity that is external to human life and as "natural resources" that can be converted into inputs for production. They exercise forms of sovereignty that are rooted in care for and connection with the land, rather than in its possession, and forms of knowledge-making that uncouple expertise from structures of domination.

The longest river in the United States, the Missouri runs through the ceded and unceded treaty lands of the Yankton Sioux and the six other tribes of the Oceti Sakowin (Great Sioux Nation), and also provides drinking water for millions of people in its basin. The river today is formally managed by an array of federal agencies, including the US Bureau of Land Management, the US Environmental Protection Agency (EPA), and the

US Army Corps of Engineers, which was responsible for erecting several colossal dams on the upper region of the river beginning in the 1940s, causing catastrophic flooding of hundreds of thousands of acres of Oceti Sakowin treaty lands. These dams, reservoirs, and irrigation systems severely degraded the water quality and floodplain habitats, and severed the complex and interdependent relationships that the Yankton and other Oceti Sakowin had developed with the river and its ecosystem. Catastrophic floods continue to threaten towns on the Yankton reservation, destroying roads and damaging homes.[33]

Judith LeBlanc, a member of the Caddo tribe of Oklahoma and an organizer with Native Organizers Alliance (NOA), explains that Mni Wizipan Wakan was an outgrowth of the assertion of tribal elders "to regain the moral, inherent and legal right to co-manage the Missouri River's hydroscape and bioregion" in accordance with traditional values and teaching. In addition to collecting water samples and surveying medicinal plants in the region, members work with their tribal governments to establish water codes and emergency water management protocols that are far more stringent than those of the EPA. They have set out to build a database of social, natural, geographic, and scientific information and maps rooted in both Western science and Indigenous practices and knowledge, including ceremonial and spiritual practices grounded in the Yankton Sioux's historic role as caretakers of the river.[34]

Regular water talks by the river bring together tribal governments, tribal scientists and researchers, and non-Native people including local ranchers and farmers, combining ceremony with public education discussions about the roles that tribes are playing in restoring the river. Leadership trainings facilitated by NOA, like those led by Ella Baker, emphasize the roles that everyday members of the tribes can play in generating knowledge about the conditions they face and inhabit, contesting the notion that scientific and technical research capacities are the domains of elites alone. Yet the project also asserts that Western scientific research models are insufficient to ensure proper relations between human and nonhuman entities, including the water, birds, fish, and land. The integration of groups like the Brave Heart Society, a traditional society of grandmothers that was revived in the mid-1990s on the Yankton reservation, sustain and transmit intergenerational knowledge and practices about maintaining such relations. LeBlanc says that collectively, the project seeks "new emerging forms of governance that go beyond the outmoded forms of federal management that prioritizes corporate plunder of Mother Earth."[35]

Ultimately, the project builds the capacity of tribal members and tribal governments to engage in what Nishnaabeg writer and artist Leanne Simpson describes elsewhere as "process-centered modes of living that generate profoundly different conceptualizations of nationhood and governmentality—ones that aren't based on enclosure, authoritarian power, and hierarchy." Simpson explains that within Nishnaabeg intelligence systems, "governance was made every day. Leadership was embodied and acted out every day . . . Daily life involved making politics, education, health care, food systems, and economy on micro- and macro-scales." Central to this process of *governance as making* are forms of reciprocal recognition, the capacity to see "another being's core essence." Simpson holds that such recognition "cognitively reverses the violence of dispossession because what's the opposite of dispossession in Indigenous thought again? Not possession, because we're not supposed to be capitalists, but connection, a coded layering of intimate interconnection and interdependence that creates a complicated algorithmic network of presence, reciprocity, consent and freedom."[36]

LeBlanc explains that the project is grounded in the historic treaty rights of the Oceti Sakowin nations, especially the Fort Laramie Treaty of 1868, which bound the federal government to recognize the sovereignty and collective land rights in the Black Hills of the Dakotas. These treaty rights, though regularly violated by the US government, still provide the legal foundation for tribal governments and nations to assert their sovereign authority to co-manage the river and its ecosystem. But LeBlanc insists that "tribal sovereignty will never be achieved individually, tribe by tribe" within the prevailing economic and political system of the United States. The sovereignty and treaty rights of tribal nations are sites of power and collective regeneration through which wider transformations of governance and power can be won, transformations that can also serve to liberate non-Native people from the destructive practices that threaten their lives as well.[37]

These dynamics are clearest in the broad intertribal formations that have emerged in the last decade to block the development of massive fossil fuel projects in the upper Midwest such as the Keystone and Dakota Access pipelines. Both projects threatened Oceti Sakowin lands and people, and the assertion of their treaty rights were central to the efforts to block their development. Yet the pipelines, like the large-scale dam projects of the twentieth century, also threatened the environment, health, and well-being of non-Native people, including many white farmers and ranchers.[38]

As Nick Estes, a citizen of the Lower Brule Sioux tribe, demonstrates in *Our History Is the Future,* at stake in the water protector's struggle against the Dakota Access Pipeline was a vision of freedom premised on "the amplified presence of Indigenous life and just relations with human and nonhuman relatives, and with the earth." These forms of relationality constitute "the core of an Indigenous lifeworld." The dominant settler colonial narratives position Indigenous existence and polities as simplistic, singular, and frozen in time—outside the motive forces of history—or inevitably succumbing to the forces of progress and unable to survive in a modern world. Such narratives belie the tremendous sophistication with which Indigenous societies have maintained forms of relationship, governance, and kinship with human and nonhuman societies. Native people do not exist in a static, magical, or more natural relationship to the environment. They have instead developed complex and dynamic sets of practices that are far more capable of governing the broad range of relationships and dynamics in which human societies are embedded than the forms of governance produced by Caucasian democracy. In seeking "the emancipation of earth from capital," they demonstrate that tribal sovereignty, leadership, and treaty rights are essential to the broader health and well-being of the environment, society, and social health.[39] "Far beyond the project of seeking equality with the colonial state," Estes writes, "the tradition of radical Indigenous internationalism imagined a world altogether free of colonial hierarchies of race, class, and nation."[40] The water protectors at Standing Rock, like the Mni Wizipan Wakan project, work to realize a wider type of freedom.

The Standing Rock struggle against the Dakota Access Pipeline, which won global attention in 2016, built on a resurgence of mass mobilizations, including a successful decade-long struggle against the Keystone XL pipeline led by Indigenous nations that included non-Native people. Joye Braun of the Indigenous Environmental Network points out that a break in the pipeline would pollute more than half of South Dakota's drinking water. "How can rubber-stamping this project be good for the people, agriculture, and livestock?" Waniya Lock, a Standing Rock descendent, argues that "the Missouri River gives drinking water to 10 million people. We are protecting everyone. We are standing for everyone. . . They are violating not only my people of Standing Rock, but they are violating ranchers and farmers and everybody else who lives along this river."[41]

On first blush such formations might seem to stem entirely from an opportunistic coalition, in which ranchers concerned about property rights temporarily align their interests with those of tribal governments. To be sure, it was the property interests of ranchers and farmers that brought them to the table. And Indigenous organizers are quick to point out that getting non-Natives to acknowledge their relationship to the land and their obligations to the tribes does not substitute for the actual restoration of Indigenous lands or the fulfilment of treaty obligations. Yet rather than simply forge a short-term coalition based on mutual interests, Indigenous organizers have used these struggles to educate non-Natives in the region about the history of tribal sovereignty treaty rights and violations, and the role of Indigenous spirituality, belief systems, ceremony, and practice in the protection of the water.

Ojibwe journalist Mary Annette Pember described the "consciousness-shifting among non-Natives" that has occurred through this process. Non-Native participants came to understand Indigenous practices that treated "the land, water and wildlife" as "relatives" that are afforded care, reciprocity, and respect.[42] Settlers who had been historically socialized into one understanding of governance rooted in dominance over Native people and supremacy over the land came to understand new practices that linked their well-being and futurity to the protection of Native treaty rights and sovereignty. As one rancher who participated explained, "A lot of us have given more consideration to their Native American treaty rights and see things more from their perspective now."[43]

These efforts have many parallels in Indigenous North America. In Northern California, the Karuk and Klamath tribes have reasserted management over forests and fisheries, attempting to reverse the trends toward catastrophic fires and the devastating decline in salmon populations that are central to tribal food systems and spiritual practices. The Muckelshoot Food Sovereignty Project in the Pacific Northwest centers tribal governance over food systems as central to its social and political health. Through the project, the Muckelshoot tribe has bought back nearly 100,000 acres of ancestral land in Washington to provide the material basis for the hundreds of foods that historically nourished Muckelshoot people before colonial settlement imposed far less diverse and unhealthy food practices.[44] Indigenous governance over sacred sites, such as the Bear Ears National Monument in Southeastern Utah and Yucca Mountain in Nevada, is similarly rooted in principles of non-domination over the land; Indigenous efforts to protect such sites serve, in the words of Dina Gilio-Whitaker (Colville Confederated Tribes), not only to contest "endless expropriation of their lands by multinational forces driven by market fundamentalism but also to produce a paradigm shift that acknowledges their worldview as a legitimate and necessary basis for understanding the world we all live in."[45]

Caucasian democracy has left us with a diminished account of the ways humans can and should relate to the land, and social structures that determine what counts as knowledge. The legacies and ongoing violence of colonialism have made Indigenous nations acutely aware of these threats and limitations. The coronavirus pandemic reminded the world in lethal terms that while Western scientific knowledge is necessary to protect human lifeworlds, it is far from sufficient. The novel coronavirus that moved from nonhuman to human animals in 2019 demonstrated the interdependence of all life forms and the grave danger of presuming human dominance over the so-called natural world. Like the climate crisis, it reveals the profound deficiencies of governance systems rooted in the primacy of private property, which alienates people from everyday acts of managing their relationships to their surroundings. The Mni Wizipan Wakan project in the Missouri River basin foregrounds far more capacious ways to inhabit such relations and use existing sites of legal sovereignty to protect the world from Caucasian democracy.

ABOLITION DEMOCRACY

On Halloween morning 2019, thousands of Chicagoans marched through the streets near City Hall, brandishing parkas and umbrellas to protect themselves from a mid-autumn squall. They came from many different parts of the city and held many different jobs and roles—teachers, nurses, bus aides, custodians, landscape workers, lifeguards, park attendants, and special education assistants who worked for Chicago Public Schools and Chicago Park District, as well as many parents and students. Most did not know one another personally. Yet their actions together were an act of collective governance, the impossible kind of democracy that Du Bois anticipated 100 years earlier. They made the education and development of hundreds of thousands of overwhelmingly Black and brown Chicago students a part of their desperate desire, and acted collectively to provide the material resources and conditions for their development. In doing so, they envisioned a transformation of the priorities and structures of public finance, away from the accumulation of capital in the hands of a few, and toward a model of equitably shared communal resources that enable full participation in democratic processes.[46]

Eleven days earlier, 35,000 members of the Chicago Teachers Union (CTU) and two other unions representing school district and park district employees had announced their intention to strike. Under federal labor law, most labor actions and organizing deal narrowly with the wages and working conditions of a narrow classification of workers, be they pilots, plumbers, nurses, or janitors. The law specifically bans general forms of solidarity and collective action between different groups of workers, such as sympathy strikes. That is, for most workers to address their own wages and working conditions, they must first disavow an interest in anyone's lives but their own.

The thousands of workers who walked off their jobs in Chicago certainly cared deeply about their wages, benefits, and working conditions, particularly as the cost of living in Chicago had skyrocketed. Yet they also asserted that winning better benefits and wages within a system that consistently fails to provide adequate resources and learning conditions for the students and families they serve would be a hollow victory. Their demands were far more expansive: funding for homeless students; smaller class sizes; sanctuary schools that would protect students and families from immigration police; restorative justice programs to oppose the criminalization of students; affordable housing for teachers; nurses and counselors in every school to meet students' mental, physical, and emotional health needs. They asserted a mandate to govern broad areas of social life.

Social studies teacher Stacy Davis Gates, the CTU's vice president, explained that workers assumed it was their responsibility "to figure out how to get the nearly 20,000 homeless students in our schools housed." Gates made clear that the issues they were addressing were structural and dealt directly with questions of governance. "It's about the systems of white supremacy that persist in every American institution and that must be dismantled in order for real justice and real equity to take place. And what we are seeing in this moment is that the institution is reluctant to release the resources that a school district with over 90 percent students of color deserve."[47]

The social relations that underscore Caucasian democracy do not lend themselves easily to these forms of solidarity. The logics of market competition counsel us not to tie our fates to others, holding that individual uplift is the best way to receive fair remuneration for one's labor. Why would a teacher walk off their job and risk their income and security so that a student in another part of the city has a nurse in their school, or an aide on their bus, or shelter if they lose their homes? Such actions require an unshakable belief in the capacity of all students to learn and a conviction that everyone shares in the obligation to provide the resources and conditions to make such development possible. These are commitments that need to be forged through the methods counseled by Ella Baker—group study, deliberation, and organization building as everyday practice.

In the mid-2000s, a group of rank-and-file Chicago teachers set out to transform their union through these very methods. They convened study groups to better understand the roles that a burgeoning school privatization movement was playing in promoting vouchers and charter schools as solutions to the endemic crises facing public schools, and the attacks on teachers and their unions that accompanied such projects. They spent years developing relationships with community organizations in predominately Black and brown neighborhoods that were mobilizing to fight plans to close dozens of neighborhoods schools. They formed a series of caucuses and organizations within the union to build relationships between teachers, parents, neighborhood organizations, and other school employees around a vision of well-funded public education, rejecting the elite-driven school reform measure championed by then mayor Rahm Emanuel. At a 2010 rally, Karen Lewis, a longtime high school science teacher who played a central role in this organizing and served for four years as union president, explained:

> Corporate America sees K-12 public education as $380 billion that, up until the last ten or fifteen years, they didn't have a sizable piece of. This so-called school reform is not an education plan. It's a business plan ... fifteen years ago, this city purposely began starving our lowest-income neighborhood schools of greatly needed resources and personnel. Class sizes rose, and schools were closed. Then, standardized tests, which in this town alone is a $60 million business, measured that slow death by starvation. These tests labeled our students, families, and educators failures, because standardized tests reveal more about a student's zip code than a student's academic growth.[48]

Lewis offered a sophisticated analysis about governance, capitalism, taxes, and race and class subordination that was forged through countless hours of study, discussion, and relationship building among teachers, one that would increasingly become the common perspective of thousands of educators and other school staff. Jane McAlevey explains that Lewis, in this role, "was reclaiming the identity of teacher as not just worker, but teacher, parent, community member, citizen activist."[49] In 2012, the CTU's 26,000 members led a historic seven-day strike that contested Emanuel's school closure plan, as parents and community members enthusiastically joined local picket lines and cheered teachers' efforts. They won hundreds of millions in new funding for Chicago schools and students. After the strike, the CTU continued to expand its methods of democratic governance through an intensive process of relationship building among diverse groups of workers, parents, unions, and community organizations, rooted not in a single set of shared experiences but in a consciousness and vision about avowing their obligations to one another and to young people in the city.

In the midst of the 2019 strike, the abolitionist geographer Ruth Wilson Gilmore explained to a packed lecture hall at DePaul University that "the work being done by the Chicago Teachers Union is the work of abolition," referencing the social forces and collective action historically associated with the abolition of slavery, and in the contemporary period, the abolition of prisons.[50]

In this context, abolition is often associated with an ending, a process of termination. But Gilmore explains that "abolition is not *absence*, it is

Striking teachers protest in downtown Chicago, September 2012. Credit: Atomazul/
Shutterstock.com.

presence. What the world will become already exists in fragments and
pieces, experiments and possibilities . . . Abolition is building the future
from the present, in all of the ways we can." This analysis returns to Du
Bois's account of abolition democracy during the 12 years following the
Civil War. Tens of thousands of newly freed people organized churches,
schools, and structures of governance based on the conviction that, in
Angela Davis's terms, "a host of democratic institutions are needed to fully
achieve abolition—thus abolition democracy."[51] Rejecting the assumption
of Caucasian democracy that private property forms the basis of democratic capacities and participation, abolition democracy foregrounded the
shared and public provision of "the material resources that would enable
[freed people] to fashion new, free lives."[52]

Du Bois noted that before the Civil War, education in the South was
understood as the province of elites alone, and publicly financed schools
were rare. White workers, Du Bois explained, "accepted without murmur
their subordination to the slaveholders, and looked for escape from their
condition only to the possibility of becoming slaveholders themselves.

Education they regarded as a luxury connected with wealth."[53] Instead, it was "the other part of the laboring class, the black folk, who connected knowledge with power" and who understood that "wealth, without education, was crippled." This produced the "extraordinary mass demand on the part of the black laboring class for education" and for "the establishment of the public school in the South on a permanent basis, for all people and all classes." For the first time, in states across the South, many thousands of public schools opened, producing the "first great mass movement for public education at the expense of the state."[54]

Abolition democracy produced other "presences" as well. Reconstruction governments also demanded "the redistribution of public lands, including distribution of public lands, public buildings, and appropriations for rivers and harbors" across the South, and newly elected Black representatives "opposed the restriction of Chinese immigration, arraigned our selfish policy towards Indians." Black Reconstruction lawmakers also worked to eradicate property-owning requirements as a condition to hold office and to expand voting rights for all men.[55] Du Bois described the 12-year period as "the finest effort to achieve democracy for the working millions which this world had ever seen."[56]

Du Bois argues that this vision and practice of multiracial governance, which regarded no one as degraded or disposable, and in which state programs, institutions, and capacities would be organized around this commitment, produced a powerful "counter-revolution of property." Planters opposed schools for both poor whites and all Black people, viewing the proposition as "absurd" because, they contended, freed people could not learn, and thus "their education involved an unjustifiable waste of private property for public disaster."[57] Struggles against taxes and public financing mechanisms became central to this opposition, as white elites recruited white workers to embrace the proposition that public funding for Black education and development was against their interests and status. The end of Reconstruction dismantled many of the revenue systems that had funded these programs, rooted in the very modern notion that taxes should not betray the basic principles of property, and are wasted if spent on someone else. Du Bois argued that by consenting to planter-led regimes of Caucasian democracy, white workers not only betrayed the cause and freedom of Black people, they also undermined the most powerful force of democratic and egalitarian governance for themselves.[58]

The practices of state-building and governance that emerged from the post-Reconstruction South instead hardened the commitments of Caucasian democracy. As Joy James points out, while the Thirteenth Amendment outlawed a private citizen's right to enslave another human being, it permitted "slavery and involuntary servitude" as "punishment for a crime wherof the party shall have been duly convicted" and thus asserted the state's authority to enslave, legitimating the "public ownership of racialized humans." This public authority to enslave is premised on a mode of state power focused on the management of allegedly degraded populations—the management of death and disposability—the framework that gives rise to the modern prison industrial complex.

This genealogy of Black Reconstruction and abolition democracy illuminates Gilmore's argument that Chicago's striking teachers and school and park workers engaged in profound acts of abolition. In the middle of the strike, thousands of people rallied at the planned sites for two luxury residential developments that had been granted $2 billion in tax subsidies by the city. These genuflections to the interests of property and capital by the state, along with the city's long history of police violence and its sprawling jail and prison system, reproduce the very forms of state power that Black Reconstruction sought to dismantle. "Broke on purpose," the strikers asserted, insisting that the city's disavowal of its young people was rooted in a parochial vision of governance that presumed their degradation.

Black and brown communities had weathered generations of such state violence and abandonment. Yet they could still imagine and demand an alternative vision of public governance and life rooted in mutuality and care that contested the ways that privatization strengthens elite interests and undermines life possibilities for many people. They advanced an antiracist vision of the state focused not on the management of death and disposability but on the presumption that the government can play a role in facilitating, advancing, and even guaranteeing human health, dignity, and possibility. This question of whose life, health, and education the state advances—and whose are neglected or destroyed—also plays out through a framework of citizenship, itself structured by the logics of white supremacy.

In the narratives that follow, young organizers propose alternative models of recognition and belonging for undocumented migrants in the United States.

UNDOCUMENTED AND UNAFRAID

In early March 2012, 20-year-old Daniela Cruz walked into the middle of 75th Avenue in West Phoenix, just outside the campus of Trevor Browne High School, which has a large immigrant and working-class student body. She locked arms with five others, all high school and college age, and sat in the street. More than a hundred supporters, including many Browne students, called out, "Undocumented and unafraid." One sign read, "Jail the worst you have? Because Our Organizing Starts in Jail!" A hundred police officers eventually arrived on the scene, bearing helmets and shields, and several dozen soon encircled the group. Cruz was arrested and taken to the Fourth Avenue jail. She later told a reporter, "I have never felt as free as when I was sitting in the middle of the street and when I was chanting 'undocumented and unafraid.'"[59] Cruz and her companions created a sense of freedom that was rooted in collectivity, rejecting a model of citizenship that was bestowed by the state and whose terms of inclusion are implicitly founded on violence and exclusion.

At the time of Cruz's arrest, the Obama administration declared that its immigration enforcement priorities would target "felons, not families," leading to the deportation of a record-setting 400,000 people each year. The same taxonomy of danger and innocence led Arizona lawmakers in 2010 to pass the Show Me Your Papers Law (Senate Bill 1070), which permitted law enforcement agencies such as the notorious Maricopa County Sheriff's office, home to Joe Arpaio, to stop, question, and detain any person suspected of being out of compliance with immigration law. Republican state senator Russell Pearce declared he proposed the law because "I saw my fellow citizens victimized by illegal alien criminals."[60]

Obama, Arpaio, and Pearce rehearsed the long-standing commitments of US immigration law, in which the state alone grants freedom on an individual basis by conferring citizenship or other legal status to individual subjects who prove their worth. To secure this individual recognition, one does not defy the state but obeys it, to demonstrate moral, social, economic, and political fitness for citizenship.

Yet Cruz, like Ella Baker, defined freedom as a feeling and presence generated through collective action rather than a status bestowed by the state to a worthy subject. It was a sovereignty one inhabited with others, rooted in a transformation of the material conditions of life. And in rejecting the state's demand for noncitizens to prove their worth and obedience, Cruz and her companions departed in critical ways from the mainsprings of political organizing for immigrant rights in the US.

US citizenship offers specific material benefits. A right to enter and leave the country. The right to vote. Authorization to work. Formal protection against immigration raids and deportation. Access to some of the social programs offered by the state, related to food, health care, housing, and income support, as limited as they may be. Since the first immigration act in 1790, immigration and citizenship law has focused primarily on identifying those who could contribute to the nation and were worthy of the "gift" of citizenship, and those who were not. Until 1952, these criteria were explicitly tied to race and natural origin, and often to sexual orientation and gender as well. Yet even after 1965, when those exclusions were replaced by preferences for family reunification and certain occupational skills, immigration laws remained grounded in discerning individual fitness and worthiness. As President Lyndon Johnson explained at the signing ceremony on Ellis Island for the 1965 Immigration and Nationality Act, "Those who can contribute most to this country—to its growth, to its strength, to its spirit—will be the first that are admitted to this land."[61]

In this framework, people seeking such benefits from the state must demonstrate that they are the taxpaying, hardworking, law-abiding, patriotic, properly domesticated subject favored by the law. The neoliberal subject par excellence, the devoted holder of the American Dream. The political discourse of immigrant rights has long reflected these obligations, from the ubiquitous signs at rallies declaring "I'm a worker, not a criminal" to fact sheets produced by advocacy groups declaring that immigrants on aggregate pay more in taxes than they take in public services and commit fewer crimes than their native-born counterparts. Good subjects.

When Daniela Cruz and the other students locked arms and sat in the West Phoenix intersection, they abandoned such appeals. Initially, the

"Dreamer" movement that gave rise to many dozens of similar acts of civil disobedience focused on creating a legislative path to citizenship for undocumented youth who arrived to the US as children, drawing on familiar tropes of innocence, hard work, and respectability as justifications for inclusion. Yet in the youth organizers' hands, it quickly morphed into a far more transgressive political movement, one that refused the "gift" of citizenship on such partial grounds.[62] They asserted rights to family and kinship, to education, to safety, to freedom from police violence, to work, and to life, without grounding them in claims of exceptionality or deservingness. In this way, they articulated a basis for citizenship and collective governance much different from the underlying basis of Caucasian democracy. Elizabeth Rubio and Xitlalli Alvarez Almendariz describe such efforts as no longer being "solely invested in chasing after those gifts granted by the state" because to "yearn for or accept the gift of citizenship is to admit something about the legitimacy of one's own domination and to allow the state to set the rules of the game."[63] In deploying the narrative of "coming out" as undocumented, they also drew upon and identified with a tradition of queer political formation that contested the dominant categories of "normal" social life. Indeed, queer, trans, and gender nonbinary organizers have been at the forefront of new immigrant organizing, challenging the "good immigrant" narratives grounded in patriarchal family formation.[64]

In demanding and creating social, political, and economic life and possibility beyond the framework of state recognition and its gifts, the contemporary youth-led immigrant rights movement has joined a long history of migrant world-making in the US that does not simply genuflect before the Statute of Liberty and the shibboleths of American exceptionalism. For example, on the West Coast in the later nineteenth century, nativist forces often depicted migrant workers from China as sojourners who drained the US state and economy of resources and failed subjects whose loyalty to a foreign land meant they lacked the autonomy and self-possession to claim a place in the US polity. White workers regularly resorted to mob violence and attacks to protect their democracy from such incursions. Yet many migrants operated from much different political terms and consciousness. They simultaneously campaigned for the rights to public education, struck for higher wages and formed unions, and demanded respect from customers and clients in Chinatowns, even as

Youth-led civil disobedience in support of the DREAM Act in Phoenix, 2012. Credit: Jack Kurtz.

they also sent remittances to their families in China, continued Chinese language and religious traditions, and returned to China at the end of their lives or arranged to have their remains sent for burial to family villages. In this way, they rejected the US nation-state as the sole arbiter of rights or protections from racist persecution. As historian Jean Pfaelzer writes, "They point to a transnational people claiming their rightful status in the United States" who forged relationships that spanned "legal, familial, economic, religious and political borders."[65] In this way, their conception of governance far exceeded the dominant mode of US citizenship.

The contemporary youth-led movement for immigration justice has similarly sought to disturb a core feature of US political formation by rejecting the implicit anti-Blackness that often animates immigrant claims to civic inclusion. Within US histories of white supremacy, to declare oneself to be a "worker, not a criminal" and a seeker of the "American Dream" is also covertly to announce one's distance from American Blackness, long imagined as the epitome of the failed national subject. In seeking recognition from the state and the gift of citizenship, immigrants to the US, even from Black-diasporic nations in the Caribbean and Africa, become incentivized to signal that unlike African Americans, they are fit to be included in the US market and state.[66]

As one youth organizer explained to sociologist Ala Sirriyeh, by "saying 'I'm not a criminal, I'm a student,'" the dominant Dreamer narrative was "criminalizing others," because "if we are not the criminals then who is the criminal?"[67] The organizing led by undocumented youth has consciously resisted those appeals, and increasingly orients their work toward dismantling broad forms of racist criminalization and policing. A youth organizer with the Immigrant Youth Coalition (IYC) in California explained that in the context of fighting immigrant detentions, "people were saying, 'they were unjustly detained.' No. Detention itself is unjust so it's an oxymoron. What you are choosing to say is that this particular person should not, but others should, and we know who that means. It's black people. This country has made that very clear."[68]

Youth-led immigrant justice work has also become far more multiracial, led by groups like the UndocuBlack network, that trace the interconnection and independence of regimes of criminalization and immigration enforcement. Demands for "sanctuary cities" in which local police refuse to cooperate with federal immigration enforcement officers have expanded to include sanctuary from all forms of racist policing, especially those that target Black communities.[69] In Chicago, groups like Organized Communities against Deportation (OCAD), which emerged out of the first set of youth to come out as "undocumented and unafraid" in 2010, have joined with organizations like the Black Youth Project 100 on the Erase the Database campaign to demand the dismantling of the gang lists maintained by the Chicago Police Department, which include the names of tens of thousands of overwhelmingly Black and brown people. In Los Angeles and Oakland, immigrant rights organizing includes campaigns against jail expansion, gang injunctions, police violence, housing justice, the criminalization of homelessness and street vending, and gentrification.

Taken together, the last decade of youth-led immigrant justice organizing and collective action has produced concepts and practices of citizenship and political subjectivity that reject the gift of legal recognition offered by the state in favor of an anti-racist notion of freedom that sets out to abolish much wider forms of domination. It has been attendant not just to the logics of *exclusion* that structure US immigration law and citizenship, but also the violent practices of *inclusion* that weaponize the vulnerability and precarity of noncitizens against the interests and lives of subordinated Black communities. Further, it has offered a much more sober critique of US citizenship itself, and the failings of the nation-state. Citizenship, they have demonstrated, has not protected many African Americans, other non-Black people of color, and even many white people from the impacts of state violence.[70] Nor has citizenship protected tens of millions of households and families from the ravages of hunger, poor health care, and economic instability, conditions brought into painful relief by the Covid-19 pandemic.

The political theorist Joy James writes that "emancipation is *given* by the dominant, it being a legal, contractual, and social agreement." By contrast, "freedom is *taken* and created . . . a practice shared in community."[71] James was describing a very specific context—freedom within and beyond enslavement and captivity—and calling attention to the everyday practices of enacting sovereignty that reject the idea that freedom is a condition that can only be bestowed on subjects regarded as virtuous and worthy. To be clear, the struggle of undocumented youth extends from much different historical conditions and relations of power than the struggle to abolish slavery in the US in its many enduring forms. Yet when Daniella Cruz describes freedom as a feeling and condition produced in collective opposition to state violence, she is drawing from a genealogy and practice of governance and freedom much more closely aligned with W. E. B. Du Bois and Ella Baker and Karen Lewis than with Thomas Jefferson.

CODA: ABOLITION AND RECONSTRUCTION

Together, the narratives gathered in this chapter propose a radical transformation of democratic governance. Enacting reconstruction democracy, with its promise of more equitable rights and freedoms, requires sustained acts of imagination, courage, and organization. It also requires a reworking of the dominant structures of knowledge-making and education, public finance and private property, citizenship and belonging—removing one by one the pillars of Caucasian democracy so that participation in self-governance, and the sense of freedom that it cultivates, becomes open to all.

The economic, social, and health crises produced by the Covid-19 pandemic revealed both the failures and the potential of democracy in the US in the twenty-first century. On the one hand, dramatic miscarriages of governance were exposed. Elected leaders and administrators at all levels failed to respond to the threat of widespread infection, influenced in part by a broadly held and deeply racialized belief that that viruses only circulated among populations marked as nonwhite and deviant: the Middle East (MERS); West Africa (Ebola); Asia (SARS and Avian Flu); Haiti (HIV/AIDS). Desperately needed medical equipment and protective gear were in short supply. The patchwork health-care and health insurance system left many exposed to sickness and disease. Electoral systems faced grave uncertainty, and access to voting varied widely. Prisons and detention facilities failed to safeguard the health of millions of incarcerated people. The virus raged with particular lethality through Indigenous nations, which had long been denied adequate health care, sanitation, and infrastructure. A deep distrust of government and state power, primarily on the political right but from other quarters as well, left many deeply suspicious of orders to shelter in place. Even the public health strategy to maintain social distance and to stay at home—which disproportionately protected households with stable incomes and living arrangements while requiring others to labor outside the home and risk exposure and death— reflected a hierarchical conception of public health. Nearly all of these inequalities moved through the legacies and realities of racism and colonialism. Covid-19 exposed the many faults of Caucasian democracy.[72]

On the other hand, the government in many ways proved to be the only institution with the capacity to protect human life and meet human needs. Billions in direct federal stimulus payments permitted countless households to pay mortgages, buy groceries, and cover other basic needs. State and local agencies protected renters and home owners from eviction. Thousands of public schools delivered food to hungry children and their families. Without social insurance programs like unemployment, Social Security, Medicaid, and Medicare, millions would have faced far graver consequences. And where public systems did not meet human needs, mutual aid efforts formed to distribute food and medicine, to share services and information, and to protect people from premature death.[73] These efforts remain much more closely aligned to the democratic methods articulated by Du Bois. At their best, they follow Angela Davis's counsel that "we need to insist on different criteria for democracy: substantive as well as formal rights, the right to be free of violence, the right to employment, housing, healthcare, and quality education."[74]

The crises laid bare by both Covid-19 and the rebellions and movements to end state violence against Black people have also generated renewed calls for greater inclusion of Black and other people of color within the governing structures of Caucasian democracy. Davis is clear on the dangers posed by such incorporations alone, writing that the "challenge of the twenty-first century is not to demand equal opportunity to participate in the machinery of oppression. Rather, it is to identify and dismantle those structures in which racism continues to be embedded."[75] The episodes and formations discussed in this chapter point to a much larger genealogy of collective organizing that can meet the imperatives of abolition and reconstruction.

3 Internationalism

"I believe the Black Lives Matter movement can benefit greatly by learning about struggles outside of the U.S., but particularly the Palestinian struggle." So explained Patrisse Cullors, one of three Black women who cofounded Black Lives Matter after George Zimmerman was acquitted of Trayvon Martin's murder in 2013. In late 2014, soon after a grand jury concluded that Officer Darren Wilson had violated no laws when he took the life of 18-year-old Michael Brown that summer, Cullors joined other organizers from groups including Black Youth Project 100, Hands Up United, and Dream Defenders, for a 10-day trip to Israel and the occupied Palestinian Territories. The trip followed a visit by a delegation of Palestinian organizers to Ferguson, to learn from and engage with organizers in the St. Louis suburb. Cullors's observation, that anti-racist organizers in the US might find new insights into their political struggles many thousands of miles from their homes, builds on a long history of internationalism that has viewed white supremacy in the US as inextricably linked to colonial domination in many other parts of the world.[1]

As Cullors and others on the trip reported when they returned, those solidarities rest on demanding political labor. Forging connections between conditions in Palestine and Ferguson requires attention to both similarities and difference. More than simply proclaiming mutual support or shared experiences, it compels a tracing of the complex structures of policing, political regulation, and cultural hegemony that link these disparate sites. It requires the shaping of new identifications and frameworks outside the nation-state and its uninterrupted militarism—what Ruth Wilson Gilmore describes as "the continuum from policing and prisons to war."[2] And it demands the invocation of new political imaginaries that link peace and the cessation of violence to transformations in the political economy and the social fabric.

In traveling to Palestine and engaging the history of Palestinian social movements and their relation to racial violence within the US, Cullors and her comrades demonstrated many of the practices capable of realizing these ambitions. Following this example, the stories in this chapter, from struggles against the occupation and militarization of Hawaii and Puerto Rico to resistance against US wars of imperialism in Asia, the Caribbean, and Latin America, to opposition to the nuclear economy, make visible the relationships between and among different modes of militarized violence. They do not simply announce their distaste for war or assert vague platitudes for peace. Instead, they seek to disrupt the forms of incorporation and consent that US militarism requires. And rather than rendering these sites as exceptional or "un-American"—that is, at odds with a national history of inclusion, peace, and global democracy—they link militarism to everyday forms of economic exploitation, social domination, and liberal governance, offering a far more robust and radical critique of US state violence.

Militarism, the permanent and ongoing use of organized violence by the state as a universal solution to address all social problems and conflicts, is a central and enduring feature in US national development. Since 1890, the military has intervened in the affairs of other sovereign nations more than 100 times. Indeed, from the nation's founding in 1776 to 2019, there have only been 21 years when the US has not been involved in a military conflict.[3] Military conquest has been central to settler colonialism, and the violence directed toward sovereign Native nations. Militarism functions as an ideological framework regulating a broad range of institutional, social, cultural, and economic concerns. It is both a set of material interests and a worldview; an ideology rooted in presumptions of hierarchy and disposability. Throughout the history of the United States, military conflict has been framed as a vehicle of civilization and freedom. The theft of Indigenous land and life, military occupation in the Philippines, Hawaii, Puerto Rico, and Vietnam War, and recent occupations in the Middle East have all been justified in these terms. This chapter probes the contradictions of, and charts resistances against, a political ideology of freedom that is predicated on violent control and the expendability of human life. The hierarchies of race perpetuate a national ethos in which near-constant violence is required for the preservation of rights and liberties, and for defense against barbarism or depravity.

AGAINST THE IDEOLOGY OF BARBARISM

The spectacles of militarization—the politician's tour of the border wall, the public display of offenders in a "tent city" or chain gang, the menacing political ads warning of Black and brown transgressors, the recitation of the enemy's barbarity—are integral to the normalization of its material effects and moral implications. In a 1967 essay in the Black political and cultural journal *Freedomways,* the writer and organizer Jack O'Dell linked these sites together, explaining that "the road which leads from the 'Indian massacres' of the last century to the Pentagon and another from the oppressive slave plantation to the ghetto are the major conjunctive highways running through the very center of US life and history. In turn, they shape the mainstream contours of American national development."[4] For O'Dell, writing at the height of the Southern-based Black Freedom movement, these forces represented "the main social cancer in the body politic of the nation," which resulted in "manipulative control over the lives of millions."[5]

If militarism requires perpetual enemies, then racism provides the political vocabulary of differentiation and diminishment necessary to transform populations into such enemies. Race performs crucial political labor by marking those persons who are antithetical to civilization itself, whose devalued and inferior status designates them for sacrifice and elimination. The disenfranchisement of the felon, the torture of the enemy combatant, and the strip search of the migrant enact and reproduce these distinctions. The very categories of the "illegal," the "criminal," and the "terrorist" require the deployment of "racial violence as an instrument of public safety."[6]

At the same time, militarized economies, regimes, and modes of governance in the US also constitute the terrain on which racially subordinated people are invited to prove their fealty to the nation and their fitness for citizenship. The surest way to demonstrate that one is not the enemy is to join the attack on another racialized foe. And the capacity of the militarized state to incorporate the subjects of racialized and colonial violence into its ranks and leadership serves to legitimate the claim that US militarism is animated by a vision of expanding liberal freedoms and rights to other corners of the world rather than by desires for empire, power, and authority. Militarism thus links disparate people together in relationships of violence, domination, and control. It recruits people into one another's dispossession and loss.

O'Dell described the antithesis to these traditions of militarism as lying within "the world's rejection of empire as a category of life."[7] This dissenting view has long criticized the suppositions and logic of militarism, and the forms of national and racial identity it produces and legitimates, insisting that reconciliation, peace, and redistribution are realizable and necessary to save humanity. O'Dell described these struggles to "rescue human life" from the "juggernaut" of war as rooted in an assertion of "a new social morality in America: a civilized morality which asserts the primary value of *human life* and its right to survive as the basis for liberty and the pursuit of happiness."[8]

To secure consent and participation in these relationships, military conquests must mask or erase the violence and loss that are inevitably produced. It must make killing honorable. It must offer concrete incentives— wages, political rights, status, honor, recognition—to those recruited into its structures, and impose consequences on those who refuse. As the historian Simeon Man recounts, during the Vietnam War, the choice posed to young men in the multiracial Crenshaw neighborhood of Los Angeles was as follows: "Do you want to join the army, or do you want to go to jail?"[9]

A central and recurring strategy among racial justice movements has been to demonstrate the links between empire-building and militarization abroad and racial dispossession and violence at home. Making such connections has been a frequent theme in challenges to US racialized

---

militarism, contesting the dominant narrative, often espoused by mainstream peace groups, that US military interventions bear no connection to structures of racial and colonial domination. It has meant challenging what O'Dell called the "ideology of barbarism" that militarism both hides and naturalizes. By invoking an alternative vision of interdependence and human advancement that rejects the permanence of war, they summon an extended memory of racial justice action committed to universal disarmament, internationalism, and peace.[10] In lieu of the affective investments in militarism, they highlight relationalities, obligations, and affinities that exceed national boundaries and interests.

THE WAR AT HOME: "LA BATALLA ESTÁ AQUÍ"

On an October day in 2002, Elizabeth "Betita" Martínez stood before a crowd of 15,000 gathered at San Francisco's Civic Center for one the largest anti-war protests in the United States since the Vietnam War. It was just six months before a US-led military invasion dubbed "Operation Iraqi Freedom" would rain tens of thousands of missiles and bombs on Baghdad. More than 600,000 Iraqis died in the next five years in this peculiarly American brand of liberation through ordnance and death.

Martínez, a few months away from her seventy-sixth birthday, had wavy black hair down to her shoulders and a broad smile. She was no stranger to this scene. In 1965, she left a budding career in journalism to become the New York City coordinator for the Student Nonviolent Coordinating Committee (SNCC). Shaped by many decades of labor in the Black Freedom movement, solidarity work with Cuba and Central America, and Chicanx-led struggles in the Southwest, Martínez had long understood the mutual dependence between the making of war and the making of race. As she concluded her speech, she recalled an anti-war chant that summoned this analysis, one she later explained would "emphasize the importance of seeing the threatened war on Iraq in terms of this country's racism here and around the world."

She called out to the crowd, "One, two, three four/We don't want your racist war!"

The chant was met largely by silence; the raucous energy that had coursed through most of the protest dimmed. Few joined in or applauded. Their restraint was no accident or anomaly. Following the dominant pattern of peace activism in the United States, most at the gathering in San Francisco saw little connection between the pending invasion of Iraq and what Martínez and others called the "War at Home."[11]

Prominent white anti-war leaders at the time would not deny their ambivalences about making such connections. The scholar Shampa Biswas notes that the anti-war movement in the United States often relies on "foundational myths" about national identity to argue that wars of aggression are somehow "un-American."[12] But this suggestion misrepresents the long history of US militarism and state violence within and outside the country's borders—in part, allowing predominantly white peace activists to obscure public complicity in this violence, which is carried out through democratic structures of governance.[13]

Martínez similarly noted the failure of "peace activists . . . to recognize that there is a 'war at home' along with the wars abroad." Martínez described this war as defined by "an unending struggle with racism as shown in the criminalization of youth, the expanding prison industrial complex, ongoing inequality in social institutions like schools and housing, and a constant stream of actions to take back the gains of the 1960s like affirmative action and bilingual education."[14]

Chicanx organizers who opposed the US war in Vietnam insisted, "La Batalla está aquí" (The war is here), asserting that the drafting of thousands of poor and working-class Mexican American soldiers into the war extended directly from failures to provide education, employment, and life possibilities at home. The Detroit-based organizer James Boggs similarly wrote that "the peace movement cannot save humanity as long as it refuses to face the inhumanity that exists inside this country toward other racial and national groupings and that exists in the relations of this country to other races and nations. Nor can it ever get a peacetime economy in this country until it clashes with the war economy and the reason why such a war economy exists." For Boggs, celebrations of American exceptionalism and virtue hampered, rather than advanced, the peace movement. "The same people who are for war in this country are those who are for discrimination against races and nations. They are the ones who are for the continuation of American superiority over other nations and other areas of the world."[15]

In May 1915, as the United States was moving toward entering the Great War, W. E. B. Du Bois explained in an essay titled "The African Roots of War," published in the *Atlantic*, that "hitherto the peace movement has confined itself chiefly to figures about the cost of war and the platitudes on humanity. What do nations care about the cost of war, if by spending a few hundred millions in steel and gunpowder they can gain a thousand millions in diamonds and cocoa? How can love of humanity appeal as a motive to nations whose love of luxury is built on the inhuman exploitation of human beings, and who, especially in recent years, have been taught to regard these human beings as inhuman?" Du Bois explained that at a recent meeting of pacifists in St. Louis, he posed the question, "Should you not discuss racial prejudice as a prime cause of war?" The group, according to Du Bois, refused to even discuss the proposition, dismissing it as too controversial.[16]

Undeterred, Du Bois explained that "we, who want real peace, must remove the real causes of war." He located such causes in the plunder of Africa's civilization, resources, and people. Du Bois argued that the great revolutions of the nineteenth century among the European working class that challenged the "divine right of the few to determine economic income and distribute the goods and services of the world" had begun to broaden access to wealth in Europe by "the dipping of more and grimier hands into the wealth-bag of the nation." In other words, these forms of economic redistribution also broadened the popular constituency for imperialism. He explained, "It is no longer simply the merchant prince, or the aristocratic monopoly, or even the employing class, that is exploiting the world: it is the nation; a new democratic nation composed of united capital and labor." In order to broaden the access to wealth and accumulation among an expanding and politicized working class, Europe would have to increase the exploitation of labor and resources "primarily from the darker nations of the world—Asia and Africa, South and Central America, the West Indies and the islands of the Seas."[17]

Du Bois sought to advance what Biswas describes as an anti-war practice that engages and confronts the "complicity of Americans in enabling, in a variety of ways, the militarism and aggression." Such an oppositional response had to be "predicated on a global ethic" that moves "beyond the limited boundaries of a nationalist position" that was often rooted in a desire to "to reclaim American goodness."[18] As one Japanese American who became involved in the movement against the US war in Vietnam stated, "A lot of us felt that the white anti-war movement had these slogans like 'Bring the boys back home,' as if what was wrong with the war was that American boys were dying—not that the U.S. was an invasive force in an Asian country and that there were Asians dying too." It was a struggle over the questions of identification, recognition, and reciprocity. As he explained, "Who do you identify with? Do you identify with the Vietnamese, or do you identify with oppressed people in this country? Or do you identify with the U.S.?"[19]

These efforts disrupted the moral authority on which US military interventions rested. They repeated a call made in 1848 by the abolitionist Fredrick Douglass in his condemnation of the pending US invasion of Mexico for the American public to "forsake the way of blood" and reject "the mad spirit of proud ambition, blood, and carnage, let loose in the land."[20] Douglass noted that the war was led by a slaveholding president and was premised on "Anglo Saxon cupidity and love of domination" and "our appetite for fiery conflict and plunder."[21] For Douglass and others who embraced this anti-imperial legacy, the mythology of American exceptionalism and innocence was not a resource to be harnessed against war-making, but a structure of identification that had to be contested and undermined. By tracing the connections between what Nikhil Singh calls "the inner and outer wars," this thrust of anti-war organizing sought to form new identifications between minoritized groups in the US and colonized populations abroad, rooted in a shared recognition of what Douglass described as "the sacredness of human life."

If practices and relationships of violence, especially military service, "make" people into worthy national subjects through martial citizenship, then experiences of violation (from the "war at home") produce a different form of political subjectivity that reject the mythologies of US militarism in favor of identifications that link seemingly disparate places and sites. For example, when Betita Martínez moved to New Mexico in the late 1960s to join the burgeoning Chicanx movements, she noted that "a lot of the women in northern New Mexico were like the women I had met in rural Mississippi [working for SNCC]. They were Fanny Lou Hamers—only they spoke Spanish—in northern New Mexico." And Martínez used the newspaper in New Mexico she helped start, *El Grito del Norte* (Cry of the North) to trace the connections between women's lives in Mississippi and New Mexico with those in rural Vietnam. US militarism and nationalism sought to continually sever and deny such relationships and mutuality; Martínez worked within a tradition committed to foregrounding and enlivening such connections. Similarly for Du Bois, peace could only be realized if anti-war forces in the US came to identify with African workers and their collective struggles against imperial plunder and control.

If militarism is rooted in a set of material and symbolic practices of identification with the nation and with state violence as the guarantor of freedom, figures like Martínez and Du Bois committed themselves to a set of counterpractices premised on global identifications and solidarities. This analysis is remarkably ubiquitous across a range of times and places, and was particularly evident on the editorial pages of Black newspapers at the turn of the twentieth century amid US military incursions into Cuba, Hawaii, Puerto Rico, and most especially the Philippines.

THE US OCCUPATION OF THE PHILIPPINES: IDENTIFICATION AS CRITIQUE

US militarism and imperialism has not simply been fueled by racism. Militarism itself also *makes* race. Racism furnishes the indispensable vocabulary of virtue and degradation required to legitimate wars of invasion and occupation by democratic nations. Contesting these traditions of race-/war-making and empire has often required new imaginations of "international relations" premised on a sense of lateral identification and association among subordinated groups that reject nationalism and its violence.

At the turn of the twentieth century, advocates for US imperial occupations of Hawaii, Puerto Rico, Cuba, and the Philippines linked the hardening of white supremacy within the nation to military expansion abroad. The US military defeated Spanish forces in the Philippines (as well as Cuba and Puerto Rico) in 1898, wars ostensibly fought in the name of liberating colonized subjects from Spain's imperial rule. But the US government had no intention of ceding military and political control over these territories, which provided key nodal points within the increasingly global reach of the US military and economy and secured new markets, resources, and sources of low-wage labor for US corporations.[22]

Race provided the crucial vocabulary of diminishment and degradation necessary to rationalize an ongoing occupation of these areas, a dynamic that was particularly striking in the Philippines. As Indiana senator Albert J. Beveridge thundered in a 1900 address on the "Philippine question" on the Senate floor: "God has not been preparing the English-speaking and Teutonic peoples for a thousand years for nothing but vain and idle self-contemplation and self-admiration . . . He has made us adept in government that we may administer government among savage and senile peoples."[23] Two years later, as a US military occupation turned large expanses of the Philippines into killing fields, President Theodore Roosevelt told a crowd gathered at the newly opened Arlington National Cemetery, "The warfare that has extended the boundaries of civilization at the expense of barbarism and savagery has been for centuries one of the most potent factors in the progress of humanity."[24]

The "administration" of government envisioned by Beveridge over a "barbarous race" was rationalized by the same forces of Manifest Destiny that rationalized the conquest of the continental US, a calling not limited to "territory on this continent only but any territory anywhere belonging to the nation." The mission was the same: "subdue the wilderness, revitalize decaying peoples, and plant civilized and civilizing governments all over the globe." Beveridge drew directly on the experiences of "our Indian wars" to argue for a full-throated military conquest of the Filipino people, who were similarly "not a self-governing race."[25] The economic structures and unequal tiers of citizenship organized through racial difference within the nation—the plantation economy, the reservation, Jim Crow, and Chinese exclusion—provided a template for US expansion abroad. Indeed, as the military extended its reach into the Philippines, the dominant framework of racial subordination in the United States came to frame the status of the newly "liberated" Filipino people. The journalist Henry Loomis Nelson reported in 1902 that "our troops in the Philippines . . . look upon all Filipinos as of one race and condition . . . and entitled to all the contempt and harsh treatment administered by white overlords to the most inferior races."[26]

War-making required and reproduced race-making. Many white anti-imperial champions opposed military occupation of the Philippines on the grounds that the newly colonized subjects would despoil and degrade the Anglo-Saxon character of the US. They too disavowed the lives of Filipinos and embraced the logics of white supremacy.

By contrast, a long tradition of Black internationalism and anti-imperialism sought distinct forms of identification with Filipino people and with their armed struggle against US imperialism.[27] While some Black leaders, including Booker T. Washington, viewed these conflicts as an opportunity to prove African American fitness for citizenship, many others sought to trace out the connections between racial and colonial violence within the nation and imperial wars abroad.[28] A particularly violent regime of white supremacy gripped the nation in the 1890s, witnessed in the rise of the lynch mob, the tightening of segregation, and the retreat of commitments to abolition democracy that arose after the Civil War. Many Black journalists and leaders linked these developments and the long histories of Native genocide and treaty violations with the rise of imperial occupations abroad. Unlike most white anti-imperialists, their critique focused on the hollow claims that the ships of the US Navy were sent to bring "civilization" and "self-government" to faraway lands, and foregrounded an identification with other colonized people around the world. If racism facilitates militarism through a process of disidentification, anti-racism in this context rested precisely on appeals for global identification, rooted in experiences of subordination at home.[29]

For example, the journalist Lewis H. Douglas noted in 1899 that "whatever this government controls, injustice to dark races prevails. The people of Cuba, Porto Rico, Hawaii and Manila know it well as do the wronged Indian and outraged black man in the United States." It was "hypocrisy of the most sickening kind to try to make us believe that the killing of Filipinos is for the purpose of good government and to give protection to life and liberty and the pursuit of happiness."[30]

An 1899 editorial titled "Bayonet-Imposed Civilization" in the Indianapolis *Recorder* explained that the "officers in command of the American forces are old Indian fighters, who owe their success to the close adherence to the theory that 'a dead Indian is the best Indian.' They will employ the same methods in dealing with the Filipinos."[31] The same year, the Coffeyville *American* explained that "the matter of the treatment of these people who belong to the dark-skinned races is a matter which concerns us ... Experience and not promises weighs more potently in these matters, and the treatment which the Indians, the Chinese, and the Negroes have received at the hands of white Americans speaks in no uncertain tone—it would be deplorable to have inhabitants of the Philippine Islands treated as the Indians have been treated or the people of Cuba or Puerto Rico ruled as the Negroes of the South have been ruled." Imperial wars, the editors argued, represented a degraded form of governance: "This kind of civilization has very little to commend it and it is doubtful whether it ought to be extended to our newly-acquired territory." The government should instead "remedy our own scandalous abuses rather than to extend the system under which they have arisen to other people."

At times, the Black press narrated their connections to the Filipinos through a language of solidarity, connected by a shared experience of domination and resistance. The Kansas City *American Citizen* announced its opposition to Black soldiers enlisting to fight in the Philippines, insisting it was "pitting Negro against Negro," forging a global concept of blackness in struggle against a globalizing white supremacy. "God forbid the sending of a single negro soldier from this country to kill their own kith and kin for fighting for the cause they believe to be right."[32]

Julius F. Taylor, publisher of the Salt Lake City *Broad Ax*, emerged as one of the most forceful and insightful critics of US imperialism, a half-century before the idea of Third World solidarity was introduced into the global political vocabulary. The *Broad Ax* editorialized consistently against the war, urging its readers not to be complicit in the dispossession of another people, insisting that the "black man" who dies fighting in the Philippines will "go to meet his Maker feeling that he was an accessory to a great land-grabbing scheme not of his own will."[33] The paper asserted its "sympathies, which are as broad as the universe, are with the Filipinos, and it is perfectly clear to our mind that the war upon them is contrary and antagonistic to the fundamental principles of liberty and justice ... This war now being waged is unhuman, blood-thirsty, wrong and is conducted for conquest only and not in the interest of humanity."[34]

The pull of national identification and disidentification would be particularly vexing for the four regiments of African American soldiers deployed to the Philippines in 1899. On the one hand, their military service was premised on the proposition that by demonstrating their bravery, national loyalties, and qualification for American citizenship, they could escape some of the worst violence and dispossession at home. On the other hand, their experiences in a brutal war of counterinsurgency in the Philippines, which included the wholesale slaughter of hundreds of thousands of combatants and noncombatants alike as well as the destruction of homes and food sources, made visible the ways that the violence that enforced Jim Crow in the US was brought to bear against the Filipino people. Soon after segregated Twenty-Fourth Infantry landed in the Philippines, Sergeant Patrick Mason wrote to the *Cleveland Gazette*, "I feel sorry for these people and all that come under the control of the United States. I don't believe that they will be justly dealt by. The first thing in the morning is the 'Nigger' and the last thing at night is the 'Nigger.' You have no idea the way these people are treated by the Americans here."[35] These soldiers experienced firsthand Cedric Robinson's observation that "racism has the advantage of being able to move and transfer its disaffections from one group to another without being held accountable."[36]

Filipino insurgents also took notice of the relationship between their experiences fighting US colonialism and regimes of white supremacy and segregation that were hardening within the United States. A Black veteran suggested that Filipino soldiers had been "told of America's treatment of the black population" and thus were "made to feel that it is better to die fighting than to become subject to a nation where, as they are made to believe, the colored man is lynched and burned alive indiscriminately." Another journalist suggested that "all prominent Filipinos" believe that "if the status of the negro, as they understood it, was to be theirs in the new system, they would have to leave the islands anyway, and they had concluded to make a fight before going."[37] Indeed, some in the Black press called for African Americans to take notice of the anti-colonial spirit expressed in the Filipino effort to expel the United States army from its homelands. "The backbone displayed by the 'ignorant, uncivilized' barbarians as termed by the Americans, is what the Negro of the United States needs. Take pattern, ye black sons of America!"[38]

Such experiences served as the basis for new modes of identification and solidarity between African American soldiers and Filipino insurgents. Emilio Aguinaldo, the first president of the Philippines following the cessation from Spain and subsequent leader of the military resistance against the US, issued this broadside to Black soldiers fighting in the US military, drawing comparisons between racial lynchings in the US and the violence unleased in the Philippines: "'To the Colored American Soldier.' It is without honor that you are spilling your costly blood. Your masters have thrown you into the most iniquitous fight with double purpose—to make you the instrument of their ambition and also your hard work will soon make the extinction of your race. Your friends, the Filipinos, give you this good warning. You must consider your history, and take charge that the Blood of Sam Hose proclaims vengeance."[39] The reference to Hose, who was brutally tortured and lynched in Georgia in 1899, was part of a larger effort of propaganda targeting Black soldiers that underscored the wave of racial violence gripping the US South at the time and offering commissions to soldiers willing to defect from the US Army.

Among the 2,000 Black soldiers deployed to the Philippines, only a few dozen, disturbed and upset by US military tactics, responded to Aguinaldo's entreaty. The most famous, Private David Fagan, defected from the segregated Twenty-Fourth Infantry and joined Filipino military forces, eventually becoming a high-ranking leader and a mythical figure within the Filipino resistance struggle, leading dozens of guerilla assaults against US forces.[40]

Other soldiers who did not defect made their identification with the Filipinos clear. Sergeant Major John W. Calloway, also of the Twenty-Fourth Infantry, expressed deep regret for the US imperialist endeavor, declaring "the feeling of what wrong morally we Americans are in the present affair with you." Sensing the inevitability of US military occupation and domination, he stressed the role of mass education as a counterpoint. "What you young men must do is Educate, Educate, Educate! . . . Bring up the masses, teach them. The capacity of a people is measured by its masses, not its exceptionals." Calloway's counsel here harkens directly to the ethos of collective Black political formation and advancement during Reconstruction, rooted in the principle and practices of mass uplift.[41]

At work across the editorials in the Black press and the actions of Black soldiers lay a rigorous critique of imperialism developed through the experiences of fighting racism within the US and an identification with Filipinos facing US imperialism abroad. It was the insights forged through experiences of Jim Crow violence, exploitation, and segregation that developed a capacity to comprehend the twisted meaning of "civilization" and "democracy" that the US claimed to be exporting to the world. Moreover, this critique made connections between disparate places in the world—the US, Hawaii, Puerto Rico, Cuba, and the Philippines—and the practices of collective sovereignty and autonomy that are violated. Imperialist expansion, they understood, was rooted in a degraded understanding of governance and democracy, as it functioned through the belief that there existed categories of humanity not fit for self-government, and with whom US citizens shared no common purpose. Black internationalists rejected such a contention, insisting that self-determination and collective sovereignty were universal conditions of all of humanity.

These identifications constituted a wider type of freedom, one that rejected an ideology of barbarism and did not require, as Dr. King would say nearly 70 years later, "massive doses of violence to solve the world's problems." By linking together geographically disparate sites that shared experiences of devastation and suffering produced by state violence, they contested the dominant narrative of US benevolence that has always been central to securing consent for militarism. And they imagined and enacted modes of identification and solidarity that exceeded the national parochialisms on which militarism thrives. Indeed, it was through an analysis of racism and white supremacy in the US that they came to such global identifications, in stark contrast to many white anti-imperialists who rejected such commitments.

The global anti-colonial identifications witnessed in African American opposition to US imperialism in the Philippines anticipated a flourishing practice of Black internationalism in the twentieth century that confronted the particular structures of recruitment and affinity on which militarism thrives. W. E. B. DuBois, for example, took to the pages of the NAACP's the *Crisis* to condemn the US Marines' 1915 invasion of Haiti, insisting that the US recognize and respect the sovereignty of the Western Hemisphere's second oldest democracy.[42] In the early 1950s, as President Truman accelerated the war in Korea, political figures including the actor

Paul Robeson, the Los Angeles–based journalist Charlotta Bass, and the Communist leader Claudia Jones worked to build popular consciousness among civil rights supporters in the US around the imperative of peace in Korea.[43] And a rich history of mutual identification and exchange has linked minoritized communities within the US to self-determination struggles in Palestine, Egypt, and the Arab world.[44]

All of these commitments and politics were rooted in an identification with subjects, groups, and nations whose alleged violence and degeneration threatened the foundations of freedom in the US. Yet even as such groups sought to build alliances and identifications abroad, they still had to contest the potent ways that militarism secured consent and popular legitimacy at home.

THE STAR-SPANGLED BANNER: CONTESTING SYMBOLIC PARTICIPATION

On a blustery January day in 1973, a crowd of 20,000 people listened intently as 40-year-old Ethel Ennis hovered on the last note of "The Star-Spangled Banner." Ennis, a supremely talented if underappreciated jazz vocalist, had been invited to sing the anthem at President Richard Nixon's second inauguration by Vice President Spiro Agnew, who like Ennis hailed from Baltimore and was a jazz enthusiast. Dressed in a light purple overcoat and fur hat, Ennis was the first Black woman to sing the anthem at a presidential inauguration and the first to sing it without an accompanying military band. She took this opportunity to improvise on the melody, playing with the song's phrasing and scooping up or down to related pitches to embellish the standard melody.[45]

About a month before Ennis's performance, Nixon had authorized a massive 11-day aerial bombing campaign across a wide swath of North Vietnam. "Operation Linebacker II," as it was dubbed by military planners, heaped 15,000 tons of ordinance on civilian areas around Hanoi and Haiphong, destroying large parts of the country's infrastructure and killing more than 1,500 civilians. The "Christmas bombings" were particularly shocking because Nixon had pledged during his reelection campaign

Ethel Ennis sings the national anthem at Nixon's second inauguration, January 1973. Credit: The Richard Nixon Presidential Library and Museum (National Archives and Records Administration).

to end the war; Secretary of State Henry Kissinger had promised a few months before the election that "peace is at hand."[46]

Ennis was no conservative ideologue. A registered Democrat, she explained later that she accepted the invitation to sing the anthem amid a period of national turmoil over the war in order to "lullaby and cradle America."[47] And at a time when few Black singers or artists reached a national stage in this way, she embraced the chance to represent her music and style and to make the anthem her own. She later told an interviewer that she had decided, in accepting the invitation, that she would be "singing for the people."[48]

As Ennis drew out the phrases of the anthem, recalling the playful and improvisatory approaches of singers like Louis Armstrong and Ella Fitzgerald, a multiracial group of 60,000, many of whom had gathered at Washington, DC's Black churches, protested outside the inaugural ceremony, demanding an immediate end to the war.[49]

The protesters targeted the administration, some chanting, "Nixon, Agnew, you can't hide; we charge you with genocide."[50] But the inauguration inspired the 36-year-old poet June Jordan to address Ennis, rather than Nixon. Jordan's "Poem to My Sister, Ethel Ennis, Who Sang 'The Star-Spangled Banner' at the Second Inauguration of Richard Milhous Nixon, January 20, 1973," began:

> *gave proof through the night*
> *that our flag was still there*
> on his 47th inauguration of the killer king
> my sister
> what is this song
> you have chosen to sing?

For Jordan, neither Ennis's artistic virtuosity nor her aspirations to unify a shaken populace redeemed her appearance "for the second coronation of the killer king." Amid an imperial war opposed by colonized and formerly colonized people from around the world, Ennis's presence on that national stage could not be neutral. Willingly or not, she was being conscripted—incorporated into a project that sought popular consent for a brutal war. The national anthem, whose lyrics recall a US military triumph over British forces in 1812, remains a potent affective emblem of American militarism.[51] The ritual requiring audiences to stand in silence, sometimes with hand over heart, while the anthem is played symbolizes and reproduces popular consent to militarism and nationalism.

Jordan's haunting verse continued as a series of questions to Ennis, linking Nixon and the militaristic rituals of the anthem to the "homicidal holiday shit" that left the "silence of the children dead on the street." Jordan asked Ennis:

> After the ceremonial guns salute the ceremonial rifles saluting the ceremonial
> cannons that burst forth a choking smoke to celebrate murder
> Will it be clear
> In that red that bloody red glare
> My sister
> That glare of murder and atrocity/atrocities
> of power
> strangling every program
> to protect and feed and educate and heal and house the people

The poem was not an act of condemnation. Jordan did not, in today's terms, seek to "cancel" Ennis. Instead, in addressing Ennis repeatedly as "my sister," Jordan acknowledged and affirmed their connection, their dependence, and their kinship. Rather than dismissing Ennis, she asked the singer "to see," to notice the violence and suffering she had been recruited to both conceal and celebrate.

Jordan's entreaty to Ennis illuminates the contradictory relationship between racism, anti-racism, and militarism.[52] On the one hand, Jordan's poem laid bare the enduring and devastating impact of US militarism and imperialism, and its central role in distributions of life and death and across the globe. Her descriptions of "incinerated homes and Bach Mai Hospital blasted" invoked the military's capacity to extinguish life at an industrial scale, and linked it to the ways that investments in militarization suffocate alternative visions of social progress and human sustenance. And as Jordan's larger body of poetry and essays makes evident, she understood militarization, colonial violence, policing, and prisons as interconnected and interdependent. The hollowed-out countryside of Vietnam was linked to the hollowed-out neighborhoods of Newark. The colonial vision that organized apartheid South Africa was linked to the colonial vision that led to the seizure of land and the elimination of Indigenous life in the United States. Distinctions between the colonizer and colonized, between the occupier and the occupied, between white and nonwhite, are produced through relations of violence; race-making and war-making always travel together.[53]

At the same time, Jordan addressed the powerful and complex performances of national virtue and righteousness that perpetually accompany US military action: the claim that all US wars are fought in the name of liberation, a heavy but necessary burden borne by a freedom-loving populace. These ideological seductions are as important to the military as any fleet of tanks, helicopters, or bombers. Jordan recognized the ways such ceremonies address collective desires and secure popular assent, and how the longing for national inclusion can make all of us complicit in "homicidal holiday shit." Her encounter with Ennis was a rumination on such complicity, and the silences demanded in exchange for national belonging. Indeed, since the late nineteenth century, military service and participation in the military economy have been one of the central means by which subordinated groups have secured employment, civil rights, and political standing within the United States. Even as militarization has been vital to the production and reproduction of racial hierarchy, people of color have been essential to the military's functioning and operation. Militarization, paradoxically, makes use of both racial domination and racial incorporation.

Yet for Jordan, there was still hope that Ennis could claim and inhabit a political tradition different from the one offered by Nixon and Agnew. She concluded the poem:

Can you see
my sister

say can you see
my sister

and sing no more of war

The poem's final line recalls "I ain't gonna study war no more," from the nineteenth-century Negro spiritual "Down by the Riverside." Referencing themes in the Old Testament about emancipation and the rejection of military and national violence, "Down by the Riverside" gestures toward a history of refusal—a cessation of consent. When Dr. King preached for the first time about his opposition to the war in Vietnam at his home Ebenezer Baptist Church in Atlanta in 1967, he situated himself directly in this genealogy, concluding the speech: "I don't know about you, but I ain't gonna study war no more."[54]

As historian Kimberley Phillips argues, Jordan's poem to Ennis "drew its righteous tone from people who understood that while they struggled for their own freedom, they were also compelled to turn their collective power to demand justice for others."[55] For Jordan and many others who mobilized to end the war in Vietnam, "speaking out against war had become a fundamental part of the struggle for racial justice."[56] And by challenging and subverting the celebration of militarization represented by the anthem, Jordan sought to interrupt the affective responses the performance is designed to recruit.

Jordan's decision to address herself to Ennis as her "sister" also invokes a mode of accountability that works independently of the hierarchies that militarism upholds, decentering the power of the state in favor of a lateral form of accountability between two Black women. This commitment to contest the conscription of other minoritized groups into militarized culture and institutions was a central practice of Black-led anti-war organizing. It was rooted not in demonization or distinctions in morality but in the interruption of the material and symbolic sites of recruitment and conscription. As the Third World Women's Alliance (a multiracial feminist organization founded by members of the Student Nonviolent Coordinating Committee [SNCC]) explained, "We want equal status in a society that does not exploit and murder other people and smaller nations ... fully aware that we will never be free until all oppressed people are free."[57]

Well before Dr. King's pronouncements against the war in Vietnam, Black organizers in the South had already been making the links between the domestic front and the international front: the dogs and firehoses and torture they faced as they attempted to cast ballots, ride the bus, and find decent work, and the bombs and napalm that showered the Vietnamese countryside. It was an understanding and analysis forged in the crucible of violence and death, shaped by the experiences of watching friends and loved ones die, in Tuskegee and in Hanoi.

In 1965 SNCC developed the Black anti-draft program, which included organized actions at military recruitment offices to dissuade Black soldiers from enlisting.[58] A leaflet passed out in McComb, Mississippi, that year explained, "No one has the right to ask us to risk our lives to kill other Colored People in Santo Domingo or Viet Nam, so that the white Americans can get richer. We will be looked upon as traitors by all the Colored People of the world if the Negro People continue to fight and die without a cause."[59] These actions unfolded as a growing number of soldiers who defied draft orders linked their opposition to the war to their opposition to racial violence at home; they understood the military as the guarantor of domination rather than of freedom.[60]

SNCC organizers also made political education materials, including a comic book authored by Julian Bond in 1967 and mailed to chapters around the country to use in encouraging draft-eligible men, especially high school students, not to register or enlist.[61] The comic book, which was intended to be used in community education settings, followed the model of Freedom Schools in the South, rejecting heavy-handed propaganda in favor of positing questions rooted in identification and consent. Its closing line reads "The war is fought in your name . . . What do you think?"[62]

Anti-racist efforts to confront conscription into the military peaked in 1968 when Gwen Patton, a Montgomery, Alabama–based organizer with SNCC, helped to found the National Black Anti-War Anti-Draft Union (NBAWADU). Its inaugural conference in Washington, DC, that year drew 700 people. Three years later, more than 300 delegates attended the Emergency Summit Conference of Asian, Black, Brown Puerto Rican and Red People against the War in Gary, Indiana.[63] If draft resistance in the popular imagination is associated with young white men burning their draft cards, these efforts were rooted in commitments to educate communities of color about the relationship between racist violence in the US—whether in Detroit, East Los Angeles, or Mississippi—and the war in Vietnam.[64]

RAYTHEON DINÉ: RACIALIZED MILITARISM AND MILITARIZED ANTI-RACISM

On April 6, 2017, President Donald Trump announced from his Mar-a-Lago estate in Florida that US warships in the Mediterranean Sea had launched of 59 cruise missiles at Al Shayrat airfield in Syria.[65] Initial reports indicated that more than a dozen people were killed in the attacks, including some civilians. Between 2014 and 2019, in the name of bringing freedom and democracy to the region, US coalition–led airstrikes in Syria killed nearly 14,000 people.[66] June Jordan's poetic cry from 1973 about "American shit vomit dropping down death and burying the lives the people" extended far beyond Vietnam.

The 3,000-pound missiles were named Tomahawks. The US military often references Native nations and people in branding its armaments and missions. There are Black Hawk, Apache, Lakota, and Chinook helicopters. The Gray Eagle drone. Huron and Ute airplanes. In its 2011 mission to assassinate Osama bin Laden, the military assigned him the code name "Geronimo." Many dozens of military bases are named after Native people or those who led military assaults against them. "Welcome to Injun Country" is a regular refrain from US soldiers stationed abroad, as are references to the "civilizing" and "democratizing" mission of the nation's military interventions on the "frontier."[67] Here, the colonial tropes that ratified the military conquest of the eighteenth and nineteenth centuries—the noble savage succumbing to the march of civilization—get renewed for the global cavalry of the new millennium.

Given this history, it is perhaps surprising to learn the provenance of some of the components of the Tomahawk cruise missiles that rained down on the Al Shayrat airfield: a facility in Farmington, New Mexico, known as Raytheon Diné. A partnership between Raytheon, one of the world's largest private military contractors, with annual sales of $24 billion, and the Navajo Nation, the plant employs more than 350 workers, 90 percent of whom are Navajo. The facility expanded in 2017, opening a $5 million warehouse to store missile components, a project paid for almost entirely by the tribe's economic development fund, which brought an additional 70 jobs to the Raytheon Diné facility. In this corner of northwest New Mexico at the edge of the Navajo reservation, the contradictory labor and history of colonialism, racialized militarism, and a militarized anti-racism come into full view.

The Navajo Nation entered into a partnership with Raytheon in 1989 to bring employment and revenue to the tribe and the reservation, where more than 40 percent of the households lived (and continue to live) below the federal poverty line. Yet long before that, the Navajo had already been radically transformed by the military's presence and impact. As Anishinaabekwe (Ojibwe) writer Winona LaDuke explains in *The Militarization of Indian Country*, "Militarization and national violence has defined the relationship between the U.S. and indigenous nations" from the removal and extermination policies imposed by the US army to the forms of cultural violence and assimilation secured by Indian boarding schools, which were founded by a military leader, Colonel Richard Pratt.[68]

In the infamous "Long Walk" during the Civil War, the US Army forced thousands of Navajos to trek 400 miles from their ancestral lands in present-day Arizona to Bosque Redondo, an internment camp in western New Mexico. The historian John Grenier argues that military actions like these, targeting "insurgent" civilian populations, were central to the military's development. This specific form of anti-Indian violence served as a precursor to the "irregular wars" subsequently fought in the Philippines, Korea, Vietnam, and in the "war on terror" today.[69]

In the 1930s, after the discovery of uranium and coal on Navajo lands, hundreds of mines opened over the objections of tribal leaders. Tens of thousands of Navajo mineworkers and others in surrounding communities were exposed to radiation poisoning and radioactive waste at the same time the US Bureau of Indian Affairs actively worked to reduce livestock on the Navajo reservation under the guise of modernization. The Bureau severed "social and material relations formed around sheep herding [and] preempted the entry of Navajos into the wage economy."[70] By the late 1980s, the Navajos' growing dependence on revenues from uranium- and coal-mining leases made the tribal government more vulnerable to the fluctuation and collapse of those industries, even as tribal communities witnessed the poisoning of their drinking and irrigation water because of the mining.[71]

At the same time, military service and the military economy have become a site for some people to escape the same economic and social vulnerabilities produced by this long history of military dispossession and colonial rule. There are today between 160,000 and 190,000 Native American military veterans, or an estimated 22 percent of the Native adult population, a proportion three times as high as the non-Native population.[72]

In a national culture that valorizes militarization and patriotism, military service has continually offered an opportunity for members of subordinated groups to claim rights and protections by demonstrating their loyalty and belonging by struggling for "the right to fight" or what some scholars have described as "martial citizenship"[73] and "warrior patriotism."[74]

In this context, in which other possibilities for communal life, relationships, and sustenance for Navajo people become constrained or eliminated, military contracting emerges as a strategy for the tribe's economic survival; private defense companies and the US military more generally become valorized as crucial allies in the tribe's struggle for self-determination. As Navajo Nation president Ben Shelley explained at the groundbreaking eremony for the new Raytheon warehouse in 2014, "Not only do we make the best Tomahawks in the world, but we are also working together to advance lives of Navajo people through employment and economic development."[75]

The Raytheon Diné case is important because it reveals the capacity of a militarized economy and polity to incorporate a diverse range of racialized and colonized subjects into a global circuit of militarized violence, control, and profit. LaDuke notes that because of the history of uranium mining in the Southwest, Indigenous people and their lands and labor are indelibly "linked to the Hiroshima and Nagasaki bombs, as well as to more than a thousand nuclear tests undertaken in the Pacific and in Nevada."[76] And those places are linked to facilities like the Hanford Site in central Washington, located entirely within the territory of the Yakama Nation, which stores much of the radioactive waste produced by generations of nuclear weapons systems.[77] So too does militarization today connect Navajo engineers and manufacturing workers in New Mexico with bombing sites in Syria. As one group of Diné and other Indigenous people organizing against these military contracting arrangements explained, these deals are best understood as "a reflection of capitalist expressions of tribal sovereignty."[78]

Militarized and nuclear economies work across time and space, linking places and moments of extraction to places and moments of production, detonation, and disposal. Raytheon Diné severs and denies those relationships, imagining only a connection to job and income gains, corporate prosperity, or national security. Yet a rich history and contemporary practice of Indigenous organizing, theorizing, and creative work has refused these militarized incentives and imperatives. Indigenous theorizations of relationality, reciprocity, and refusal account for some of the most generative and far-reaching practices and frameworks to resist and undermine racialized militarization. They yield ways of understanding relationships between entities, peoples, and nations, as well as nonhuman animals, landscapes, and other life forms that are rooted in mutuality rather than exploitation and demonization.

Indigenous experiences with militarism and settler colonialism have produced visions and practices that have asserted a necessary relationship and dependence on other colonized peoples, sometimes in distant parts of the world. For example, some of the uranium in the nuclear weapons used by the US military to kill 200,000 people in Hiroshima and Nagasaki in 1945 was mined in the Northwest Territories in Canada by members of a First Nations group known as the Dene. The men who mined and transported the uranium were also exposed to radiation; many later died of radiation-related illnesses.

Decades later, Dene leaders sought to come to terms with their conscription into the militarized and radioactive economy, and their role in the annihilation of 200,000 people in a distant land. The Dene Uranium Committee published a report called "They Never Told Us These Things." Anthony Burke explains that they sought to "draw a cosmic circle between the events and connect their two communities in a shared discourse of mourning and experience."[79]

Diné scholar Lou Cornum writes that in 1988, six Dene elders "came to Hiroshima to apologize and to recognize the shared radioactive reality between people touched by the detonation of the bomb and those who unwittingly touched the materials that would make such a weapon." Cornum observes that "nobody from the Canadian government was present, none among those who had exploited the miners' bodies and their home lands and willingly aided the construction of the atomic bomb ever made the journey." Cornum asks, "What does it mean to ask forgiveness for something that was forced upon you?" The material relationships of mining, radiation exposure, and detonation produced an "irradiated international" that could seek "to protect themselves from harm without reproducing harm for others."[80]

The Dene delegation to Japan deserves attention not because it secured a particular policy goal or political realignment but because it brings forward a mode of relationality and mutual accountability across place and time; a connection rooted in shared experiences of domination and visions of liberation rather than of national belonging.[81] Indigenous literary works, including Leslie Marmon Silko's (Laguna Pueblo) *Ceremony* and Marie Clements's (Métis) play *Burning Vision* similarly explore the complex relationships between disparate sites linked by militarism and violence, in which one can be both the victim and the victimizer.[82] Silko and Clements invoke a practice in which relationality and solidarity must be forged across great distances and many decades in order to interrupt the material and affective appeals of nationalism.

Today, Diné groups including Tó Nizhoni Ani, the Black Mesa Water Coalition, Diné CARE, and coalitions such as the International Indigenous Environmental Network continue to challenge efforts to draw the Navajo tribal government into the militarized and resource extraction economy. Their capacity to think across scales of time and place is central to their critique. As Leona Morgan (Diné) of Diné No Nukes, explained, "Colonization isn't just the theft and assimilation of our lands and people, today we're fighting against nuclear colonialism which is the theft of our future." Tom Goldtooth, executive director of the Indigenous Environmental Network, insists: "Our Native Nations are on the frontlines fighting a colonial energy system that does not recognize treaties and Indigenous rights, our spiritual cosmologies and the protection of water of life."[83]

This collective refusal to be incorporated into a "colonial energy system" is rooted in a wider type of freedom (and sovereignty) for Indigenous groups in particular but has resonances and articulations within other racially subordinated groups in the US. For example, Claudia Jones was also part of an early movement of organizing efforts to counteract popular support for the atomic bomb, joining figures like civil rights leader Bayard Rustin, who led a team in Ghana to stop the French from testing a nuclear weapon in the Sahara.[84] Thirty years later, Black mayors like Harold Washington in Chicago took forceful collective stands against the expansion of the US nuclear arsenal, linking Reagan-era austerity measures devastating Black communities with nuclear proliferation and militarism.[85]

PAZ PARA VIEQUES/PROTECT KAHOʻOLAWE ʻOHANA

On a spring day in 2000, two organizers named Kyle Kajihiro and "Aunti Terri" Kekoʻolani boarded a small fishing boat in Vieques, Puerto Rico, some 5,300 miles away from their home in Honolulu. As for others on the boat, it was death that had brought them to this place.

A year earlier, a Marine Corps F/A 18 Hornet flew in low off the horizon and dropped two 500-pound Mk 82 bombs on this island municipality six miles east of the mainland. For the 9,500 civilian residents of Vieques, this was unremarkable. Since the mid-1940s, two-thirds of the 52-square-mile island had been controlled by the US Navy, including a 900-acre Live Impact Area (LIA) carved out of the white sand beaches and former sugar cane plantations. In the previous 15 years, US Navy pilots had dropped nearly 15,000 tons of bombs on this range, about the size of New York's Central Park. On this April day, however, the pilots missed their target, and the bombs landed near a naval observation post outside of the range. David Sanes, a 35-year-old civilian employee of the navy on patrol near the post, was knocked unconscious from the impact of the bomb, and quickly bled to death from his injuries. Sanes had been born in Vieques, and like all Puerto Rican citizens, was also a citizen of the United States. Sanes was killed by his government.

Kajihiro and Keko'olani exited the boat on the beach abutting the range, the shoreline of eastern Puerto Rico visible a few miles away on the horizon. With others in their small delegation, they began making their way into the LIA. Immediately after Sanes's death, a group of family, friends, and longtime activists decided to occupy the bombing range, essentially becoming human shields in order to realize their goal: "Ni una bomba más." Monte David, the encampment they built to honor Sanes, soon drew hundreds of supporters; a dozen other nearby protest camps, populated by groups of labor unions, religious communities, and political parties followed.

Kajihiro and Keko'olani walked through a field of white wooden crosses planted in the range, moving carefully around a maze of rusting bombs, trucks, tanks, and mortar shells, the remnants of five decades of war games. The area reportedly had more craters per square mile than the surface of the moon. Kajihiro described the "shock of seeing this beautiful place— white sand, blue water—and then stepping around orange flags to mark unexploded ordinance." The white crosses represented the casualties of the navy's presence, not just those killed by errant bombs but also those who had died of cancer, an effect of decades of toxic exposure and pollution.

At Monte David, they were greeted by Carlos Zenon, one of the main organizers of the occupation and a leader in the Vieques Fishermen's Association, a group that has challenged the navy's presence for decades. Zenon glanced at the shirt Kajihiro was wearing: "Protect Kaho'olawe 'Ohana."

Zenon smiled. He told he told Kajihiro, "I know your people." In the 1970s, when Zenon began organizing with others to evict the US Navy from Vieques following the death of another civilian, Ángel Rodríguez Cristóbal, he met a delegation from Hawaii that was involved in a similar effort to end the military's occupation on the small island of Kaho'olawe, seven miles southwest of Maui. Indeed, just as protesters had occupied the naval range in Vieques to stop the bombing exercises, so too had Kanaka Maoli (Native Hawaiian) protesters, including Kekoʻolani, occupied Kahoʻolawe in 1976 to defend it from the navy's ordinance. Kajihiro would explain that across a great distance and many years, Zenon's recognition of the Protect Kahoʻolawe ʻOhana struggle illustrated the critical connection between these two small places, and their shared struggles to realize a world beyond militarism and imperialism.

Indeed, Vieques and Kahoʻolawe share a significant history. During World War II, the US military seized significant parts of both islands as wartime exigency, and never returned them to civilian control. Over the next 60 years, both places became indispensable in the geopolitical vision of the US military for training, testing, and instruction, precisely because these sites were imagined to be severed and unrelated to anywhere else or anyone else. Like other islands occupied by the US military, they became "zones of sacrifice," linked by the status imposed upon them as "nonsovereign territories"[86] subject to military control. Kajihiro says that "small places become important for projecting power. They are easy to maintain and dominate without the friction of resistance."

The movements that emerged to contest the military's control over Vieques and Kahoʻolawe understood them quite differently as sites rich in relationalities and life possibilities. For the people of Vieques, this meant invoking their relationship to the land and water as food sources and habitats, as well as to many thousands of people in mainland Puerto Rico, other parts of the United States, and elsewhere who did not regard the island and its inhabitants as disposable. Indeed, the many hundreds of delegations of religious and political leaders, cultural figures, and antimilitary organizations who came to Monte David to join the human shield embodied these relations, as did the many thousands who participated in protests against the navy's presence outside of Vieques. Their presence both challenged the military's contention that places like Vieques operated with the consent of the Puerto Rican public (and the US public more generally) and demonstrated the many rich relationships in which Vieques and its people were embedded.

Protect Kahoʻolawe ʻOhana (PKO) began organizing in 1976 as part of a broader resurgence in Native Hawaiian organizing for sovereignty, land control, language rights, traditional cultural practices, and power. PKO similarly made use of unauthorized occupations to publicize and interrupt military bombing exercises there. Kahoʻolawe had for centuries been a central and revered spiritual site to the Kanaka Maoli. Beginning in the nineteenth century, large-scale ranching operations took over large parts of the island, before the US military assumed control in 1941.[87] At the heart of Kanaka Maoli resistance to the military in Kahoʻolawe is an analysis of ways that militarism, tourism, and the plantation economy disorganized relationships to land and kinship structures and the very capacity of families and localities to reproduce and sustain themselves.[88] This critique extends to nearly every part of Hawaii, as nearly 20 percent of lands in Hawaii remain under US military control.

This status, and the shared experiences to contest military control and power, undergird the many decades of reciprocal identification, exchange, and relationality between places like Vieques and Hawaii. The longtime Kanaka Maoli scholar and organizer Haunani-Kay Trask explained to scholar activist Rebekah Garrison that since her early involvement in the PKO and Hawaiian sovereignty movement, she had been aware that "people in Vieques helped us understand that we had so much in common." Trask said that every time she would give a speech or attend a rally, she "would always bring [Vieques] up, and it's kind of like comradeship." She continued: "What happens is that little archipelagos are swept up by gigantic nations . . . so everybody who suffers it is from a small place." As different colonizing nations imposed their languages on these places, it further separated them from one another, particularly in the Pacific. This required the Kanaka Maoli and other Indigenous people from Pacific island nations—New Zealand, Tahiti, Guam, the Northern Marinanas and other parts of Micronesia, the Marshall Islands, Okinawa—to "start visiting people . . . We are in an ocean that makes us very aware that we are small countries in a big place, and that place is controlled by the United States. So, we're all comrades in that moment." It was this practice of visiting and shared identification that brought Kajihiro and Aunti Terri to Mount Sanes, and that led Zenon to recognize and embrace them so instantly.[89]

The efforts in Vieques and Kahoʻolawe were also notable because their relentless protests and arrests brought international attention to these small places and compelled the US military to relinquish their authority over those places.[90] Today, organizers continue to address issues of environmental cleanup and ordnance removal, and restoring the lands of the former bombing ranges so they can sustain new life and new relationships. Broad-based networks have formed to link disparate sites of US military control and ensure that closed bases are not simply relocated to another place. Many of these efforts, including the International Women's Network against Militarism, emphasize a gendered analysis of the impact of US militarization, including the increased prevalence of sexual assault in and around the bases and the impact the military economy has on women who labor in low-wage positions.[91]

These efforts must also reckon with what scholar Sasha Davis describes as the "regime of feelings" closely tied to military and tourist economies that "establishes a certain ideological, political, and cultural order that normalizes the presence of the military, prioritizes its needs, and defends its central role in defining 'national security.'"[92] In Hawaii, the military's presence is so ubiquitous and pervasive—it's present everywhere—that it's hidden in daily life, and its cumulative impact and authority can be difficult to grasp.[93]

To reveal the military's presence and to contest the regimes of feeling upon which it relies, Kajihiro and Keko'olani have organized with the Kanaka Maoli and allied groups, including Hawai'i Peace and Justice and DMZ-Hawai'i/Aloha, to invoke a future of Hawaii that is not founded in militarized economies, control, and environmental degradation. To educate visitors and Hawaiians alike about the military's continued impact on all aspects of Hawaiian life, Kajihiro and Keko'olani created the "De Tour," a multi-hour guided tour across Honolulu that demonstrates the connections between more than a century of US military and political occupation of Hawaii and the present regime of "mila-tourism" that posits the military and tourist economies as beneficial, permanent, and inevitable features of Hawaiian life. After touring several sites that demonstrate the long reach of the military's control of Oahu's housing, economy, environment, and history, the tour ends at the Hanakehau Learning Farm, in a valley 10 miles from downtown Honolulu, on the crown lands of the Hawaiian Nation.[94]

Over lunch, longtime Hawaiian organizer Andre Perez, who spent seven years living on Kaho'olawe working on environmental restoration

Rally at global conservation meeting to address the environmental damage from US military bases. Credit: Ann Wright.

after the navy left, explains that the restoration of the farm, as a site to grow traditional foods and to support balanced and ethical relations to the land, represents the possibilities for "a little kīpuka of Hawaiian critical consciousness that is in the shadow of militarization, in the belly of the beast, but serves as a beacon of hope for the future."[95] Perez is also a military veteran; Native Hawaiians continue to be overrepresented in the military, and many leaders in the Kanaka Maoli movement today have served in the military, as it represented one of the few possibilities outside of the low-wage tourist economy. Perez, Kajihiro, Kekoʻolani, and others have organized to build this "kīpuka," a zone of new possibility for peace, restoration, relationality, and flourishing that if nurtured properly may be spread to other places in the world. In a world overrun by militarism that can only imagine a freedom predicated on violence and war, their organizing, practices, and vision invoke an alternative and wider vision of freedom.

CODA: DAVID CEMÍ PRESENTE

Following the death of David Sanes Rodríguez in 1999, a widely circulated photo showed the lifelong Vieques resident in his civilian naval uniform, shoulders back, his hand at the brim of his cap in full salute. The
image captures many of the contradictions that haunt other places dominated by the US military. As the navy's control of two-thirds of the island
eradicated other possible economies and livelihoods, employment in the
military became one of the few viable ways to earn a living; Sanes was
proud of his service on the naval base. As two-thirds of the island had been
off limits to most civilians for more than 50 years, even amid the protests
against the navy's presence, it was difficult to imagine other futures.

Yasmín Hernández's portrait of David Sanes reckons with these con-
straints. The Puerto Rico–based artist, who has familial connections to
Sanes, sought a way to preserve his life, memory, and spirit as captured by
the photo without reproducing or naturalizing his relationship to the military as inevitable. Hernández's work, titled "David Cemí," preserves his
posture and straightforward gaze from the photo. But both his hands now
rest by his side; the salute removed. "Cemí" names an ancestral spirit in
the language of the Taino, the Indigenous people of the Caribbean. He is
now rendered in fluorescent blue-green hues, erasing the trappings of his
military uniform and invoking instead the famed bioluminescent bay on
the island's southern shore, which during certain times of the month
alight with a bright blue glow emitted by billions of single-cell microscopic
organisms. The colors invoke for Hernández an "indigenous cosmology,
particularly the belief that the ocean is the dwelling place of spirits." The
portrait reimagines Sanes as a transcendent figure of peace and justice,
connected to the West African and Indigenous presence in Vieques that
long proceeded the US military's control of the island. Hernández thus
summons identifications that are not oriented toward state violence and
militarism but are rooted in other forms of relationality—to the land and
environment and to ways of knowing and being—that remain ever present
in Vieques and in all places now under military control.[96]

No form of broad-based redistribution—of resources, social power,
rights, or standing—can take place without addressing the fundamental
ways that militarization configures social and political life in the United

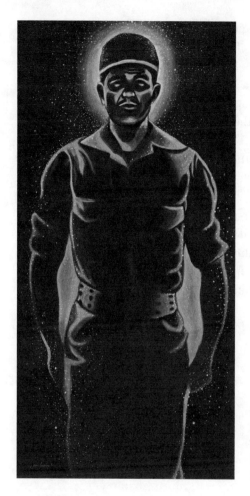

Portrait of David Sanes Rodríguez.
Credit: *David: Cemí*, 2009, Bieké
Tierra de Valientes series. Yasmín
Hernández. Acrylic on black fabric,
60" ≈ 30". yasminhernandezart.com.

States today and recruits diverse subjects into its structures and logics.
The legacy of US military incursions and operations—in Africa, Asia, the
Middle East, Central and South America, the Pacific, Europe, and across
many places in the US, is ongoing. One cannot, for example, comprehend
the crisis driving millions from their homes and communities across the
globe today without reckoning with the long impact of US militarism. At
home and abroad, militarization fuels the ecological crisis, consumes tremendous material resources, enables immense corporate profiteering,

and makes preemptive violence and premature death the necessary conditions of an impoverished notion of freedom.

And as figures such as W. E. B. Du Bois, Betita Martínez, June Jordan, and many others have argued, a robust movement for demilitarization cannot be built without reckoning with the way racism and the elaboration of racial meaning secures the popular consent and material conditions on which militarism relies. The ideology of race produces and legitimates what Jordan describes as the "conversion of a stranger's land into a killing field"[97] even as it deploys forms of multicultural incorporation that justify empire.

And yet this long record of war-making, invasions, and occupations has produced collective practices and strategies that imagine and enact new forms of relationality, vulnerability, and flourishing necessary to abolish "empire as a way of life." This means following the example of draft resisters and those working against militarism in Vieques and Hawaii as well as rebuilding a society after militarism.

There are no final blueprints for this work—only sketches and poems and impulses and notes. But they provide us with a starting point.

4 Labor

"TO ENJOY AND CREATE THE VALUES OF HUMANITY"

On a Saturday in mid-June 2001, a group of farmworkers marched down South Wilmington Street in Raleigh, North Carolina. Many labored in the state's cucumber fields for dozens of farmers that sold their product to the Mt. Olive Pickle Company, one of the largest independent pickle producers in the country. Most were classified as "guest workers" by the federal government, among the roughly 100,000 migrant farmworkers that toiled across more than 20,000 farms in the state, harvesting cucumbers, tobacco, watermelons, and sweet potatoes.[1] They worked amid dangerous pesticides for low wages, forced to keep up a backbreaking pace with few enforceable workplace rights. Poor medical care, ramshackle housing, and sexual harassment and discrimination from supervisors were common. Two years earlier, the workers had turned to the Farm Labor Organizing Committee (FLOC), a 25-year-old union based in northwest Ohio, to organize. They soon launched a consumer boycott of Mt. Olive to demand that the company recognize the union and sign a collective bargaining agreement with the workers and the pickle growers in the state.

Yet the farmworkers who made their way through downtown Raleigh did not seek a fair contract and decent working conditions just for themselves. They did not simply demand a share of the "American Dream" or a

Juneteenth Black and Latino Unity March in North Carolina, June 2001.
Credit: UE150.

pathway to the spoils of US citizenship. The political genealogy they summoned that day was not the US Constitution, but a celebration of
Juneteenth, and the legacy of Black struggle for emancipation and the
forging of new conditions of freedom. Indeed, the 300 marchers who
chanted, "Don't spend a nickel on a Mt. Olive pickle" were not farmworkers alone. The march was co-organized with FLOC by Black Workers for
Justice, a group that emerged from a campaign led by Black women who
worked for K-Mart, and UE Local 150, a militant union of public employees founded by housekeepers at the University of North Carolina, Chapel
Hill, in the early·1990s. Their collective platform and demands included
not only a fair contract for farmworkers, but also an end to racial profiling
by police. They called for reparations for African Americans in general
and for payments to Black farmers and Mexican braceros in particular.
They demanded union organizing rights and a living wage for all workers,
and amnesty for the undocumented.[2]

For FLOC, the Juneteenth march and the solidarities it summoned were
not simply rooted in the formation of a temporary coalition to support
their campaign. FLOC understood that the very foundations of the agricul-

tural economy that farmworkers encountered in the South were enmeshed with the legacy of slavery and the way it transformed people into commodities. And in order for farmworkers to transform the conditions they faced, they needed to learn from and contribute toward Black-led struggles for power and economic justice. They needed to draw from an "abolitionist consciousness" that found life possibilities not from employers or elites but from one another.[3] The fate of the worker harvesting the cucumber crops was tied to the housekeeper laboring in the UNC dorms, and to the driver racially profiled by the police. For farmworkers' conditions to change, everything had to change. As FLOC president Baldemar Velásquez explained at the march, the farmworkers' campaign compelled the powerful company they confronted to change their "entire lifestyle, the way they live and the way they're used to thinking about things."[4]

This chapter surveys efforts of groups—workers rushing to keep pace with the assembly lines in Detroit; those laboring in the grocery stores of Koreatown in Los Angeles; domestic workers in Atlanta—that have forged social relations, solidarities, and power to make possible lives and worlds beyond the imperatives of private accumulation and domination. It traces a genealogy of anti-racist labor thought and collective action around work and economic life that has sought not only to raise wages or benefits but also to reorient the broader political economy toward care and the meeting of life needs. These accounts center on the leadership of Black and immigrant organizers, exploring how those most exposed to the violence of capitalism are best positioned to understand, and radically transform, the relations of power around labor and the material conditions of life in the United States. These individuals and collectives, exploited as workers or pushed into the wageless "surplus" by increasing demand for efficiency, used their experience to develop sophisticated ideas and practices of resistance, powerful visions for a society free of exploitation, and vital solidarities across boundaries of class, race, language, and place.

A PERSON IS NOT A THING

Nearly 25 years before the Juneteenth marchers laid claim to the streets of downtown Raleigh, Dr. Martin Luther King Jr. declared in an Atlanta speech that "a nation that will keep people in slavery for 244 years will 'thingify' them and make them things."[5] King echoed a famous assertion by the Martiniquan writer and poet Aimé Césaire, who in 1950 wrote: "My turn to state an equation: colonization = thingification."[6] For King and Césaire, it was the transatlantic slave trade that structured and engendered this process of turning human life into a "thing" and that produced the necessary social ideas of degradation to sustain such a diminished understanding of human capacity. King and Césaire rejected the assumption that thingification ended with the abolition of slavery and colonial rule. These relations were most visible and devastating for the descendants of the enslaved; they were witnessed in the hierarchies that emerged in the South at the end of Reconstruction and in the sharecropping, domestic labor, chain gangs, and convict labor leasing programs that arose in its place.[7] Thingification shaped distinct forms of violence and social control against Black people; much of contemporary policing and carceral power is devoted to this specific end.[8]

King and Césaire also made clear that the alchemy that turns people into objects was a generalized attribute of the modern world order, always nourished through anti-Black racism, but never limiting its violence and discipline to Black people alone. The declaration that one is a "worker, not a criminal," sometimes heard in immigrant rights marches is made in the hope that it will protect one from thingification; that it permits an escape from the forms of exploitation and abandonment deemed permissible against those racialized as Black.[9] Yet contemporary wage labor indemnifies few people from thingification. This is not to suggest that wage work today, even in the most exploitative settings, is historically analogous to slavery and enslavement. That is not true, and such comparisons distort rather than expand our capacity to understand these relationships. It is instead to reject the deep-seated white supremacist assumption that explains exploitation and violence as *caused* by the particular ideas attached to Black people, as if there was some inherent condition associated with Blackness that explained their exploitation. Such a formulation transfers culpability from the motives and actions of the exploiter to some alleged condition of the exploited. It exonerates, in Toni Morrison's terms, "the hysteria and greed of those whose business it is to manipulate us."[10]

To contest thingification requires a transformation of the order on which it rests. It mandates a shift in the social relations that facilitate the private control and ownership of land and human labor, centering on three conditions foundational to the modern world economy.

First, for capitalism to function and profit to accumulate, existing forms of collectivity, protection, social relations, and the means for people to support themselves must be discredited, dissolved, and destroyed. Thus, at the dawn of the modern era, communally held lands in Europe were privatized and enclosed. In the Americas, long-standing and complex relations between Indigenous peoples and lands were condemned as primitive, and the land was taken by speculators and put under private control. The taking and privatization of communal lands continues to this day. When Portuguese enslavers arrived in West Africa in the 1500s they encountered forms of governance, kinship, and mutuality not rooted in thingification; within those relations, people could not be turned into inputs for investors from Liverpool. Only after being torn from those safeguards and incorporated into regimes of labor could they be subjected to such commodification and violence.[11] Colonialism and slavery had to destroy the commons, in all its forms, to leave people only with the possibility of turning their labor power (both waged and unwaged) over to capital in order to survive.[12]

Second, stripped of the protections of the commons and the collective, dispossessed subjects must be put into competition with one another. Race, gender, colonialism, and nation are central to this process of alienation and partition. The literary scholar Jodi Melamed argues that "capital can only be capital when it is accumulating, and it can only accumulate by producing and moving through relations of severe inequality among human groups," requiring "loss, disposability, and the unequal differentiation of human value."[13] The historians David Roediger and Elizabeth Esch have demonstrated that racial differentiation has been a central facet of labor management since industrialization.[14] Capitalism cannot function through an undifferentiated workforce; race and gender provide the critical social vocabulary of inherent worth and degradation that market competition requires. It organizes employment and the social relations of work around the allegedly unequal capacities for freedom that designate people for particular kinds of work. Indeed, white supremacy has bequeathed diverse and complex modes of racialization and differentiation. It has produced various figures—the enslaved, the migrant, the Indigenous, the alien—different not only from the native-born white, but also from one another.

Prevailing notions of national citizenship that sort people into good and bad subjects—those with the fitness to practice democratic citizenship and those without, similarly partition or alienate people from one another. To declare oneself a worker and not a criminal is a response to this division, a declaration that in the distinction between the fit and the unfit, the migrant worker pressing for her survival belongs to the former and not the latter.

Third, as in all dominant social relations, these conditions of wagelessness, competition, and alienation must be understood as natural and inevitable rather than the result of specific relations of power. That working for a wage for someone else, in competition with others, or exploiting the labor of another person, is the only means to live and to survive. That without such competition, and without the incentive of private accumulation and wealth around which it is organized, society will fail, as the loafers and indigent among us will bring everyone down. Racism is central to producing these distinctions, and to facilitating the feelings of distrust and suspicion that prevent alternative relations and solidarities from taking hold.

Yet the conditions that produce and facilitate thingification are never inevitable; other ways of relating, other visions of economic and social life, and other solidarities are always present. There are possibilities for freedom beyond mutual exploitation and preying on the vulnerabilities of others. There are visions of economic life that are not centered on the right to work for the profit of others, but in the social and collective potential to organize work, production, and consumption differently. These are imaginaries we learn from people like James Boggs and groups like the Dodge Revolutionary Union Movement—those who question what seems natural, refuse the logic of competition, and forge collective visions based on the right of every person to enjoy full humanity.

MISFITS AND RENEGADES

James Boggs could see it coming. He could see then what we know now. Fifty years before the Covid-19 pandemic revealed it to so many, he could see that this economy—this way of organizing work, of distributing income and wealth, of turning people into things—was heading toward disaster. That having one group of workers in a warehouse, a tomato field, an auto assembly plant, or a retail sales floor race against one another and the machines they worked alongside to meet a quota, while another group sat idly at home, without work and threatened by hunger, diminished us all. That labor, technology, production, and consumption could be organized around ends other than private accumulation and hoarding, in ways that would be far more sustaining of human life and creativity and of the world we inhabit. And that because racial subordination and differentiation were central to reproducing this treacherous order, the leadership and collective action necessary to abolish it would originate from those who comprehended capitalism's unwavering reliance on racism. People like James Boggs.

Born in a small town in central Alabama in 1919, Boggs as a teenager joined millions of other Black Southerners who journeyed north in the first part of the twentieth century, though his life partner, Grace Lee Boggs, would explain that he never surrendered his Alabama twang. In the late 1930s he settled in Detroit, where he worked at a sprawling Chrysler assembly plant for 28 years, joining tens of thousands of Black and white workers laboring in the city known as the Arsenal of Democracy. (For in this country, democracies have arsenals). He was an organic intellectual in the fullest sense. Following his shift on the assembly line, he would write, organize, and build political community, often with Grace, an equally formidable intellectual and movement builder.[15]

Boggs's experience on the assembly line, as a rank-and-file leader with the United Auto Workers (UAW) and the militant strikes it led in the 1940s, and as a journalist and organizer immersed in Detroit's vibrant milieu of Black radicalism, shaped the questions central to his writing, analysis, and organizing. What sectors of society would ultimately prove capable of leading the most far-reaching challenges to corporate power in the US? What "radical concepts" might such movements assert based on the "principle that people should be able to enjoy everything in life and from life, without being fettered or limited by any system"?[16] How could Black social movements ensure that their energies would not be incorporated into an order that incentivizes people to exploit, disavow, and abandon one another? And what he described as the "burning question" of how to create the kind of human responsibility in the distribution of material abundance that would allow everyone "to enjoy and create the values of humanity"?[17]

For Boggs, the means by which employers secured the incorporation, consent, and deference of workers to their imperatives lay at the center of these questions. Racism shaped and limited the contradictory orientation of the UAW and other industrial unions. On the one hand, white workers often joined in multiracial labor actions, including wildcat strikes, to raise wages and benefits and assert control over conditions on the line. On the other hand, white workers also organized to defend and reproduce racial hierarchies and divisions within the plants that employers had long fostered. For example, in the summer of 1943, some 25,000 white workers walked off the line at Ford's Packard plant to protest the promotion of three Black workers, one of dozens of white-led "hate strikes" that unfolded at plants across the country.[18] In the late 1940s, the passage of the Taft-Hartley Act and the purging of Communists and other radical elements from the US labor movement accelerated these dynamics, as labor leaders increasingly linked the well-being of workers with that of their employers. The confrontational labor actions of the 1930s and 1940s gave way to a sustained period of acquiescence on the part of the nation's most powerful unions in the 1950s, secured through a steady increase in wages and benefits for union members. As long as the assembly lines kept moving and consumer demand continued to grow, labor leaders like UAW president Walter Reuther were content to cede control over the speed of the line and the organization of the workforce to employers.[19] These modest increases in wages and protections against state violence and predation recruited many white workers into an identification with their employers and the existing economic order. These "bribes of whiteness" diminished the capacity of many white workers and white-led labor unions to press for a more fundamental transformation of that order.

Yet this transaction—labor peace in exchange for a cut of the profits, had a downside, even for white workers. The long-term contracts between the UAW and the automakers had not prevented the back-breaking speedup of the assembly lines, and the rash of injuries it produced, or addressed the waves of layoffs that regularly visited the plants. It largely reinforced the racialized and gendered division of labor, as Black male workers were assigned to the lowest-paying and most dangerous positions while most women (and especially Black women) were altogether excluded. And it had not provided anything close to full employment for Detroit's working-class communities. In the 1950s, as automakers moved their plants to the surrounding suburbs and white working- and middle-class families followed, hundreds of thousands of Black Detroiters were left with two unseemly options: find a place among the dwindling number of auto production workers and try to keep up with the line, or join the growing ranks of the abandoned, left to the terrors of police abuse, segregated and dilapidated housing, and meager state benefits.

For Boggs, there had to be another way. He argued in his 1963 book *American Revolution: Pages from a Negro Worker's Notebook* that rather than racing to prove themselves fit for exploitation by an intensifying regime of work and production, workers should instead demand a social order in which the accumulation of wealth made possible by technology should be enjoyed by all. He wrote, "Now that our productive machinery has been developed to the point that it can do the tasks that have heretofore been done by men, everyone, regardless of class, regardless of background, is entitled to the enjoyment of the fruits of that development, just as all men are entitled to warm themselves in the heat of the sun."[20]

For Boggs, a wider type of freedom could not be found in trying to get more people into the workforce or to turn those exploited by the market into exploiters themselves. The fight must not be simply for "access to the system" but for "the means and resources to have a decent living—a new concept of the system, a new vision of society."[21] Work could be organized around a basis other than competition and fear of destitution, and human needs—for food, shelter, kinship, health, medicine, work, reproduction, movement, creativity—could be claimed by all without qualification or ranking.

James made the stakes of the moment clear, writing that Black people should organize "not only to fight for jobs that soon will not exist but also ... to demand the equivalent income that would be derived from work if work is not available." Simply advocating for more work or full employment, as many liberals might, was not the answer, for it presumed that employment itself, even under the most dire conditions, had some inherent dignity. But more work under the same terms would not address this crisis. Indeed, the very notion that tied people's value to their capacity to labor for wages was itself rooted in the "18th-century philosophy that . . . anyone who can't or doesn't work (unless he happens to own property) is a misfit, an outcast, and a renegade from society."[22] Mainstream labor leaders, Boggs noted, were largely uninterested in transforming these conditions or organizing such "misfits." The white-led labor movement, for the most part, had "in effect become partners with management in a system of corrupting the population" and maintaining production levels in service of private profit and control, provided that some jobs were afforded to its members.[23]

Moreover, under these conditions, waged workers, predominantly but not exclusively white, laboring faster and harder for their survival, would channel much of their political frustration against the wageless and the expendable, rather than the exploiters. Anticipating the revolts in the 1970s and 1980s against property taxes, welfare benefits, and other social services, Boggs warned that "one section of the population will be pitted against another, not only the employed against the unemployed but those who propose that the unemployed will be allowed to starve rather than continue with such a drain on the public against those who cannot stand by and see society to generate into such barbarism."[24]

No one was wholly immune to the inducements to abandon these expendables and align with the ranks of the exploiters. Boggs maintained that "inside each American, from top to bottom, in various degrees, has been accumulated all the corruption of the class society that has achieved its magnificent technological process first and always by exploiting the Negro race, and then by exploiting the immigrants of all races."[25] Moreover, even those who bore the brunt of this exploitation would be "constantly encouraged to attempt to rise out of their class and themselves become exploiters of other groupings and finally of their own people."[26] That is, within this system, the dominant way to protect oneself from exploitation would be to join in the exploitation of others. Boggs warned of the pain and violence that would accompany "the struggle to rid themselves and each other of this accumulated corruption."[27]

Like C. L. R. James, whom he met and befriended in the late 1940s, Boggs argued that Black political and labor struggles constituted the most promising sites of radical organizing.[28] Black workers had a much more

sober and sophisticated understanding of the totality of the system's violence and its innate tendency to intensify and expand production as much
as possible with the fewest number of workers. For Black workers in particular, this meant some would race against steady accelerations of the
assembly line while others would be abandoned by a "system that creates
and multiplies the number of expendables."[29]

It would be for those displaced from this system and left without work
"to struggle for a society in which there are no displaced persons."[30] It was
these outcasts, rendered obsolete to the interests of capital, that could provide a new social vision in which the benefits and profits of automation
would be shared by all. With less need to work, everyone could apply their
talents, labor, and creative faculties to ends other than the private accumulation of wealth. Black people in cities like Detroit, abandoned by capital and subject to growing violence and surveillance by the state, were best
positioned to assert "a new declaration of human rights to fit the new age
of abundance."[31] Boggs explained, "We must look to the outsiders for the
most radical, that is, the deepest thinking after the changes that are
needed. What ideas will they have?"[32] It was a formidable task, as this
"new generation, the outsiders, the worthless people" for whom there was
no wage work would "now have to turn their thoughts away from trying to
out wit the machines" as traditional labor unions had done, and instead
focus their energies "toward the organization and reorganization of society and of human relations inside society." Boggs described this task as a
"revolution . . . directed not towards increasing production but toward the
management and distribution of things and toward the control of relations among people, tasks that up to now have been left to chance or in the
hands of an elite." It was their historical imperative to "pose radical concepts beyond the imagination of us."[33]

Boggs was not calling simply for a legislative fix, like universal basic
income, which provided a stipend to the wageless in order to maintain
consumption and protect and inure the current system. He anticipated
instead a process in which those most violated and abandoned by the economic order—both those toiling on the assembly line and those who were
jobless and wageless—would organize to struggle for a new form of economic life altogether. It would soon become clear to Black workers and
organizers in Detroit that their position within the hierarchies of labor—

and within the workplace—gave them particular power to disrupt production and push for radical change.

ORGANIZING BLACK POWER AT THE
POINT OF PRODUCTION

In May 1968, five years after Boggs published *American Revolution,* a multiracial group of 4,000 workers at Chrysler's aging Dodge Main Plant in Hamtramck, ten miles from downtown Detroit, walked off the job and halted production, demanding an end to the back-breaking speed-ups and perilous working conditions on the line; it was the first work stoppage at the plant in 14 years.[34] Many of the Black leaders who had organized the unplanned, or wildcat, strike had already been organizing within the plant against demands for speed-ups and increased productivity, the rash of workplace injuries, and the racism of plant managers. They were also deeply connected to Black-led organizing and consciousness-raising formations at campuses like Wayne State University and in community and neighborhood organizations in Black Detroit.

The company eventually fired two Black workers, Major Baker and Bennie Tate, for their alleged role in leading the wildcat strike. No white workers were disciplined, though many had also participated. In response, Baker, Tate, and a group of other workers at the Hamtramck plant founded the Dodge Revolutionary Union Movement (DRUM). For the Black workers who led the strike at Hamtramck, the violence of the assembly line and the pervasive racism in the allocation of jobs and authority within the plant mirrored the violence of the police baton, of the racially restrictive housing covenant, and of the unequal ordering of life in the city as a whole. Like Boggs, they asserted that work on the assembly line and the wages it provided was not the realization of freedom and autonomy but an extension of the long tradition of thingification. As explained in the *Inner City Voice,* a community-based newspaper edited by DRUM leaders, "Black workers are tied day in and day out . . . to a massive unending assembly line . . . that one never sees end or the beginning of but merely fits into a slot and stays there, sweating and bleeding, running and stumbling, trying to maintain a steadily increasing pace. Adding to the severity of the working conditions are the white racist and bigoted foreman, harassing, insulting, driving and snapping the whip over the backs of the thousands of black workers who have to work in these plants in order to eke out an existence." Black workers, largely abandoned by the UAW leadership, had come to "realize that the only method of pressing for their demands [was] to strike and to negotiate at the gates of industry."[35]

The 1968 rebellion at the Hamtramck gates was but one episode of a larger sweep of Black insurgency in the city. On a hot July night 10 months earlier, a police raid of an afterhours club in northwest Detroit had instigated one of the largest urban rebellions in the nation's history. Tens of thousands of Black Detroiters took to the streets for four days. More than 1,700 members of the National Guard imposed martial law on the city; 43 people lost their lives, the large majority killed by the police. The "Great Rebellion" was a revolt against the totality of the social order—not only racist policing, housing, and employment practices, but also the broad failure of the state and the market economy to produce conditions that would preserve and protect life. That is, at the height of the US postwar economic boom, a period that commentators today celebrate for its relative economic equality and shared prosperity, it was Black workers and community members who could best discern the inherent violence on which this system of prosperity rested.

DRUM, and an aligned group of Revolutionary Union Movement chapters that emerged at other auto plants in the area, sought to bring the consciousness and social vision of the Black Power movement to the point of production in one of the economy's most profitable industries. As John Watson, one of the founders of the umbrella League of Black Revolutionary Workers (LBRW) would explain in a 1969 interview, "Our analysis tells us that the basic power of black people lies at the point of production, that the basic power we have is the power as workers." Black workers, Watson explained, "have historically been and are now an essential element in the American economic scene. Without black slaves to pick the cotton on the southern plantations, the primitive accumulation of capital which was necessary to develop industry in both Europe and America would never have been accomplished. Without black workers slaving on the assembly lines and automobile plans in the city of Detroit, the automobile companies would not be able to produce cars in the first place, and therefore, wouldn't be able to make the tremendous profits which they have been making."[36] The masthead of a newspaper edited by Watson and other DRUM supporters at Wayne State University put it this way, "One class-conscious worker is worth 100 students."[37]

Their social vision was centered a classless society, one in which "all forms of exploitation and oppression are eliminated within the community," made possible by the abolition of an economic system of predation by elites. Marxism in their hands was a far more sophisticated and dynamic framework and practice, as it proved much more attentive to the ways capitalism and the organization of labor worked in practice, and the ways it relied so heavily on racial differentiation and the nominal incorporation of white workers. Groups like DRUM asserted that politically conscious Black workers could exercise a kind of leadership for the liberation of all workers that white workers and liberal labor leaders could not. Watson stated plainly that "white workers should prepare to accept leadership from the most advanced section of the proletariat."[38]

As skilled labor organizers and unionists, DRUM's leaders understood the fundamental necessity of building power and organization at the worksite, challenging the employer's control over working conditions, and organizing to improve pay and benefits. DRUM also contended that organized and politically conscious Black workers had a far more sophisticated and expansive ideological analysis about the ways that capitalism undermined the militancy of organized labor through the bribes of whiteness. By contrast, the growing workplace organizing and strike activity among Black workers underscored not only struggles over wages and working conditions but also broad regimes of social control. Black women hospital workers led strikes in in Charleston, South Carolina, and New York City, foregrounding a centuries-long white dependence on Black health and caregiving labor. The declaration of striking sanitation workers in Memphis, Tennessee, "I am a man," similarly exposed and contested the thingification of Black workers.[39]

For DRUM as well as Boggs and C. L. R. James, the leadership for that struggle would depend on politically conscious and organized Black workers and would take place both within and beyond the workplace. The League of Revolutionary Black Workers (LRBW) began organizing in other plants, and at other local worksites, including hospitals, newspapers, and the United Parcel Service (UPS).[40] When DRUM led wildcat strikes, they

DRUM flyer for wildcat strike and rally, 1969. Credit: Walter P. Reuther Library, Wayne State University.

recruited people who did not work in the plants, including high school students, to walk the picket lines and help with other organizing activities, putting into practice Boggs's call for a labor-led movement that organized well beyond the shop floor and linked workplace issues like speed-up's and discrimination to wider concerns like housing, police violence, and US militarism.[41] A Black-led labor movement would be at the forefront of a movement to liberate all workers, and those who had been abandoned by the system of work altogether. The LRBW pledged in its founding constitution in 1968 to "help organize D.R.U.M.-type organizations wherever there are Black workers, be it in [Chrysler CEO] Lynn Townsend's kitchen, the White House, White Castle, Ford Rouge, the Mississippi Delta, the plains of Wyoming, the mines of Bolivia, the rubber plantation of Indonesia, the oil fields of Biafra, or the Chrysler Plant in South Africa."[42]

And like Boggs, DRUM put political education and consciousness-raising at the center of its organizing work. Boggs had warned earlier that as long as Black workers "demand integration and democracy they are demanding the right to become capitalist exploiters, first of each other and then, if this is not enough, imperialist exploiters of the underdeveloped world."[43] Leaders like Watson, Baker, and Tate had participated in study groups for several years before the group's founding; several traveled to Cuba in 1964 and met with Che Guevarra. *Inner City Voice*, whose monthly circulation reached 10,000, featured stories about organizing and working conditions on the shop floor, police violence in Detroit, and resistance to US imperialism and influence in Vietnam, Cuba, and Latin America, as well as regular columns by C. L. R. James and James Boggs. RUM chapters at other auto plants also had their own newsletters.[44]

LRBW leaders also collaborated with a group of white filmmakers based in New York to produce a remarkable documentary, *Finally Got the News*, that offered a profound critique of the capitalist mode of production rooted in the experience of Black workers. In an early scene, Watson describes the historic role of Black labor in the development of the US economy from slavery through industrialization as "the transformation of sweat and blood, literally, into finished products." He continued, "There are certain other groups that if they stopped working tomorrow, the whole system is going to cease to function. Bus drivers, mailmen, truck drivers, workers of steel . . . People who play a crucial role in the money flow, and the flow of commodities, and the flow of raw materials, and the creation of finished products throughout the entire society. And by and large, black people are overwhelmingly employed in those kinds of jobs." Watson and RUM reasoned that a politically conscious formation of Black workers and community members would be at the forefront of challenging a despotic economic order led by "investment bankers, stockbrokers, insurance men, it's motherfuckers who don't do nothing." Another LRBW organizer explained that the "ruling clique" that benefited from this order "is parasitic, vulturistic, cannibalistic, and is sucking and destroying, man, the life of motherfucking workers. And we have to stop it because it's evil."[45]

At its height, LRBW organized chapters in dozens of worksites across Detroit involving thousands of workers, and reached tens of thousands through its newspapers, study groups, and community organizing efforts. All of this activity was rooted in the contention that Black people's labor was as indispensable to the wealth of the country as it was during slavery, and that organizing at the point of production was essential to realizing greater power for Black workers and communities over the conditions of their lives. Just as W. E. B. DuBois had described Black collective activity, escape, and flight to the North before and during the Civil War as a "general strike" to win abolition, so did LRBW contend that the nation's dependence on Black labor made workplace organizing essential.[46] In 1970, the League convened the Black Workers Congress, drawing 500 participants from across the country.[47]

Their efforts also encountered broad-based opposition, from right-wing groups in Detroit, to the employers whose worksites they organized, to local municipal and business leaders, to the leadership of the United Auto Workers, who accused the group of fomenting division between Black and white workers and actively undermined their efforts. By the early 1970s, this repression, and splits among the group's leadership over political and ideological questions, led to the group's collapse.

Fifty years later, though, their political analysis and organizing practice continue to hold important lessons. The Covid-19 pandemic and the subsequent economic shutdown brought all of these issues to the fore, as millions of "essential workers" toiled for long hours and risked their lives to keep the economy running, while millions of others lost work, avoiding destitution only because of emergency relief from the federal government. The conditions almost exactly realized James Boggs's account, in which there was not enough work available to provide everyone with an adequate income and in which the benefits of automation and technological development accrue almost entirely to a small elite. (Amazon's Jeff Bezos's net worth increased by almost $50 billion in the first six months of the pandemic.)[48]

Today there are renewed discussions of a guaranteed (if minimal) income for those who are wageless. But these policy discussions never disrupt broader control over the means of production and the organization of the economy. They are instead a way to maintain consumer demand without fundamentally reorienting the balance of power and authority over those resources. If a handful of companies—Amazon, Disney, Apple, and so on—continue to dominate particular markets, any influxes of cash ultimately will accrue to the fortunes of the oligarchs. The reorganization of profit, work, and production, and the centering of the analysis and consciousness of those made disposable are imperative. In this context, DRUM's legacy of wildcat strikes, political education programs, and demands for a new economic order are more salient than ever—as is their analysis that the essential nature of Black workers' labor confers transformative power.[49]

LOS ANGELES, 1998

You could hear the rhythmic thumping from the Janggu—the traditional Korean drum shaped like an hourglass—from blocks away, before Assi Market was even in sight. But also the chants. In Spanish, English, and Korean, matching the picket signs. "Unión só, pobreza no." "Justicia trabajadores de Assi." Then the dozens of people walking the picket line (sometimes they danced too). On the bigger days, their numbers reached into the hundreds. Families with children. Allies from local labor and immigrant rights groups. Students from Asian American studies classes at UCLA. The chanting, singing, and laughing led one observer to describe the demonstrations as "angry, but so full of hope."[50] And the Assi Market workers—sushi cutters, parking lot attendants, boxboys, butchers, and cashiers—at the center of a novel multiracial organizing experiment to confront the human estrangement and segregation on which racial capitalism thrives. Just as James Boggs and leaders of the DRUM urged Black workers to throw in their lot with the wageless "outcasts" of capitalist production, rejecting identification with white-led unions and employers, so too did Korean and Latinx workers at Assi Market support each other despite pressure on the former to align with their Korean employers' interests. For these immigrant workers, the workplace became a space of solidarity forged across racial lines and despite differences of culture and language. In refusing to be exploited, they also refused to exploit each other.

The pickets at Assi Super in Los Angeles Koreatown emerged in response to a wildcat strike in November 2001, not unlike the one led by

DRUM 33 years earlier that brought production at Hamtramck to a halt. Assi was the largest supermarket in Koreatown, a densely populated, two-square-mile area of markets, restaurants, apartments, and single-family houses a few miles west of the office towers and rooftop bars of downtown Los Angeles.[51] The market's owners suddenly cut the weekly hours for dozens of workers, most of whom already toiled at minimum wage with no benefits and few workplace protections. In response, about two dozen workers in the produce section, all immigrants from Mexico and Central America, dropped their box cutters, aprons, and work gloves, and walked off their jobs.[52]

The fluctuation in hours was accompanied by constant demands from supervisors to work faster, also recalling the conditions workers faced on the assembly line in Detroit. Elodia Martinez, who worked in the Assi kitchen preparing sushi and kimbap, would later explain, "The managers are constantly hurrying us, shouting at us and even screaming . . . I once saw a manager of the kitchen hit a worker, but we couldn't do anything."[53] One striking worker, Gabriel Perez Galavan, a "boxboy" charged with unpacking and folding produce boxes, explained that "there were 15–20 boxboys and there was a lot of competition for each of us to keep our jobs . . . It was rumored that whoever didn't pull their weight would not last for long, and we probably wouldn't see them after that week." Managers similarly pushed parking lot attendants to help customers load their cars at a crushing pace in withering heat, often with few breaks. Galvan described their experience of thingification: "We cannot stand to be treated like any old object, we are human beings as well."[54]

More than a thousand workers, nearly all immigrants from Korea, Mexico, El Salvador, and other parts of Central America, worked in Koreatown's large supermarkets, which earned profits comparable to the large supermarket chains like Safeway. Assi itself was owned by a Korean American businessman named Daniel Rhee, and was part of one of the largest Asian food-importing enterprises in North America. Yet workers at Assi and Koreatown's other markets, unlike the cashiers, butchers, and shelf stockers at Safeway, labored without a union or a collective bargaining contract. Large private-sector unions had largely ignored the tens of thousands of new immigrant workers from all corners of the globe—Asia, Africa, the Caribbean, and Latin America—that arrived in Southern

California in the 1980s and 1990s, working in car washes, restaurants, garment factories, warehouses, supermarkets, construction, and as domestic workers. Low wages, few benefits, long hours, and the constant threat of immigration raids were the norm. The dominant union organizing models and strategies focused on larger workplaces and established industries marked by less turnover and instability.[55]

Thus, when these migrant workers entered the region's sprawling economy, they did so isolated from other workers who had already joined together to contest the power of employers. Nor could they turn to the state for protection—laws governing minimum wage, overtime, and workers' compensation were rarely enforced. These labor laws, secured by the polity over many years of struggle to ensure that the power of the state would guarantee minimal protections to some workers, were unevenly enforced in these sectors of the economy, another form of estrangement from social protection and solidarity.

Denied the power and protection they might have gained from other workers in their industry or the protections against workplace abuse promised by the state, the workers who walked off the job at Assi had to find new sources of solidarity. They walked a block away from Assi to the small offices of Korean Immigrant Worker Advocates (KIWA). KIWA was founded in early 1992, only a few months before a jury exonerated the police officers who beat Rodney King, instigating a multiracial rebellion across many hundreds of blocks in South Los Angeles. KIWA was among dozens of community organizing groups, immigrant rights formations, and independent worker centers that took shape in the aftermath of the rebellion. By the late 1990s, KIWA had already begun developing multiracial organizing campaigns among Latinx and Korean workers over low wages and workplace harassment in Koreatown's restaurants.[56]

KIWA's founders, Danny Park and Roy Hong, were young Korean immigrants shaped by the militant labor organizing and unionization campaigns that erupted across South Korea in the 1980s. In the US media, the dominant image of post-1965 Korean immigration was the figure of the striving small business owner, running a liquor store, dry cleaner, or grocery store, often set in opposition to the Black and Latinx neighborhoods in which they operated. This narrative erased the significant class differences within Korean immigrant communities; an estimated 70 percent of Korean immigrants were low-wage workers in restaurants, markets, and other businesses owned by Koreans. In Koreatown's restaurants and at markets like Assi, they labored alongside Latinx immigrant workers, though often separated by the language they spoke and the work they performed. (Most Latinx workers were assigned to "back of the house" duties that involved fewer interactions with customers.)[57]

In this way, employees at Assi confronted a central feature of racial capitalism; the constant partitioning of workers from one another to undermine their capacity to collectively resist. Predation is always attached to a condition of isolation or separation from collective life. And when the foreman or manager barks an order to work faster, longer, and harder, it is this threat that lurks behind their every command: if you don't like it, I'll find someone to take your place. The task for the striking Assi workers was to overcome this partitioning and alienation. They would ultimately initiate a six-year organizing effort to build a new formation—the Immigrant Workers Union—to win concrete improvements in the working conditions at the market and to establish a new model of a multiracial independent union.

The organizing challenges were formidable. The Korean workers at Assi made up roughly half of the 150 total employees and suffered many of the same insults faced by Latinx workers: low wages, inconsistent work schedules, gender-based harassment, and threats and abuse by managers. At the same time, they faced immense pressure to identify with their employers in the name of ethnic solidarity, compelling them to disavow Latinx co-workers whose conditions mirrored their own.

The produce workers who led the original walkout formed the basis of the two-dozen member organizing committee, and with the support of KIWA's staff, led the campaign to demand recognition of their union. They printed union materials in Korean, Spanish, and English, and conducted meetings in all three languages to facilitate these connections. They organized delegations to their boss to demand regular work schedules, and filed a complaint with the US Equal Employment Opportunity Commission over Assi's discrimination against Latinx workers. In fall 2001, the organizing committee filed a petition with the National Labor Relations Board (NLRB), the federal entity that oversees union recognition campaigns, and a secret ballot election was set for the following spring.[58]

Workers and supporters rally in front of Assi Market, August 2002. Credit:
Koreatown Immigrant Worker Alliance.

A community support campaign quickly emerged, another strategy to
build social relations and solidarity that had been denied to low-wage
workers. Immigrant rights, labor, and Asian American community organizations, as well as student groups, helped lead pickets, leafleted customers, organized delegations to Assi managers, and raised money for the
union effort. These direct actions, joined by many Korean and Asian
American supporters, also publicly challenged the authority of the market's owners as the sole spokespersons and leaders of the Korean
community.

While this solidarity work was critical, the focus of the organizing campaign remained on building new forms of solidarity and leadership among
the workers themselves. One group of student supporters described the
forms of worker-led organizing they witnessed while interning on the
campaign:

> Workers planned the campaign strategy, organized their co-workers,
> planned press conferences and actions, and oversaw all the components of
> their struggle. In this process, KIWA staff, community supporters, students,
> and activists relinquished their traditional positions of power as those with
> the privilege of English language skills, citizenship, and higher levels of edu-
> cation. Instead of a top-down, authoritarian decision-making process (like

the one the workers encounter at the workplace) this campaign subverted traditional hierarchies by deferring to the decisions of the worker committee. The movement in support of Assi workers sought to respect the decision-making abilities of immigrant workers as they took the lead in this dynamic campaign.[59]

Much of this organizing focused on recruiting Korean workers at Assi to join the IWU and to publicly support the campaign. Several such workers, including Chin Yol Yi, who worked in the Assi fish department, became outspoken leaders, testifying to the harsh treatment they faced and condemning the forms of racial abuse they witnessed against Latinx co-workers. At one meeting, Yi bowed and apologized to his colleagues for the treatment they suffered at the hands of Korean managers, explaining in Korean, "I will do anything to help the Latino workers."[60] Yi later explained in a union flyer, "I joined this effort because after working in Korean supermarkets for fifteen years I realized that there will be no improvement in working conditions if workers don't do anything about it."[61] Supporters and staff also described movingly the ways that Latinx workers made use of the Korean phrases and language they had learned during many long hours in the market as a way to engage, support, and even comfort Korean co-workers who joined the union campaign.[62]

The election in March 2001 ended in a tie, and the IWU failed to garner the majority necessary to win recognition of their union. Assi's management retained a notorious union-busting law firm to discourage workers from joining the union; they eventually suspended 56 workers (50 Latinos and 6 Koreans) who had been active in the campaign, including Chin Yol Yi, insisting that they did not have proper work authorization because their Social Security numbers did not match a federal database.[63]

As the IWU continued to pressure Assi to recognize their union and to rehire the suspended workers, they called for a boycott of the market. For the next four years, boisterous daily pickets greeted shoppers; on some days, they had the feeling of a street party.[64] Many of the suspended workers paced the line for eight hours a day, nourished by food brought by volunteers. Other Assi workers joined at the end of their shifts.

In 2007, a legal settlement was reached. Assi paid nearly $1.5 million into a fund to be split among current and former employees as compensation for discrimination and wage and hour violations. The settlement and the end of the boycott were celebrated by KIWA and the campaign's supporters, but the outcome was bittersweet. The IWU was never recognized, and the 56 suspended workers were never rehired. A broad range of challenges, from the weak enforcement of federal labor law to the difficulties of sustaining an organizing and boycott campaign over several years, proved vexing. In the end, workers could not match the economic, political, and social power of their bosses.[65]

Yet the Assi campaign and the IWU's nascent organizing model hold important lessons in the ways that workers can build the solidarity, social relationships, and power needed to contest and overcome the conditions of competition and estrangement on which labor exploitation thrives. In this approach, solidarity isn't constituted by issuing statements, giving endorsements, or declaring oneself an "ally." It is instead rooted in the daily practices of listening and exchange, of recruitment and base building, so that people can enter into one another's lives. It means constituting new social relationships—between workers within and across different workplaces, as well as between workers, customers, and communities—to transform conditions of isolation into relations of solidarity.

In 2006, KIWA changed its name from Korean Immigrant Worker Advocates to the Koreatown Immigrant Workers Alliance, formalizing its model of building power and social relations among a broad range of low-wage workers. KIWA continues to organize many such workers, especially in the restaurant industry, disrupting the dominant vision of Koreatown and Korean Americans as a singular, business-focused community aspiring only to join the ranks of the US bourgeois. Putting into practice the insights and principles counseled by Ella Baker, KIWA's campaign focused on developing the leadership, skills, and political analysis among the workers themselves, seeing in everyone a potential organizer and leader.[66] KIWA's programs have been an important site of political education, organizer training, and anti-racist political formation for many hundreds of Asian Americans in the area who came became involved in the organizing campaigns, as well through an annual Summer Activist Training for young adults. And with a host of other worker centers in the area, including the Black Worker Center, National Day Laborer Organizing Network, and the Filipino Workers Center, they have, like DRUM, asserted the primacy of work and labor organizing as central to rebuilding a new social order.[67]

ATLANTA, 1968: FREEDOM BUSES

For the members of DRUM, it was the shop floor—beneath the whirring and humming of the vast assembly line—where autoworkers first encountered one another and came to understand that their best futures would be realized through solidarity and mutual avowal. For the produce workers and sushi cutters at Assi market, it was the break room, the parking lot, and later the KIWA office where these relationships were forged. In almost all labor organizing, it is the workplace that is the first site of reciprocal recognition and shared consciousness. But that was not the case for the thousands of Black women who did domestic work—caring for children, shopping, cooking, cleaning—in private households in Atlanta in the late 1960s. They shared an experience of low wages, insecure jobs, and temperamental and sometimes abusive employers. But they did not share a single workplace. The "shop floor" for them was spread out across tens of thousands of private homes in the region, as many domestics worked for multiple households at the same time. To find one another, and to build collectivity and power, they needed other strategies, and other means of connection. And they needed Dorothy Bolden.

Born in Atlanta in 1920, Bolden took on her first domestic work when she was nine years old, doing household chores, childcare, and washing dirty diapers for $1.50 a week.[68] She briefly tried other trades in her adult life—as a waitress, an elevator operator, at a laundry named the National Linen Service, in the mail room at Sears, Roebuck, and moving freight with a hand truck at a railway company. But working with children was her passion. As was the case for nearly all Black women at the time, caring for her own children—she raised six—was not considered worthy of compensation, or even a form of work. Only by taking care of other families' children—white families' children—could she earn a wage, and she spent most of her working life as a domestic with childcare responsibilities. "I should have been a teacher," she later told an interviewer.[69]

When Bolden was in her early 20s and preparing to leave work at the end of the day, the white woman who employed her insisted she stay to wash more dishes rather than return to her family. When she refused, the woman called the police, who took her to a mental institution for five nights, concluding that a Black domestic who rejected the orders of a white employer was revealing signs of mental illness.[70] The expectations that Black women domestic workers would show absolute deference to the families that employed them were rooted in racist and sexist expectations about Black women's "natural" propensity for servitude and caregiving work, as well as deference to the white women who controlled the conditions of their employment. This was a relationship that grew directly from the violence of racial servitude and slavery. Black women's labor was vital to the reproduction of white propertied and slave-owning households, a dynamic that abolition and emancipation did not end. A 1912 testimony by an anonymous domestic worker titled "More Slavery at the South" in the *Independent* described the constant and uninterrupted barrage of chores she was expected to complete. "I am not permitted to rest. It's 'Mammy do this,' or 'Mammy, do that,' or 'Mammy, do the other' from my mistress all the time." She continued: "You might as well say that I'm on duty all of the time—from sunrise to sunrise, every day in the week. I am the slave, body and soul, of this family."[71]

Comparisons to slavery appeared in accounts of domestic work well into the twentieth century. In 1935, Ella Baker and Marvel Cooke wrote a short investigative article in the NAACP's the *Crisis* titled "The Bronx Slave Market" about two street corners in the South Bronx where Black women lined up each morning seeking domestic work. "Rain or shine, cold or hot, you will find them there—Negro women, old and young— sometimes bedraggled, sometimes neatly dressed—but with the invariable paper bundle, waiting expectantly for Bronx housewives to buy their strength and energy for an hour, two hours, or even for a day at the munificent rate of fifteen, twenty, twenty-five, or, if luck be with them, thirty cents an hour." In describing these sites as "slave marts," Cooke and Baker made clear the continuities with involuntary servitude, and the gender and sexual exploitation that animate white supremacy. One block, they noted, "exudes the stench of the slave market at its worst" as "human labor [is] bartered and sold for slave wage" and "human love is also a marketable commodity."[72]

In the twentieth century, as industrialization and economic expansion permitted more white households to rely primarily on a male breadwinner and gender discrimination limited all women's access to well-paying jobs, the reliance on women of color to perform domestic labor increased. More than 60 years after abolition, a growing number of white women and households fed at this trough. Baker and Cooke noted that "paradoxically, the crash of 1929 brought to the domestic labor market a new employer class. The lower-middle-class housewife, who, having dreamed of the luxury of a maid, found opportunity staring her in the face in the form of Negro women pressed to the wall by poverty, starvation, and discrimination."[73]

Baker and Cooke illuminated the ways that long-standing structures of race and gender domination and involuntary labor created the material conditions of desperation and precarity that made domestic workers so vulnerable to exploitation. As the sociologist Evelyn Nakano Glenn has argued, diverse forms of coercion undergird caregiving labor, and this coercion has operated through patterns of racial and colonial power distinct to different regions of the country. For example, well into the mid-twentieth century, thousands of Native American women and girls were removed from their tribal communities and lands and sent to boarding schools and other institutions for placement as domestic workers in non-Native households.[74] In Hawaii and along the West Coast, the caregiving economy drew in Japanese American women and girls. In the Southwest, Anglo households employed Mexican Americans in such roles.[75]

Across all of these sites, domestic workers individually resisted the terms of their employment as they could, rejecting the subservient roles to which they were assigned. They abandoned or deserted households that abused them, contested race and gender norms, and returned to their communities and families of origin when possible.[76] Yet absent coordinated action, these workers' ability to change their conditions of employment was limited. Domestic workers had attempted such collective action for decades. In 1881, Black women workers in Atlanta formed the Washing Society and led a brief but successful strike of hundreds of laundry workers across the city.[77] In the 1930s, the National Negro Congress formed the Domestic Workers Association in New York.[78] But the lack of a single employer made recognition of a collective bargaining agreement all but impossible, and domestic workers were also excluded from a range of labor laws and protections, including the Fair Labor Standards Act, the 1938 legislation stipulating minimum wage, overtime, and child labor safeguards.[79] These exclusions, and the denial of other forms of income support and assistance to women of color, made it difficult for

Dorothy Bolden speaking at National Domestic Workers Union of America event, 1970s. Credit: Southern Labor Archives, Georgia State University.

many workers to altogether withdraw their labor through a traditional strike, as they and their families were denied other means to survive. All of these dynamics were on Dorothy Bolden's mind in the mid-1960s as she contemplated a strategy to build power and recognition for domestic workers in Atlanta.

Bolden's political consciousness was shaped by many years of laboring as a domestic, as well as through her participation in the early Civil Rights movement. She was friends and neighbors with Dr. Martin Luther King Jr. and Coretta Scott King, became active in local school desegregation campaigns in the early 1960s, and supported the efforts of the Student Nonviolent Coordinating Committee. Bolden came to realize that desegregation efforts would be profoundly limited if the many thousands of Black women who worked as domestics continued to struggle to meet their basic needs.[80] Bolden appealed to Dr. King to organize domestic workers, and he urged Bolden her to lead the effort herself.

Dorothy Bolden turned to the bus. Every morning, city buses from Black neighborhoods like Vine City would transport thousands of domestic workers through downtown Atlanta and into white suburbs and homes, where they helped raise children and run households. The bus was one of the main sites where domestic workers encountered one another, where they could talk about their wages and working conditions, and their experience with different employers. Bolden came to realize that if domestic workers were to be organized, it would happen in transit; she rode the bus for many hundreds of hours across the city to meet and organize such workers. "I decided then I was going to start communicating. I would go around in the bus and ask the maids how they would feel about joining if we would organize, and they would say, 'Oh, I'm for that.'"[81] Scholar Premilla Nadasen described the encounters on such "freedom buses" as "venues where poor women could share grievances and concerns, trade stories of abuse, exchange" much like the Freedom Schools and citizenship schools established across the rural South, which were sites of connection, consciousness-raising, and organizing.[82]

Together with several workers, Bolden announced on the radio that they were forming the National Domestic Workers Union of America (NDWUA). Bolden explained that her task was to meet with domestic workers "every week to keep them encouraged, to keep the strength up."[83] Hundreds soon joined. The group began meeting weekly at the Fleet Street Baptist Church education building; a young lawyer named Maynard Jackson, who eventually became the city's first Black mayor in 1973, provided early legal advice. To join, one paid a dollar in membership dues and signed a voter registration card. Bolden was elected to serve as the group's first president.[84]

Much of the NDWUA's early work focused on teaching workers to negotiate with their employers—setting a standard wage of $13.50 per day plus carfare, and $15.00 per day if they worked once a week, when more labor was often expected. They started an employment referral service and training programs as a way to regularize working conditions. They advocated for vacation pay, Social Security deductions, trial periods, transparency in hiring arrangements (temporary vs. permanent), access to meals, overtime, and additional pay for the caring of children. They published a booklet for domestic workers that detailed information about

Social Security, unemployment benefits, and minimum wage laws, and listed the particular chores, like climbing ladders and scrubbing floors on knees, that domestic workers should refuse.[85] Another demand that emerged at an early meeting was that employers cease addressing domestic workers by their first names, a practice that one observer noted "was designed to keep the women subordinate" and belittle their status.[86]

While Bolden and the NDWUA understood the vulnerability faced by domestic workers, they also recognized the potential power they held within the region's economy, and as voters in local elections. They continually emphasized how valuable domestic workers were to the households that employed them, making visible the very particular types of skilled labor they provided. It was on this basis, rooted in the proficiency, intelligence, skills, and commitment of the workers themselves, that Bolden and the NDWUA organized domestic workers to take action.[87] They did not focus their energies and time on trying to shift the attitudes and consciousness of the white women who employed domestic workers, but instead sought to build the power and capacity of the workers themselves to transform the conditions of their lives and their communities.

The NDWUA soon grew to more than 10,000 members and spawned chapters in other cities. In the early 1970s, they led a successful campaign to bring domestic workers under the protections of the Fair Labor Standards Act, bringing raises and workplace protections to many hundreds of thousands of workers who had never even heard of the union. Bolden also became an important figure in Atlanta municipal politics, continually advocating that domestic workers and other poor women be included in the civil rights agenda.

The impact and legacy of the NDWUA go beyond the pay increases and workplace rights they helped to secure. Then as now, the patriarchal organization of work and the division of labor placed most of the responsibility for reproductive work and care in the hands of women. Yet in most instances, rather than mount a broad, multiracial feminist challenge to these structures, middle-class white women sought to exploit the vulnerability of women of color to avoid this labor for themselves. They sought refuge from the violence and discipline of patriarchal power by claiming some of the spoils of white supremacy, producing a truncated feminist politics rooted in the subordination of other women. In this context, the

NDWUA's focus on increasing the capacity of Black women to confront and negotiate with the white women who employed them, at the proverbial scene of the crime, had consequences that went beyond improvements in individual working conditions and pay. The NDWUA's demands directly challenged the racist and gendered expectations of servitude and deference held by white women employers. In this way, they summoned a far more expansive feminist politics of work that fundamentally challenged the diminution of caring and reproductive labor. Denied access to other forms of state protection (through labor law enforcement) and worker solidarity (though collective bargaining agreements), the NDWUA made the household itself a site of labor struggle and political consciousness, and sought to transform the whole basis on which care work was valued and compensated. Their organizing contested the hierarchies of worth and disposability that anchor patriarchal dominance, illuminating the interdependence of women's lives.[88] And their work was anchored in the power of domestic workers themselves, and the relationships they commanded as voters, church members, bus riders, and civil rights participants, to change these conditions.[89]

The NDWUA ceased its operations in the mid-1990s, unable to develop and sustain another generation of leadership as Bolden aged. Bolden passed in Atlanta in 2005 at age 81. But the group's legacy lives on.

In 2007, not far from where the NDWUA convened its first meetings, a multiracial group of 13 grassroots organizations launched the National Domestic Workers Alliance (NDWA). They came from many corners— Haitian immigrant women caring for children in New York, Latinx *domésticas* from Los Angeles, Filipinas organizing against labor trafficking globally—to transform the conditions of domestic and caregiving labor.[90] The group now includes many dozens of affiliate organizations across the country and has launched a campaign to win a national Domestic Workers Bill of Rights that would enshrine a host of workplace protections that were envisioned by Bolden and her contemporaries.

Their allied "Caring across Generations" campaign links the needs, interests, and lives of caregivers and domestic workers to those they care for. In this analysis and organizing practice, for domestic workers to assert control over their lives, working conditions, and freedom, the entire caregiving economy must be transformed. Their campaign invokes a new vision for such work, in which the needs of those who give and receive care are understood and treated as mutually dependent.

In 2015, the NDWA established the Dorothy Bolden Fellowship to recognize and train a new generation of domestic worker organizers and leaders. Much as Bolden moved across the city buses 50 years ago, NDWA organizers today rove city playgrounds and parks to meet caregivers, listen to their stories, and share with them a vision in which domestic workers control the conditions of their working lives. They seek to replace a longstanding gendered politics of labor rooted in race and class domination with a social vision in which all labor is valued and worthy of dignity. Their 2019 policy report, "Unbossed: A Black Domestic Workers Agenda," based on dozens of interviews with Black domestic workers, envisions wide-ranging transformations in the care economy rooted in raising labor standards, expanding civil rights protections, investing in caregiving infrastructure, and addressing patterns of harm and interpersonal violence. It is a vision specifically rooted in the contemporary and historical experiences of Black domestic workers that would also transform conditions for millions of care workers, recipients, and the economy as a whole.[91]

During the coronavirus pandemic of 2020, these interdependencies, especially in nursing homes and home health-care settings, were illuminated with particular force and devastation. The racist and sexist logics and practices that legitimate the disposability of health care and caregiving workers put everyone in danger. The power of such workers to control the conditions of their labor and thus the well-being of their patients and clients has profound implications for public health as a whole. They toil for a freedom wider than their own.

CODA: BEYOND THINGIFICATION

The Detroit Revolutionary Union Movement waned after a few years of existence, leaving the authority of the Chrysler and Ford plants largely intact. KIWA workers at Assi won a legal settlement and some backpay, but struggled to build a permanent organization among the workers laboring in Koreatown markets. The National Domestic Workers Union of America also had a relatively short life, fading as Dorothy Bolden aged out of her role. By traditional social movement standards, none of these efforts would register as an outright success. And we should not be surprised that within a polity constantly socialized to practice competition and disavowal over solidarity and collectivity, such efforts would face treacherous terrain. Yet they are still worthy of our attention.

The Covid-19 pandemic eliminated tens of millions of jobs in the US, and many times more worldwide. Government payments and subsidies helped some. But the long-term prognosis is grim. With ownership and authority over the economy in fewer and fewer hands, and demands for greater profits and efficiencies stretching to every industry and workplace, the conditions predicted by James Boggs nearly 70 years ago have arrived. Under the current system, there is not enough paid work to support all those who need a wage to live. The wageless life is becoming a generalized condition for many more households; economic precarity is no longer a temporary or cyclical fear but a baseline order. As Boggs warned, the constant sense of danger, vulnerability, and desperation produced under these conditions fuels greater competition, disavowal, and animus among everyone.

Here, the lessons of DRUM, KIWA, and the NDWUA are instructive. Rooted in their working experiences in the factory, the produce section, and the private home, they collectively produced new insights about the violence of thingification, and the danger it posed to the waged and wageless alike. They understood, even in fleeting ways, that there was no escape from this regime alone. The solidarities they forged in meetings, on the bus, and on the picket line directly challenged the regime of disposability and abandonment that white supremacy legitimates. Their practices of mutuality and power, anchored in the workplace but committed to a broader liberation, remain essential in our day.[92]

Conclusion

In late March 2020, as the US Congress debated the terms of the first massive economic recovery package to address the Covid-19 pandemic, shutdowns, and layoffs that left millions without the basic means of subsistence, Tea Party activist Sonnie Johnson made a startling admission to listeners of *Sonnie's Corner,* her weekly radio show. "Conservatives," she told her audience, "have no ideas to offer in the current moment. We are watching from the sidelines." The creeping socialism that Johnson had spent years warning fellow travelers on the right about had all but arrived in the form of a $2 trillion federal outlay. The principles of government restraint and free market authority were being buried among the dead in the Covid-19 crisis.[1]

Any sober analysis of the recovery legislation that eventually passed, with its hundreds of billions in tax breaks and subsidies to wide-ranging corporate interests, reveals a much more complicated story.[2] But Johnson's basic sense, that dominant market ideologies and policies were facing a popular legitimacy crisis in the face of the pandemic, had resonances across the political spectrum. In these accounts, the relentless spread of the virus and the economic chaos that ensued demonstrated the interdependences of our world, and the fallacies of borders that divide nations, classes, and racial and ethnic groups. In spite of decades of relentless corporate attacks on government, public institutions and programs proved their value and importance each hour. Everyday workers—from delivery drivers to grocery clerks to nurses and EMTs—emerged as the heroines of the crisis, fat cats be damned. More among us are finally coming to realize the dangers of living in a privatized, market-driven society.

In the summer, as the popular uprisings against police violence and everyday forms of white supremacy grew more intense, social transformation seemed imminent. Books about anti-racism soared to the top of national best-seller lists. Polling showed that support for Black Lives Matter increased sharply among every group, including self-identified white conservatives.[3] Suburban teens put Black Power fists on their social media accounts. Even Republican Senator Mitt Romney took to the street, joining a demonstration against police violence.[4] Amazon declared in a statement that "the inequitable and brutal treatment of Black and African Americans is unacceptable."[5] In a social media post that spring, Amazon CEO Jeff Bezos demonstrated his fluency in the etiquette and discourse of liberal anti-racism by acknowledging the individual white privilege he and his family enjoyed. He made no mention of his $175 billion net worth, Amazon's unflinching opposition to corporate taxes to fund affordable housing in Seattle, or the company's staunch anti-union practices.[6]

As this book has argued, an anti-racism cheered on by Bezos and other elites who have attended corporate trainings on racial privilege will do little to realize the wider type of freedom envisioned by C. L. R. James and so many others. The policy platform of the Movement for Black Lives, which demands a broad range of publicly financed and universally accessible resources and goods, including health care, housing and education, and an end to the contemporary regime of militarization, prisons, and policing, cannot be realized if the fortunes of Bezos and hundreds of other billionaires remain under private control.[7]

The concentration of resources and power and wealth in the hands of the few must be transformed if the future imagined by the Movement for Black Lives—a future in which everyone lives with greater dignity—is to be won. Yet as this book has argued, it is not Bezos and other elites alone that stand in the way of this vision. To realize a future in which no one is regarded as disposable or death-worthy requires forms of social solidarity and collective relationships that have yet to be built. We cannot presume that the problem is only "out there"—among the oligarchs, profiteers, and their ideologues and apologists. It is also "in here," within all of us. The current failure of markets, institutions, and governance cannot be met by better policies, better candidates, or better ideas alone. The deeply privatized, militarized, and nationalistic political culture and economy that sustains racial domination and that we all inhabit robs us all of the experiences, practices, and relationships we need to sustain expansive movements of solidarity. These are limits we have to acknowledge; we are not yet the people we need to be to realize a future of abundance, and the billionaire guild thrives precisely on and through these limitations.

During the first stages of the pandemic, examples of altruism and social generosity were plentiful. Tens of thousands of health-care workers rushed to care for people in dire need, often at great personal cost. The norm of physical distancing is itself rooted in an obligation to care not just for ourselves and those we know but also for those we do not know—for strangers. And there were no shortage of stories about local civic commitment, from donations of homemade masks to health-care workers to looking in on neighbors to the work being carried out in sectors that keep people alive, like food production, delivery, and home health care.

Individual acts of generosity and empathy like these are surely critical. But they won't sustain the social solidarity, collective action, and mutual obligation necessary to respond to the current crisis and its aftermath. Indeed, the limits of our shared experiences and common history of solidarity, sacrifice, and mutuality leave us ill-prepared for this moment.

Historically, the most prominent forms of social solidarity in the US have emerged during times of war, a nationalism forged to defeat common enemies, foreign and domestic. Wartime civic unity has never been universal; it has always required demonization, often steeped in racism and xenophobia. Our most notable record of public investments and infrastructure lies in a military budget that exceeds $650 billion per year and an outlay in prisons, policing, and migration regulation and detention to match.[8] Indeed, one of the longest standing figures of speech in the US invoking a community's need to come together— "circle the wagons"—references white settler conflicts against Native nations. Our political vocabulary here is impoverished. We have few shared experiences of solidarity that are truly universal and not premised on violence and exclusion.

This is not just a worldview or habit of practice that can be attributed to free market champions or self-identified conservatives. Across the political spectrum, we have a robust language to charge others with dependency, degeneracy, or unfitness. It is in the air we breathe—in every policy debate about immigration, welfare, housing, reproductive rights, family, and health care. These are concepts deeply ingrained in our political culture and easily activated to undermine broad actions of solidarity. Racism here is central; it provides the basic grammar of disavowal and blame that suppresses such solidarity. It lubricates the immense machinery that produces inequality and disposability.

These inheritances strained the collective capacity to address some of the earliest impacts of the pandemic. The first federal recovery package largely excluded undocumented immigrants and many mixed-status households from receiving benefits. The long history of weaponizing citizenship to differentiate the worthy from the unworthy that fueled this policy and has shaped all of our social relations. Thus, how many labor unions, even with progressive leadership, could mobilize their members in an all-out effort to challenge such exclusions in future stimulus bills, especially without resorting to racist arguments about immigrants as potential transmitters of disease?[9]

Similarly, prison abolitionists and a growing number of prison reform advocates called for elected leaders to release many thousands of people incarcerated in federal, state, and local prisons and jails because of the threat posed to their lives by the virus. But the legacy of becoming the global leader in prisons has not only robbed many millions of people and their loved ones of their life possibilities, it has also deeply ingrained the view that human warehousing is a precondition of community safety. Thus, how many churches, civic groups, or neighborhood associations, even in the bluest of states, would mobilize to demand the immediate release of some portion of the 2.3 million people now incarcerated in the name of protecting human life?[10]

Or consider our collective capacity to imagine obligations for life beyond the nation's borders. The US public has already proved it will largely tolerate the construction of mass migrant detention complexes on the southern border, to say nothing of the millions of people trapped in refugee camps, war zones, and regions of economic and environmental crisis. Civic nationalism and American exceptionalism have given us very little language, practice, or material relations to avow these obligations and solidarities. What movement of Democratic voters today would demand funding to protect those in detention facilities and camps from the virus's ravages or future pandemics, or call for an end to sanctions against Iran or for aid to Palestine for the same purpose? And as the vaccine was being rolled out in the US, why did so few people, even on the political left, mobilize to demand that they be made available to nations in the Global South, or challenge the blatant profiteering of the pharmaceutical companies that limited such distribution?

The material conditions and relationships we inhabit in our market economy similarly restrain our capacity to act in solidarity. Racial capitalism in its most fundamental form puts us in competition with one another, and often ties our material well-being to the dispossession of others—our neighbors, our co-workers, and many others whom we will never meet or know. Our investment in the structures and payoffs of the market must be taken into account as we try to imagine and build social life beyond the demands of accumulation and profit. With little meaningful publicly guaranteed social insurance or protection, the fortunes of many working families are tied to the market and its capacities to extract value from others. For example, even the most politically committed public school teacher in California who fights against the defunding of schools depends for her retirement income on the teachers' retirement program known as CALSTRs, an enormous public pension fund that must invest in all matter of private equities, real estate, derivative instruments, and international currencies to deliver payoffs to its members.[11] Thus, a teacher's modest retirement is tied to the fortunes of the 1 percent and the dispossessions of others it requires. This dependence is true for nearly everyone with a public pension, a 401(k), or any other investment portfolio. The provision of financial aid for working-class students at many private universities is similarly linked to the returns of the school's investment portfolios. We gain security for ourselves by joining in the exploitation of others.

Gig economy workers are put into direct competition with one another every time they open an app to look for work. It is typically only through unions, and the opportunities for collective action and struggle they provide, that workers get to experience forms of collective solidarity as an alternative to individual competition.

And while we rightfully decry the oversize and anti-democratic influence of big tech, we have become wholly reliant on its services, networks, and products. During the Covid-19 shutdown, public school teachers had little choice but to educate millions of their students through Google Classroom and other privately developed learning platforms. Nearly all community and labor organizing activity and other social justice work have been sustained through corporate platforms like Zoom and Facebook. We are more dependent than ever on Amazon and Walmart and the complex centralized delivery and logistics systems they command, even as they fuel wealth, racial, and income inequality to new heights. These are the dependencies that consumer capitalism creates; these are the material relationships that restrain our ability to act together.[12]

These conditions suggest that to realize a wider type of freedom requires not only transforming the dominant structures of violence and control that produce vulnerability. It also requires those committed to such a future to transform themselves.

In her 1982 speech, "Learning from the 60's," Audre Lorde explained that even though the era's social movements "fought common enemies, at times the lure of individual solutions made us careless of each other." She asked her audience to recognize "those oppressive values which we have been forced to take into ourselves."[13] Women-of-color feminists in the 1980s constantly reflected on the ways that our wounds and desires are weaponized against one another and constrain our ability to enter into one another's lives. The writer Cherríe Moraga contends that "we are afraid . . . to see how we have taken the values of our oppressor into our hearts and turned them against ourselves and one another." She states, "To assess the damage" this has caused is a dangerous act."[14] Grace Lee Boggs recounted an insight from James Boggs that such transformations were required of everyone, not just people who think of themselves as white. "Being a victim of oppression in the United States is not enough to make you revolutionary, just as dropping out of your mother's womb is not enough to make you human." Even subordinated groups in the US would "internalize the values of the oppressor" and lose the capacity to make moral and political choices not rooted in seeking ever-expanding access to material production and consumption. As Grace Lee Boggs asserted, "Any group that achieves power, no matter how oppressed, is not going to act differently from their oppressors as long as they have not confronted the values that they have internalized and consciously adopted different values."[15]

How do we become the people we need to be? In the spring of 2018, Loretta Ross, whose career in reproductive justice and human rights organizing spans five decades, delivered the commencement address at Hampshire College, and took up these very questions. Ross had just finished a yearlong teaching appointment at the liberal arts college in Amherst, Massachusetts, teaching a course titled "White Supremacy in the Age of Trump." She used her address to share with students her candid reflections on the capacities and consciousness they needed to develop in order to contribute to social justice formations: To understand movement building and anti-racist work as joyous and fun. To lessen their obsession with individual privilege, both theirs and others. To decenter themselves in their writing and analysis. To be comfortable with differences in ideas, strategies, and beliefs among people who want to contribute to social transformation. And most of all, to find ways to help one another develop political consciousness and knowledge without resorting to prosecution and shaming when mistakes are made.[16]

She concluded: "We've given y'all the radical politics without the radical skills to handle them."

Ross's counsel is not for college students alone. It describes the challenges that many people face in applying their consciousness and knowledge of racial domination and history toward building collective movements and capacities. Too often, such consciousness and knowledge becomes a kind of credential brandished before others, a marker of individual distinction and cultivated self-awareness. At its worst, it can license a scorn and contempt for others who have failed to achieve such insights.

Yet this outlook fails to grasp the structures and forces that legitimate and naturalize inequality. The dominant modes of economy and governance we inhabit alienate us from one another, and put us into competition. These structures make suspicion and scorn a central facet of human relationships. To be politically socialized in this country is to be continuously exposed to the norms of patriarchy, racism, nativism, war, and homophobia. These are the baseline conditions of most of our education and socialization. They are not simply moral choices. The opportunities to learn about and practice solidarity, interdependence, and vulnerability are in far shorter supply.

And yet, as the stories recounted in this book suggest, there is a rich archive of people and movements who have put those very commitments into practice, stubborn in their conviction that human misery is not inevitable. And from these traditions, we can also discern some of the radical skills summoned by Ross. The capacities to speak to strangers—in the workplace, on the bus, in our neighborhoods and schools—who may not share the same worldview, history, or social position but whom we might invite into collective projects that begin to transform the material conditions of the world. A willingness to commit labor and energy to collective development and capacity building, and, following Ella Baker, to be as invested in the leadership capacities of others as we are in ourselves. To refuse the idea that any of us can heal or repair ourselves alone or in isolation, or without changing the structures that cause harm. To recognize that systems of domination will always invite inclusion of some of the dispossessed into their ranks, incorporating the few in order to disavow the many. To popularize the understanding that racial hierarchy and differentiation are everyday features of our systems of education, work, governance, housing, and health care, rather than aberrations or excesses.

In short, the radical skills summoned by Ross are practices that enlarge these collectivities and movements, rather than serving as their gatekeepers. These abilities are acquired through shared experiences of movement, reflection, study, and practice. To develop consciousness or knowledge about the histories of racial domination and power is always a social act—even when we read or learn about them individually, we are relying on the writers, organizers, and scholars whose labor helps to produce this knowledge. They cannot be developed by individuals in isolation from one another. Anti-racism is always a collective practice. Lorde thus asked, "Can anyone of us here still afford to believe that efforts to reclaim the future can be private or individual?"[17]

Dr. Vincent Harding, the brilliant theologian, educator, and close confidant of Dr. King, noted of the Civil Rights movement's "successful challenges to official segregation" that "we have imbibed much of the spirit that [Dr. King] identified as the spirit of greed, belligerency, fearful callousness, and individualism, a spirit that makes us anti-poor people, anti-immigrants, that creates injustice, that makes for war." Dr. King, Harding counseled, "challenged us to search for a new recipe, create a new vision of what needs to be baked, develop a new pie based on compassion and human solidarity rather than on maximum profits."[18]

The shards, scenes, movements, and moments recounted in this book offer no singular list of instructions to how the new pie referenced by Harding will be baked. That is the work of so much of the racial justice organizing now under way, from Indigenous organizers using deeply rooted histories of relational politics and solidarities, to new mutual aid efforts related to health care, legal defense, and community safety that allow us to experience new social relations, to Black cooperatives remaking economic connections outside of corporate profit imperatives. But history and its narration matter.

These episodes, figures, and events provide part of the genealogy that might be summoned to upend and transform the partitions so hardened and legitimated by racism to sustain new collective movements of solidarity. They provide some of the ingredients for the new recipe, and for what is required of us all. And they remind us above all of Lorde's counsel that "within each one of us there is some piece of humanness that knows we are not being served by the machine which orchestrates crisis after crisis and is grinding all our futures into dust."[19]

Acknowledgments

"The African bruises and breaks himself against his bars in the interest of freedoms wider than his own." I was first introduced to this passage by C. L. R. James in graduate school more than 15 years ago, in a seminar taught by Ruth Wilson Gilmore. It wasn't among the assigned readings. Ruthie just summoned it from the exhaustive archive of political concepts and practices she holds in her head, the effect of many decades of careful study, reflection, and organizing. I've turned to Gilmore's work in every chapter of this book, and it is in many more places where I have not yet grasped the reach of her influence on my thinking. I'm grateful to be among many hundreds of students who have benefited from her mentorship and presence of mind. Ruthie and many other faculty and graduate students at the University of Southern California's Program in American Studies and Ethnicity, including Laura Pulido and George Sanchez, shaped many of the ideas explored in this book. Thank you.

I am grateful to several universities and organizations for hosting talks that helped me advance my thinking, including Ithaca College and Paula Iaonide, UC Merced, and Mario Sifuentez, the Othering and Belonging Institute at UC Berkeley, Oregon State University, the Yale American Studies Critical Encounters Series, the Alliance for a Just Society (LeeAnn Hall and Libero Della Piana), the Center for Third World Organizing, and the Asian Pacific American Network of Oregon.

This project originally took shape at the University of Oregon and among dear colleagues in ethnic studies and political science. At Oregon, Brian Klopotek,

Kirby Brown, and Lani Teves introduced me to important sources on Native organizing and resistance. Loren Kajikawa and Mika Tanner gave superb feedback on an early version of the preface. My ten years at Oregon with these and other colleagues in ethnic studies, including Laura Pulido, Michael Hames Garcia, Charise Cheney, Ernesto Martinez, Sharon Luk, Lynn Fujiwara, and Alai Reyes-Santos, sharpened my thinking in ways I continue to appreciate, and I dearly miss the collegiality and collaboration of that department. A 2015 writers' retreat with colleagues at Oregon helped me to launch the project. I am grateful to Raahi Reddy and Kari Norgaard for feedback on an early version of the introduction and Tanya Golash-Boza for facilitating the group and introducing me to an array of everyday writing strategies. Debra Thompson and Joe Lowndes organized a delightful race, politics, and history workshop in Eugene, where I benefited from ideas and inspiration from Glen Coulthard, Chris Parker, Michael Hanchard, Cristina Beltran, and other workshop participants.

At Yale, writing partners including Leah Mirakhor, Matt Jacobson, and Chandan Reddy helped me keep the project going even during the Covid-19 shutdown; I treasured the morning texts and words of encouragement we shared. Yale colleagues in American Studies and Ethnicity, Race, and Migration, including Rod Ferguson, Lisa Lowe, Tanja Cisja, Leah Mirakhor, Albert Laguna, Grace Kao, Mary Lui, Tavia Nyong'o, Zareena Grewal, Quan Tran, Stephen Pitti, Alicia Schmidt-Camacho, Ana Ramos-Zayas, Daphne Brooks, Michael Denning, Laura Barraclough, Laura Wexler, and Matthew Frye Jacobson have provided friendship and intellectual community. I thank Laura Barraclough, Rene Almeling, Jennifer O'Neal, Isaac Nakhimovsky, and others who joined our regular writing group at Sterling Library. Students in two iterations of my seminar on antiracism, racial justice, and freedom at Yale improved my analysis in ma™ny ways. Funding from the Frederick W. Hilles Publication Fund, the MacMillan Center, and the FAS Dean's office supported various aspects of research, travel, and production.

Midway through the project, I was introduced to a brilliant developmental editor, Florence Grant, who strengthened the organization, flow, and clarity of my writing in innumerable ways, and was a generous and attentive interlocuter. I am deeply grateful to Isabella Zou for all the contributions she made in getting the manuscript ready for submission and her impeccable organization and attention to detail, and to Alexandra Rocha-Alvarez for additional archival research.

Nancy Wadsworth, Kevin Bruyneel, Edmund Fong, Priscilla Yamin, and Joe Lowndes gave generative feedback to the chapter on governance. Warm thanks to my friends and comrades at the African American Policy Forum (AAPF), including Kimberlé Crenshaw, Luke Harris, Barbara Arnwine, Devon Carbado, and George Lipsitz, for extended feedback at the Social Justice Writer's Retreat. Francis Calpotura offered valuable insight into the framing of the book and has been a treasured friend and interlocuter for 30 years.

I thank Kyle Kajihiro for an extended interview and for sharing his collaborative work on the DeTour in Hawaii, and for allowing me to join one of the tours. Judith LeBlanc generously gave her time to discuss the Mni Wizipan Wakan project and offered other formative insights from her long history of organizing in Indigenous communities.

Several organizations and individuals kindly granted permission to reprint photos of their work, including the Koreatown Immigrant Workers Alliance, UE Local 150, Adriann Barboa, Jack Kurtz, and Ann Wright. I thank artist Yasmín Hernández for allowing me to include her beautiful portrait of David Sanes Rodríguez.

Niels Hooper at the University of California Press encouraged my pursuit of this project from the beginning and shared valuable feedback at the end. Claire Jean Kim, Dan Berger, Michael Omi, and David Roediger offered sharp-sighted advice on the manuscript for the Press. I thank Kate Hoffman and the other talented and committed staff at the Press for shepherding the manuscript through the production process.

This book is dedicated to two influential mentors. I met Gary Delgado 30 years ago as a young organizing intern at the Center for Third World Organizing in Oakland. Gary has made so many of us around him better thinkers, organizers, and writers, patiently waiting for us through our mistakes and reminding us always of the contributions we could make. My encounters with George Lipsitz across the last 20 years have been equally influential. George's scholarship on race, power, culture, and social movements has been foundational to so many of us, matched always by his investment in our development. I am indebted to George for his early encouragement of this project and the many sources and ideas he shared.

Tamara Vasquez, Niru Somasundarum, Soyun Park, Sylvia Ibarra, Loren Kajikawa, Mika Tanner, Joe Lowndes, Priscilla Yamin, Brian Klopotek, Kirby Brown, Dennis HoSang, Martha HoSang, Marjorie Brown HoSang, Robert HoSang, Judith HoSang, Elizabeth Martínez, Sylvia Martinez, Carolina Martinez, Mariana Martinez, Alex Martinez, Ceclia Martinez, and Mike Solis are with me always. Isaac Martinez-HoSang and Pablo Martinez-HoSang endured my focus on completing the manuscript with patience and grace. Umai Norris and baby Adayah are the hope for the future.

My partner, Norma Martinez-HoSang, is the most brilliant organizer I know. Many of the themes in this book about the development of group power, knowledge, and capacity I have learned from watching Norma. For listening to many iterations of analysis and argument, and for finding me places to get away and write, I am eternally grateful. With Isaac and Pablo, Norma has made our home the place I treasure most in life.

Notes

PREFACE

1. E. C. Clark, *Schoolhouse Door*. On George Wallace and the historic development of Southern conservatism, see Lowndes, *From the New Deal to the New Right*.

2. Kotsko, *Neoliberalism's Demons;* Hartman, *Scenes of Subjection;* Yamin, *American Marriage*.

3. Byrd et al., "Economies of Dispossession"; Lowe, *Intimacies of Four Continents*. See also Melamed and Reddy, "Using Liberal Rights to Enforce Racial Capitalism."

4. Baker, "Address at the Hattiesburg Freedom Day Rally."

5. MLK Jr., "Where Do We Go from Here?"

INTRODUCTION

C. L. R. James, *A History of Pan-African Revolt* (Oakland: PM Press, 2012), 106.

1. Robinson, *Black Marxism;* Kelley, *Freedom Dreams;* Ransby, *Ella Baker and the Black Freedom Movement*.

2. The pamphlets were published together as *A History of Negro Revolt* by the Independent Labor Party in Britain in 1938 and reissued by the Charles H. Kerr Publishing Company in 1939. See Kelley, "Introduction," 106. On James, see also Worcester, *C. L. R James;* Nielsen, *C. L. R. James*.

3. J. R. Johnson, "Revolution and the Negro." As Robin D. G. Kelley explains in the the introduction to *A History of Pan-African Revolt*, this essay was essentially a summary of the main arguments in the earlier *A History of Negro Revolt*. Kelley, "Introduction."

4. C. L. R. James, *History of Pan-African Revolt*, 47.

5. Meyer (C. L. R. James), "Revolutionary Answer to the Negro Problem in US." For an important discussion of this essay, see Myers, "A Validity of Its Own.

6. Meyer, "Revolution and the Negro." Emphasis in original.

7. On this argument broadly see Singh, *Black Is a Country;* Robinson, *Black Marxism;* Kelley, "Introduction."

8. Estes, "Red Deal."

9. Dunbar-Ortiz, *An Indigenous People's History of the United States;* Cobb, ed., *Say We Are Nations;* A. Simpson, *Mohawk Interruptus;* Alfred, *Wasase.*

10. This concept is drawn from and elaborated within Camacho, *Migrant Imaginaries.*

11. Committee to Stop Forced Sterilization, *Stop Forced Sterilization Now!,* 5.

12. Cited in Maulik, "Our Movement Is for the Long Haul." See also Prashad, "Day Our Probation Ended"; Nguyen, "Detained or Disappeared."

13. Desis Rising Up and Moving, "Four Levels of Solidarity," https://www .drumnyc.org/resource/.

14. Sexton, "People-of-Color-Blindness." For a critique of this position, see Annie Olaloku-Teriba, "Afro-Pessimism and the (Un) Logic of Anti-Blackness."

15. Molina, HoSang, and Gutiérrez, *Relational Formations of Race.*

16. The passages are from Audre Lorde's 1982 speech at Harvard University, "Learning from the 1960's," 138.

17. Lipsitz, "What Is This Black in the Black Radical Tradition?"

18. Du Bois, *Black Reconstruction in America.*

19. Autodidact 17, "Dr. Martin Luther King Jr."

20. See "Alabama Profile," Prison Policy Initiative, www.prisonpolicy.org /profiles/AL.html.

21. Culverhouse College of Business, "Alabama's Income: Past and Present." On this history see B. M. Wilson, *America's Johannesburg.*

22. See the website for the Poarch Creek tribal government: http://pci-nsn .gov/wordpress/.

23. Kennedy, "Radio and Television Report to the American People on Civil Rights." On the history of the Redstone Arsenal in Alabama, see US Army Materiel Command, *75th Anniversary of Redstone Arsenal.* The US Army's Missile and Munitions Center and School closed in 2011.

24. National Institute on Drug Abuse,"Alabama"; Centers for Disease Control and Prevention, "Drug Overdose Mortality by State." On this dynamic generally see Tu and Singh, "Morbid Capitalism and Its Racial Symptoms."

25. Kennedy, "Radio and Television Report to the American People on Civil Rights."

26. Kotsko, *Neoliberalism's Demons.*

27. Weiser, "What Big Business Said in All Those Anti-Racism Statements."

28. Favara, "Recruiting for Difference and Diversity in the US Military."

29. V. Harding, *Martin Luther King,* 51.

30. Ibid., 51.

31. Ibid., 48.

32. Loyd, "Race, Capitalist Crisis, and Abolitionist Organizing."

33. V. Harding, *Martin Luther King,* 54.

34. Ibid., 53.

35. Combahee River Collective, "Combahee River Collective Statement (1977)." Robin Kelley explains that in this tradition, "radical black feminists have never confined their vision to just the emancipation of black women or women in general, or all black people." Kelley argues instead "they are theorists and proponents of a radical humanism committed to liberating humanity and reconstructing social relations across the board." Kelley, "Introduction."

36. Judith LeBlanc, interview by Daniel HoSang, May 15, 2020.

37. G. L. Boggs and Kurashige, *Next American Revolution.*

38. V. Harding, *Martin Luther King,* 51.

39. See among many titles Getachew, *Worldmaking after Empire;* Prashad, *Darker Nations.*

CHAPTER 1. THE BODY

1. C. Thompson, "Chris." I use the pronoun "he" following its use in the original story. The interview is included in an archive produced by Reina Gossett's blog, *The Spirit Was . . .* On Rivera's political biography, see Gan, "Still at the Back of the Bus"; Shepard, "Sylvia and Sylvia's Children."

2. Feinberg, "Street Transvestite Action Revolutionaries"; Nothing, "Introduction." On queer liberation struggles on the West Coast, see Hobson, *Lavender and Red.*

3. On queer of color critique more generally, see R. Ferguson, *Aberrations in Black.* On trans political frameworks, see Spade, *Normal Life.*

4. Cooper, "Women's Cause Is One and Universal." See also Roberts, *Killing the Black Body.*

5. Painter, *History of White People.*

6. Blumenbach, "On the Natural Variety of Mankind."

7. Blumenbach was not the first Enlightenment scholar to be moved by the classificatory yearning to interpret human difference. The brightest minds of the age

of science and rationality averred their own typological regimes. The Swiss bota-
nist Linnaeus discovered four categories based on geography. The French natural-
ist and mathematician Buffon identified six geographic groupings. The German
philosopher Christoph Meiners found two "divisions": "(1) handsome, (2) ugly; the
first white, the latter dark." Bernasconi and Lott, eds., *Idea of Race*, 32–37.

8. Robinson, *Black Marxism.*

9. This point was developed most recently in Fields and Fields, *Racecraft*. See
also Painter, *History of White People;* Ewen and Ewen, *Typecasting;* Fields,
"Slavery, Race, and Ideology in the United States of America."

10. Reddy, *Freedom with Violence.*

11. Coates, *Between the World and Me.*

12. Fields, "Slavery, Race, and Ideology in the United States of America."

13. Du Bois, *Black Reconstruction in America*, 706. The quote also appears as
an epigraph in Lipsitz, *How Racism Takes Place*, 238.

14. Lorde, "Learning from the 60's."

15. This conceptualization originally appeared in Hall, "Race, Culture, and
Communications." It was elaborated in Gilmore, "Fatal Couplings of Power and
Difference."

16. Gutiérrez, *Fertile Matters.*

17. Thomas Jefferson, *Notes on the State of Virginia.*

18. Fanon, *Wretched of the Earth.*

19. Cited in Critical Resistance and Incite! Women of Color against Violence,
"Gender Violence and the Prison-Industrial Complex."

20. See Deer, *Beginning and End of Rape.*

21. J. King, "Mass Murders Still Unsolved in New Mexico"; Valdez, "Albuquerque Sex Workers Face Perils." Also see deMaría, "Lethal Intersections and
'Chicana Badgirls.'"

22. M. Z. Pérez, "Teen Moms Look for Support, but Find Only Shame."

23. Barboa, "Eleven Women Were Found Murdered in the Desert in
Albuquerque.

24. Zavella, "Intersectional Praxis in the Movement for Reproductive Justice."

25. Barboa, "Eleven Women Were Found Murdered in the Desert in
Albuquerque."

26. Arriola, "Accountability for Murder in the Maquiladoras."

27. Smith and Ross, "Introduction."

28. Power, "U.S. Companies Are Still Rushing to Juárez."

29. Wright, "Manifesto against Femicide."

30. Arriola, "Accountability for Murder in the Maquiladoras."

31. Fregoso, *MeXicana Encounters*, 5.

32. See MMIWG2S, "4 out of 5 of Our Native Women Are Affected by Violence Today"; Lucchesi and Echo-Hawk, "Missing and Murdered Indigenous
Women and Girls."

33. See the websites Bold Futures, https://boldfuturesnm.org/, and Forward Together, https://forwardtogether.org/programs/state-national-action/strong familiesnm/. See also Paskus, "Albuquerque Protesters Rally around a Suite of Issues, from Women's Rights and DACA to Economic Justice."

34. Diaz, *Flying under the Radar with the Royal Chicano Air Force;* Sandoval, "Chicano Park's Urban Imaginary."

35. Greene, "She Ain't No Rosa Parks."

36. McNeil, "Body, Sexuality, and Self-Defense in State vs. Joan Little."

37. A. Davis, "Joan Little"; McGuire, *At the Dark End of the Street.* See also Farmer, "Free Joan Little."

38. Gilmore, "Race, Prisons and War."

39. A. Davis, "Dialectics of Race"; McGuire, *At the Dark End of the Street.*

40. Kaba, "Free Joan Little."

41. Sweet Honey in the Rock, "Joan Little" (1976).

42. McNeil, "Body, Sexuality, and Self-Defense in State vs. Joan Little," 243.

43. Rosen and Fisher, "Chicano Park and the Chicano Park Murals"; G. Pérez, "Through Our Blood."

44. W. King, "Focus of Slaying Trial Had Humble Origins."

45. Thuma, *All Our Trials.*

46. McNeil, "Body, Sexuality, and Self-Defense in State vs. Joan Little," 255.

47. Cited in Thuma, *All Our Trials,* 674.

48. Theoharis, *Rebellious Life of Mrs. Rosa Parks.*

49. Roberts, *Killing the Black Body,* 45.

50. A. Davis, "Reflections on the Black Woman's Role in the Community of Slaves," 99.

51. Ibid., 98.

52. This analysis draws broadly from Crenshaw, "Mapping the Margins."

53. Thuma, *All Our Trials,* 1099.

54. Crenshaw and Ritchie, "Say Her Name."

55. Hernandez, "Chicanas and the Issue of Involuntary Sterilization"; *No Más Bebés.*

56. Stern, *Eugenic Nation;* Stern, "Sterilized in the Name of Public Health."

57. Espino, "Women Sterilized as They Give Birth."

58. Committee to Stop Forced Sterilization, *Stop Forced Sterilization Now!*

59. Hernandez, "Chicanas and the Issue of Involuntary Sterilization," 32.

60. Silliman et al., *Undivided Rights.*

61. Committee to Stop Forced Sterilization, *Stop Forced Sterilization Now!,* 5.

62. Carpio, "Lost Generation," 50; B. E. Johnson, "Reprise/Forced Sterilizations."

63. Carmen, "Native American Growing Fight against Sterilizations of Women."

64. McGuire, *At the Dark End of the Street.*

65. Roberts, *Killing the Black Body*, 8–9.

66. Nelson, "All This That Has Happened to Me Shouldn't Happen to Nobody Else."

67. L. Ross, *Color of Choice*. See also Silliman et al., *Undivided Rights*.

68. Mingus, "Interdependency (Excerpts from Several Talks)."

CHAPTER 2. DEMOCRACY AND GOVERNANCE

1. Du Bois, "African Roots of War."

2. Molina, *Fit to Be Citizens?* On dominant approaches to governmentality, citizenship, and race and gender, see Gardner, *Qualities of a Citizen;* Lopez, *White by Law;* Yamin, *American Marriage*.

3. Du Bois, *Black Reconstruction in America*.

4. Medovoi, "Government."

5. Van den Berghe, *Race and Racism*, 18.

6. A. Davis, *Abolition Democracy*, 101.

7. I use this term following Greg Grandin, "Caucasian Democracy." The term does not refer to a ruling oligarchy of all people considered to be Caucasians, but a specific conceptualization of the relationship between land, settler colonial law, and private property rooted in slavery and Indigenous disappearance. See also Olson, *Abolition of White Democracy*.

8. Blumenbach, "On the Natural Variety of Mankind." See also Painter, *History of White People;* Jacobson, *Barbarian Virtues*.

9. Cowie, *Great Exception*. See also L. Gordon and Fraser, "Genealogy of Dependency"; Fischel, *Homevoter Hypothesis;* Martin, *Permanent Tax Revolt*.

10. Reddy, *Freedom with Violence;* Williams, *Savage Anxieties;* Ablavsky, "Savage Constitution."

11. Dunbar-Ortiz, *Loaded*.

12. Blackhawk, "Federal Indian Law as Paradigm within Public Law"; Rana, *Two Faces of American Freedom*.

13. In the 1823 *Johnson v. McIntosh* decision, Chief Justice John Marshall wrote that Indigenous peoples were "fierce savages, whose occupation was war, and whose subsistence was drawn chiefly from the forest. To leave them in possession of their country, was to leave the country a wilderness." Cited in Estes, *Our History Is the Future*. Marshall's finding is still a part of the corpus of binding jurisprudence known as Indian Law. See Cohen, *Handbook of Federal Indian Law*.

14. A. Davis, *Abolition Democracy*, 103.

15. Waldstreicher, *Slavery's Constitution;* Jones, *Birthright Citizens;* Gilhooley, *Antebellum Origins of the Modern Constitution*.

16. Zinn, *SNCC*, 105. Carson, *In Struggle*.

17. John Lewis, Fannie Lou Hamer, Bob Moses, Jim Foreman, Howard Zinn, and scores of leaders from national civil rights groups arrived to support the effort, as did dozens of faith leaders from the North. Zinn, *SNNC*.

18. Ibid., 105.

19. Baker, "Address at the Hattisburg Freedom Rally," 685. See also Orth, "Ella Baker."

20. Marable and Mullings, *Let Nobody Turn Us Around*, 375; Ella Baker, "Bigger than a Hamburger."

21. Ransby, *Ella Baker and the Black Freedom Movement*, 86.

22. Ibid. In the 1930s, the YNCL staff provided consumer education teacher in the Workers Education Project (WEP) and took labor organizing classes at Brookwood Labor School.

23. R. E. Harding and V. Harding, "Biography, Democracy and Spirit."

24. Edwards, *Charisma and the Fictions of Black Leadership*, 16.

25. Baker, "Developing Community Leadership?," 351.

26. C. L. R. James, *Every Cook Can Govern*.

27. Baker, "Address at the Hattiesburg Freedom Day Rally."

28. Ransby, *Ella Baker and the Black Freedom Movement*, 352.

29. Payne, "Ella Baker and Models of Social Change," 897.

30. Baker, "Address at the Hattiesburg Freedom Day Rally."

31. Baker, "Black Woman in the Civil Rights Struggle."

32. Lewis, Reason, and Bradbury, "Participatory Research and Education for Social Change, 262–68; Steele, "Performing Utopia"; Robinson, *Black Marxism;* Mendel-Reyes and Hamlin, "Racial Justice in Appalachia."

33. Estes, *Our History Is the Future.*

34. Judith LeBlanc, interview by Daniel HoSang, May 15, 2020.

35. LeBlanc, interview. See also Spotted Eagle, "Brave Heart Society."

36. L. B. Simpson, *As We Have Always Done.*

37. LeBlanc, interview.

38. Grossman, *Unlikely Alliances,* 191; Lipsitz, "Walleye Warriors and White Identities," 101–22.

39. Estes, *Our History Is the Future,* 257.

40. Ibid., 204.

41. Quoted in Grossman, *Unlikely Alliances.*

42. Ibid., 186.

43. Ibid., 187.

44. Gilio-Whitaker, *As Long as Grass Grows,* 87.

45. Ibid., 144.

46. Jaffe, "Chicago Teachers Strike Was a Lesson in 21st-Century Organizing"; Jaffe, "How Chicago Teachers Built Power between Strikes"; McAlevey, "Chicago's Teachers Are Making History."

47. Jaffe, "Chicago Teachers Strike Was a Lesson in 21st-Century Organizing."

48. McAlevey, *No Shortcuts*, 119–20. On the Chicago Teachers Union, see also Uetricht, *Strike for America;* Eidelson and Jaffe, "Defending Public Education."

49. McAlevey, *No Shortcuts*, 120.

50. Gilmore, "Envisioning Abolition."

51. A. Davis, *Abolition Democracy*, 96.

52. Ibid.

53. Du Bois, *Black Reconstruction in America*, 641.

54. Du Bois, *Black Reconstruction in America.*

55. Balfour and Balfour, *Democracy's Reconstruction.*

56. Du Bois, *Black Reconstruction in America.*

57. Ibid., 641.

58. Lipsitz, "Abolition Democracy and Global Justice," 277.

59. González, "Illegal Migrants across U.S. Taking Protests to Defiant New Level."

60. Cited in Daniel Martinez HoSang, "Ideological Alchemy of Contemporary Nativism."

61. LBJ, "Remarks at the Signing of the Immigration Bill."

62. McGranahan, "Refusal and the Gift of Citizenship."

63. Rubio and Almendariz, "Refusing 'Undocumented.'"

64. Terriquez, "Intersectional Mobilization."

65. Pfaelzer, *Driven Out*, 341.

66. See Herard, "The Whatever That Survived." See also Cacho, *Social Death.*

67. Sirriyeh, "Felons Are Also Our Family," 144.

68. Ibid.

69. Mijente, *Defy, Defend, Expand Sanctuary.* See also Paik, *Bans, Walls, Raids.*

70. Herard, "The Whatever That Survived."

71. J. James, *Seeking the Beloved Community*, 121.

72. Blakeley, "Corona Crash."

73. Spade, *Mutual Aid.*

74. A. Davis, *Abolition Democracy*, 103. She describes this as socialist democracy rather than capitalist democracy.

75. Ibid.

CHAPTER 3. INTERNATIONALISM

1. Yassin, "Shortest Distance between Palestine and Ferguson"; Bailey, "Black–Palestinian Solidarity in the Ferguson–Gaza Era"; Bailey, "Dream Defenders"; Alsous and Hanf, "How Durham, NC Becomes First U.S. City to Ban Police

Exchanges with Israel"; Pennock, "Third World Alliances"; Lubin, *Geographies of Liberation.*

2. Gilmore, "Race, Prisons and War," 73.

3. Jacobson, "Where We Stand."

4. O'Dell, "July Rebellions and the Military State." Note that *Freedomways* was cofounded by Du Bois.

5. O'Dell, *Climbin' Jacob's Ladder.*

6. Muhammad, *Condemnation of Blackness.*

7. O'Dell, *Climbin' Jacob's Ladder,* 155.

8. Ibid., 159.

9. Man, *Soldiering through Empire.*

10. As Singh, in O'Dell, *Climbin' Jacob's Ladder,* explains, war-making becomes a necessary development to distinguish between "the humane, indeed the human, that is, 'we the people,' and the always already elastic category 'terrorist' containing someone who may in abstracto be a person but who has permanently forfeited the 'right to have rights,' that is the right to any meaningful civil protection" (104).

11. Martínez, "Looking for Color in the Anti-War Movement." This tension unsettled the anti-war movement throughout the period, as leaders from groups like the Black Panther Party often reported facing overt hostility from white anti-war protesters when they asserted these connections. Martínez said that after the rally, she was comforted by a veteran anti-war organizer who explained, "You got off easy," and told her that in the 1970s, Black Panther leaders were "booed when they mentioned racism at early anti-Vietnam war rallies" (iv), demonstrating a persistent ambivalence to recognize the connections to the "war at home." See also Maeda, *Chains of Babylon.* A national "Open Letter about Racism in the Movement" circulated widely in early 2003 at the height of the organizing against the invasion of Iraq—a broad coalition titled "United for Peace and Justice."

12. Biswas, "Patriotism in the US Peace Movement."

13. Ibid., 86, 85.

14. Martínez, "Looking for Color in the Anti-War Movement." The War Resisters League to its credit developed and advanced an analysis that linked militarism directly to struggles within the US around racism. There certainly are important exceptions among white peace activists, including figures like Anne Braden and others. But the reluctance of the "peace movement" to substantively engage with these issues is clear. See M. Meyer, "We Have Not Been Moved." Meyer notes the ways that anti-racist groups have continually been marginalized within the larger peace movement, including within important groups such as the Fellowship for Reconciliation and the American Friends Service Committee, as well as solidarity groups opposing US intervention in Central America. See also S. Ross, "Cispes in the 1980s"; Hutchinson, "Where Are the Black Cindy Sheehan's?"

15. J. Boggs, "Peace and War," 125.

16. Du Bois, "African Roots of War," 712.

17. Ibid., 709.

18. Biswas, "Patriotism in the US Peace Movement," 91.

19. Quoted in Pulido, *Black, Brown, Yellow and Left,* 78.

20. Douglass, "War with Mexico."

21. "By peace they mean plunder." Douglass, "Peace! Peace! Peace!"

22. Melamed, "Racial Capitalism."

23. Beveridge, "U.S. Senator Albert J. Beveridge Speaks on the Philippine Question."

24. Quoted in Kramer, "Race-Making and Colonial Violence in the U.S. Empire," 169.

25. Beveridge, "U.S. Senator Albert J. Beveridge Speaks on the Philippine Question."

26. Quoted in Kramer, *Blood of Government,* 128. Even in the face of these overtly white supremacist claims, some Black leaders argued that military service would provide an opportunity for African Americans to be shielded from the ongoing denigrations of Jim Crow by demonstrating their patriotism and devotion to the nation. As the military prepared to invade Cuba in 1896, Booker T. Washington offered to recruit 10,000 "loyal, brave, strong black men in the south who crave an opportunity to show their loyalty to our land." Washington, Booker T. Washington to John Davis Long." Even though many state militias and elected officials refused to permit African Americans to serve, particularly in the South, thousands of Black soldiers still enlisted; four all-Black regiments served in Cuba. In a national culture that valorizes militarization and patriotism, military service has continually been offered up as an opportunity for members of racially subordinated groups to claim rights and protections by demonstrating their loyalty and belonging by struggling for "the right to fight," or what some scholars have described as "martial citizenship." See Stanford, *If We Must Die.* Black soldiers known as the Buffalo Soldiers also fought wars against Indigenous people in the West. Four Black regiments served in the Spanish-American War in Cuba.

27. MLK Jr., "Beyond Vietnam."

28. White opposition to imperialist expansion during this time, consolidated through organizations like the Anti-Imperialist League and championed by public figures such as Mark Twain, William Jennings Bryan, and the industrialist Andrew Carnegie, generally did not recognize the connections that Beveridge was making clear. And while some of this opposition foregrounded issues of sovereignty and freedom for the people of the Philippines, Hawaii, Cuba, Guam, and Puerto Rico, many white anti-imperialists also expressed grave concerns that the annexation of such "tropical races" would despoil the nation's Anglo-Saxon char-

NOTES TO PAGES 88–95

acter. Even the most trenchant white critics of anti-imperialism argued that the occupation of these areas threatened to tarnish an otherwise proud tradition of American democracy, failing to acknowledge the profound forms of violence and white supremacy marking the nation at the time, or their connection to imperial ambitions abroad.

29. Du Bois took these positions as well. See also "Ida Wells-Bartlett against Expansion" (from an account of a meeting of the Afro-American Council, Washington, DC); Balce, "Filipino Bodies, Lynching, and the Language of Empire."

30. Douglas, quoted in Zinn, *SNCC*, 243; Douglas, quoted in Zinn and Arnove, *Voices of a People's History of the United States.*

31. Marks, *Black Press Views American Imperialism*, 117. (March 18, 1899)

32. Ibid., 114. (February 11, 1899)

33. Ibid., 124–25. (April 28, 1899)

34. Ibid., 123. (April 15, 1899)

35. Ibid., 124. (April 25, 1899)

36. Quoted in Ayers, *Promise of the New South*, 333.

37. Cited in Johnson and Lubin, *Futures of Black Radicalism*, 124.

38. Marks, *Black Press Views American Imperialism*, 117. (March 11, 1899)

39. Quoted in Morey, *Fagen*, 92.

40. Morey, *Fagen.*

41. Russell, "I Feel Sorry for These People," 209. It is also worth noting that after the war, over 1,200 African Americans opted to stay in the Philippines rather then return to the United States.

42. Dudziak, *Cold War Civil Rights.*

43. Beeching, "Paul Robeson and the Black Press."

44. Lubin, *Geographies of Liberation.*

45. I thank Loren Kajikawa, a musicologist at George Washington University, for these insights and description.

46. Kissinger, "Transcript of Kissinger's News Conference on the Status of the Cease-Fire Talks."

47. Himes, "Singer Ethel Ennis"; Florio and Shapiro, "The High Stakes of Singing 'The Star-Spangled Banner.'" See also Ferris, *Star-Spangled Banner.*

48. National Visionary Leadership Project, "Ethel Ennis." Indeed, Ennis was not the only Black celebrity standing by Nixon that day. The famed pianist Lionel Hampton also appeared on the inauguration program. The former football star Jim Brown as well as the singers Sammy Davis Jr. and James Brown were staunch supporters of Nixon's campaign.

49. J. S. Wilson, "It's a Banner Year for Ethel Ennis."

50. Apple, "Nixon Inaugurated for His Second Term."

51. Andrea and Sheffield-Hayes, "America's Greatness Compromised."

52. Metres, "June Jordan's War against War."

53. Singh, "Racial Formation in an Age of Permanent War."

54. MLK Jr., "Why I Am Opposed to the War in Vietnam."

55. Phillips, *War!*, 272.

56. Ibid.

57. Third World Women's Alliance, quoted in Crow, *Radical Feminism*, 463.

58. "Aug. 1966."

59. Montgomery, "Strike City."

60. The Fort Hood Three—three soldiers who refused to accept their transfer to Vietnam in July 1966—had planned to speak with Stokeley Carmichael but were detained by military officials before they could do so. They spoke about how their disidentification with the military enabled new forms of identification with Vietnamese people and their right to self-rule and democracy.

61. The Georgia House voted 184–12 to vacate Bond's election, declaring that he was a "traitor." Student Nonviolent Coordinating Committee Papers.

62. A copy of the comic book can be found in SNCC Affiliated Blacks against the Draft (BAD).

63. Sellers, "Black Power and the Freedom Movement in Retrospect."

64. Martínez, "Looking for Color in the Anti-War Movement."

65. Gordon, Cooper, and Shear, "Dozens of U.S. Missiles Hit Air Base in Syria"; Hennessy-Fiske and Bulos, "Syrians Report 15 Dead in U.S. Airstrike."

66. The estimate comes from the Syrian Observatory for Human Rights, "With Isis Ends as a Dominant Force in the East of Euphrates, the 53rd Month of Coalition Bombing Witnesses the Killing of about 185 Civilians and Fighters."

67. Vine, *Base Nation*, 329.

68. LaDuke and Cruz, *Militarization of Indian Country*, 16.

69. Grenier, *First Way of War*.

70. Cornum, "Irradiated Individual."

71. Ibid.

72. LaDuke and Cruz, *Militarization of Indian Country*, 33. An estimated 15,000 Navajos served in World War II, as new restrictions on livestock grazing in the 1930s further diminished opportunities for self-sufficiency on the reservation.

73. Stanford, *If We Must Die*, 81.

74. Mariscal, *Aztlán and Viet Nam*.

75. Raytheon Company, "Navajo Nation Honors Raytheon Diné Facility with Business of the Year Award."

76. LaDuke and Cruz, *Militarization of Indian Country*, 78.

77. Ibid., 105.

78. Estes, "Unplug Navajo Generating Station, Demand Diné Liberation."

79. Cornum, "Irradiated Individual"; Burke, *Uranium*, 98.

80. Burke, *Uranium;* Hastings, "Uranium Mining Leaves a Bitter Scar on Navajo Reservation"; WISE Uranium Project, "Impacts of Uranium Mining at Port Radium, NWT, Canada."

81. Anti-nuclear delegations from Japan, including the Japan Congress against the A- and H-Bombs, have also made trips to the Diné Nation to express solidarity and build relations, particularly after a devastating uranium spill in Church Rock, New Mexico, in 1979.

82. Clements, *Burning Vision;* Silko, *Ceremony.*

83. Estes, "Unplug Navajo Generating Station, Demand Diné Liberation." In *Landscapes of Power,* Dana E. Powell examines the rise and fall of the controversial Desert Rock Power Plant initiative in New Mexico to trace the political conflicts surrounding Native sovereignty and contemporary energy development on Navajo (Diné) Nation land. Yucca Mountain, in the heart of the Western Shoshone Nation, is also a sacred site for Shoshone and Pauite peoples.

84. Two years later, Ghanaian leader Kwame Nkrumah, joined by African American activists, held the World without the Bomb conference.

85. Opposition also came from Shirley Chisolm, Ron Dellums, and other Black congressional leaders. Intondi, "African American Leadership in the Fight for Nuclear Disarmament."

86. See S. Davis, *Empires' Edge,* chapter 1.

87. Trask, "Birth of the Modern Hawaiian Movement."

88. Silva, *Aloha Betrayed.*

89. Garrison, "Hawaiian Sovereignty and Island Knowledge."

90. In Kahoʻolawe, the federal response to demands to end bombing and begin cleanup of the island began in 1980 and has dragged on for many decades. The bombing range closed in 1990, and efforts to clean up the unexploded ordinance and restore the island's habitat have continued since then. Kanaka Maoli groups have also fought to secure regular access to the island as part of traditional cultural and spiritual practices.

91. From Lorentzen and Turpin, eds., *Women and War Reader,* 308–22. See also Kirk and Okazawa-Rey, "Making Connections Building an East Asia–US Women's Network against US Militarism"; Garrison, "Settler Responsibility."

92. S. Davis, *Empires' Edge,* 6.

93. K. E. Ferguson, *Oh, Say, Can You See?*

94. Grandinetti, "In the Shadow of the Beast."

95. Cited in ibid.

96. The work is part of Hernández's Cemí series, which debuted as an exhibit of 30 portraits and installations at the Fuerte de Vieques in October 2009. Hernández conducted dozens of interviews with residents of Vieques about their lives and experiences on the island. See her website, www.yasminhernandezart.co/bieke-cemi.

97. Jordan, "June Jordan Speaks Out against the 1991 Gulf War."

CHAPTER 4. LABOR

1. Howell, "Boycotting Pickles."
2. Ortiz, *African American and Latinx History of the United States.* On the history of FLOC, see Barger and Reza, *Farm Labor Movement in the Midwest;* HoSang, "Roots and Development of the Farm Labor Organizing Committee."
3. Herard, "The Whatever That Survived."
4. P. O'Neill, "United Front"; Wood, "Mt. Olive"; Hodges, "FLOC Pact in North Carolina 'Historic.'"
5. MLK Jr., "Where Do We Go from Here?"
6. Césaire, *Discourse on Colonialism.*
7. Blackmon, *Slavery by Another Name;* Du Bois, *Black Reconstruction in America.*
8. Camp and Heatherton, *Policing the Planet.*
9. Herard, "The Whatever That Survived."
10. Morrison, "A Humanist's View."
11. Denning, "Wageless Life"; Melamed, "Racial Capitalism"; Robinson, *Black Marxism.*
12. Linebaugh, *London Hanged.*
13. Melamed, "Racial Capitalism," 77; Byrd et al., "Economies of Dispossession"; Gilmore, *Change Everything.*
14. Roediger and Esch, *Production of Difference.*
15. Ward, *In Love and Struggle.*
16. J. Boggs, *American Revolution,* 53.
17. J. Boggs, *Racism and the Class Struggle,* 18.
18. Bates, *Making of Black Detroit in the Age of Henry Ford.*
19. On race, labor organizing, and the auto industry in postwar Detroit see D. J. Clark, *Disruption in Detroit;* Sugrue, *Origins of the Urban Crisis;* Kurashige, *Fifty-Year Rebellion;* Bates, *Making of Black Detroit in the Age of Henry Ford;* Binelli, *Detroit City Is the Place to Be;* Galster, *Driving Detroit.*
20. J. Boggs, *American Revolution,* 47.
21. Ward, "Ours Too Was a Struggle for a Better World," 76.
22. J. Boggs, *American Revolution,* 49.
23. Ibid., 54.
24. Ibid., 37. For an analysis of Detroit's broader political economy during this period, see Jay and Leavell, "Material Conditions of Detroit's Great Rebellion."
25. J. Boggs, *American Revolution,* 45.
26. Ibid.
27. Ibid.
28. Boggs and James worked closely together in the Correspondence Publishing Committee, which James helped to found in the late 1940s. Their eventual split turned on some of the assertions Boggs made about the role that Black

workers would play in advancing a challenge to capitalist authority. See Rosengarten, *Urbane Revolutionary;* Ward, "An Ending and a Beginning," 279–302.

29. J. Boggs, *American Revolution,* 37.

30. Ibid.

31. Ibid., 47.

32. Ibid., 51.

33. Ibid., 53.

34. Tarr, "50 Years since Detroit's Dodge Revolutionary Union Movement." The classic account of DRUM's history is Georgakas and Surkin, *Detroit, I Do Mind Dying.* See also Hinton, "Black Bolsheviks."

35. "Black Workers Uprising."

36. Watson, "To the Point of Production."

37. Tarr, "50 Years since Detroit's Dodge Revolutionary Union Movement."

38. Watson, "To the Point of Production," 17.

39. Debnam, "Black Women and the Charleston Hospital Workers' Strike of 1969"; Fink and Greenberg, *Upheaval in the Quiet Zone;* Honey, *Going down Jericho Road.*

40. "ELRUM!"

41. Georgakas and Surkin, *Detroit, I Do Mind Dying;* H. A. Thompson and Lyons, "Whose Detroit?"

42. Cited in Tarr, "50 Years since Detroit's Dodge Revolutionary Union Movement."

43. J. Boggs, *Racism and the Class Struggle,* 37.

44. Georgakas and Surkin, *Detroit, I Do Mind Dying,* 19–23.

45. Robé, "Detroit Rising."

46. Windham, *Knocking on Labor's Door.*

47. Geschwender, "League of Revolutionary Black Workers," 4.

48. Sardana, "US Billionaires' Wealth Grew by $845 Billion during the First Six Months of the Pandemic."

49. Marable, *Black Liberation in Conservative America,* 18–25.

50. KIWA, "KIWA 25th Anniversary Video."

51. Cho, "In Koreatown, Los Angeles Workers Center Fights for Immigrant Worker Rights."

52. Kwon, "Koreatown Immigrant Workers Alliance"; 23–48.

53. KIWA, *Assi Market: Our Stories of Struggle,* 2.

54. Ibid., 5.

55. Narro, "Sí se Puede," 65.

56. Louie, "Each Day I Go Home with a New Wound in My Heart."

57. Omatsu, "Immigrant Workers Take the Lead." See also Kang, "Activism Opens Generational Rift in Koreatown Workplaces"; Lee, "Displaced and Demanding Justice."

58. Omatsu, "Immigrant Workers Take the Lead."

59. The students came to work with KIWA from UCLA through an Asian American studies course taught by the longtime scholar-activist Glen Omatsu.

60. Omatsu, "Immigrant Workers Take the Lead."

61. Flyer reprinted in KIWA, *Assi Market*.

62. Omatsu, "Immigrant Workers Take the Lead."

63. Kwon, "Koreatown Immigrant Workers Alliance," 42.

64. Ibid., 43.

65. "Assi Market Closes after 17 Years." Assi was a holding of Rhee Brothers, founded in 1976 and one of the largest Asian food corporations in the US. In the early 2000s, Korean Americans made up 20 percent of the population in Koreatown, while the Latinx population stood at 60 percent. Sanchez et al., "Koreatown."

66. Kwon, "Koreatown Immigrant Workers Alliance"; Louie, "Each Day I Go Home with a New Wound in My Heart"; Louie, "What Did KIWA and the Market Workers Justice Campaign Accomplish?" I thank Dayle Chung for sharing these sources with me.

67. Fine, *Worker Centers;* Milkman and Voss, *Rebuilding Labor.*

68. Nadasen, "Power, Intimacy and Contestation," 204.

69. Bolden, "Organizing Domestic Workers in Atlanta, Georgia," 234–35.

70. Nadasen, "Power, Intimacy and Contestation."

71. Anonymous, "I Live a Treadmill Life.

72. Baker and Cooke, "Bronx Slave Market." See also Harris, "Marvel Cooke."

73. Baker and Cooke, "Bronx Slave Market."

74. Glenn, *Forced to Care.*

75. C. O'Neill, "Testing the Limits of Colonial Parenting."

76. Glenn, "From Servitude to Service Work."

77. Hunter, *To'joy My Freedom.*

78. Boris and Nadasen, "Domestic Workers Organize!"; Boris and Nadasen, "Introduction."

79. Nadasen, "Citizenship Rights, Domestic Work, and the Fair Labor Standards Act."

80. Slotnik, "Overlooked No More." See also Bolden, "Dorothy Bolden Oral History Interview."

81. Bolden, "Organizing Domestic Workers in Atlanta, Georgia."

82. Nadasen, *Household Workers Unite*, 42; Harrison, "They Led and a Community Followed."

83. Bolden, "Organizing Domestic Workers in Atlanta, Georgia," 236.

84. Nadasen, *Household Workers Unite.*

85. Nadasen, "Power, Intimacy and Contestation," 204.

86. Beck, "National Domestic Workers Union and the War on Poverty," 80.

87. Beck, "National Domestic Workers Union and the War on Poverty."

88. On domestic worker organizing more broadly, see Chang, *Disposable Domestics;* Hondagneu-Sotelo, *Doméstica;* Dill, "Making Your Job Good Yourself"; Boris, *Intimate Labors;* Glenn, "From Servitude to Service Work."

89. Boris and Nadasen, "Domestic Workers Organize!," 429.

90. The group came together at the World Social Forum meeting in Atlanta. See Boris and Nadasen, "Domestic Workers Organize!"; Nadasen, "Tell Dem Slavery Done."

91. Arnold, "How Trailblazing Labor Organizer Dorothy Bolden Taught Me to Fight for My Fellow Domestic Workers"; Twagirumukiza, "Unbossed."

92. The Care Collective, *Care Manifesto;* Glenn, "Creating a Caring Society.".

CONCLUSION

1. Johnson offered this analysis on her weekly show *Sonnie's Corner* on March 21, 2020. Johnson made the comment as a provocation to conservatives to offer a more forceful critique of the federal spending that was ultimately approved in the Coronavirus Aid, Relief, and Economic Security (CARES) Act, signed into law on March 27, 2020. For more on Johnson, Riehl, "Sonnie Johnson Announces 'Sonnie's Corner'"; London, "Black Conservative Warns Democratic Socialism Threatens to Gain Foothold in Black Community."

2. Sloan, "Cares Act Sent You a $1,200 Check but Gave Millionaires and Billionaires Far More"; Martindale, "9 Statistics That Show What a Miserable Failure the Cares Act Is"; Bivens and Shierholz, "Despite Some Good Provisions, the Cares Act Has Glaring Flaws and Falls Short of Fully Protecting Workers during the Coronavirus Crisis."

3. Parker, Horowitz, and Anderson, "Amid Protests, Majorities across Racial and Ethnic Groups Express Support for the Black Lives Matter Movement." By the fall, polls were suggesting this support had started to decrease. Thomas and Horowitz, "Support for Black Lives Matter Has Decreased since June but Remains Strong among Black Americans."

4. Boorstein and Natanson, "Mitt Romney, Marching with Evangelicals, Becomes First GOP Senator to Join George Floyd Protests in D.C."

5. Amazon's statement is available here: www.aboutamazon.com/news/policy-news-views/amazon-donates-10-million-to-organizations-supporting-justice-and-equity.

6. Major, "Amazon Founder Jeff Bezos Says He Supports Black Lives Matter but Activists Say Otherwise"; Paul, "Amazon Says 'Black Lives Matter'"; Press, "Amazon Is No Ally in the Fight for Racial Justice."

7. See the platform at Vision for Black Lives, https://m4bl.org/policy-platforms/.

8. Korb, *Pentagon's Fiscal Year 2021 Budget More Than Meets U.S. National Security Needs.*

9. Ibe, "Millions of Immigrants Are Being Left Out of Coronavirus Relief."

10. Sawyer and Wagner, *Mass Incarceration.*

11. "Current Investment Portfolio," CALSTRs, 2020, www.calstrs.com /current-investment-portfolio.

12. Mattioli, "Big Tech Companies Reap Gains as Covid-19 Fuels Shift in Demand." On Walmart's logistics, see LeCavalier, *Rule of Logistics;* Phillips and Rozworski, *People's Republic of Wal-Mart.*

13. Lorde, "Learning from the 60's."

14. Moraga, "La Güera," 32

15. G. L. Boggs, *Living for Change.*

16. Hampshire College TV, "Loretta Ross Keynote Address." See also L. Ross, "I'm a Black Feminist"; Bennett, "What If Instead of Calling People out, We Called Them In?"

17. Lorde, "Learning from the 60's."

18. Harding, Martin Luther King, 51.

19. Lorde, "Learning from the 60's."

Bibliography

Ablavsky, Gregory. "The Savage Constitution." *Duke Law Journal* (2014): 999–1089.

Alfred, Taiaiake. *Wasase: Indigenous Pathways of Action and Freedom.* Toronto: University of Toronto Press, 2005.

Alsous, Zaina, and Sammy Hanf. "How Durham, NC Becomes First U.S. City to Ban Police Exchanges with Israel." *Scalawag.* May 10, 2018. https://scalawag magazine.org/2018/05/how-durham-nc-becomes-first-u-s-city-to-ban-police -exchanges-with-israel/.

Andrea, Pauline A., and Elizabeth Sheffield-Hayes. "America's Greatness Compromised: The 'Star-Spangled Banner' as a Symbol of Nationalism, Identity, and Division." *Pro Football and the Proliferation of Protest: Anthem Posture in a Divided America,* edited by Stephen D. Perry. Lanham, MD: Lexington, 2019, 45–58.

Anonymous. "I Live a Treadmill Life." In *Black Women in White America: A Documentary History,* edited by Gerda Lerner. New York: Vintage, 1912, 227–29.

Apple, R. W., Jr. "Nixon Inaugurated for His Second Term: Sees World on Threshold of a Peace Era." *New York Times.* January 21, 1973. www.nytimes .com/1973/01/21/archives/nixon-inaugura-ted-for-his-second-term-sees- world-on-threshold-of-a.html.

Arnold, Jacquelyn. "How Trailblazing Labor Organizer Dorothy Bolden Taught Me to Fight for My Fellow Domestic Workers." *In These Times.* October 26,

2017.https://inthesetimes.com/article/national-domestic-workers-care-dorothy-bolden.

Arriola, Elva. "Accountability for Murder in the Maquiladoras." In *Making a Killing: Femicide, Free Trade, and La Frontera,* edited by Alicia Gaspar de Alba. Austin: University of Texas Press, 2010, 25–62.

"Assi Market Closes after 17 Years." *Koreatown LA News.* January 22, 2015. https://koreatownlanews.com/assi-market-closes-after-17-years/.

"Aug. 1966, Student Nonviolent Coordinating Committee Papers, 1959–1972." Reel 58, 2. University Microfilms International.

Autodidact 17. "Dr. Martin Luther King Jr: 'I Fear I Am Integrating My People into a Burning House.'" *New York Amsterdam News.* January 12, 2017. http://amsterdamnews.com/news/2017/jan/12/dr-martin-luther-king-jr-i-fear-i-am-integrating-m/.

Ayers, Edward. *The Promise of the New South: Life After Reconstruction—15th Anniversary.* New York: Oxford University Press, 2007.

Bailey, Kristian Davis. "Black–Palestinian Solidarity in the Ferguson–Gaza Era." *American Quarterly* 67, no. 4 (2015): 1017–26.

———. "Dream Defenders, Black Lives Matter and Ferguson Reps Take Historic Trip to Palestine." *Ebony.* January 9, 2015. www.ebony.com/news/dream-defenders-black-lives-matter-ferguson-reps-take-historic-trip-to-palestine/#ixzz3P2SqDnwi%20.

Baker, Ella. "Bigger than a Hamburger." *Southern Patriot* 18, no. 5 (1960): 4.

———. "The Black Woman in the Civil Rights Struggle." 1969. Speech. Iowa State University, Archives of Women's Political Communication. https://awpc.cattcenter.iastate.edu/2019/08/09/the-black-woman-in-the-civil-rights-struggle-1969/.

———. "Developing Community Leadership?" In *Black Women in White America: A Documentary History,* edited by Gerda Lerner. New York: Vintage, 1992, 345–51.

———. "Address at the Hattisburg Freedom Rally." In *Rhetoric, Religion and the Civil Rights Movement, 1954–1965,* edited by Davis W. Houck and David E. Dixon. Vol. 1. Waco: Baylor University Press, 99.

Baker, Ella, and Marvel Cooke. "The Bronx Slave Market." *Crisis* 42, no. 11 (1935): 330–40.

Balce, Nerissa S. "Filipino Bodies, Lynching, and the Language of Empire." In *Positively No Filipinos Allowed: Building Communities and Discourse,* edited by Antonio T. Tiongson Jr., Edgardo V. Gutierrez, and Ricardo V. Gutierrez. Philadelphia: Temple University Press, 2006, 43–60.

Balfour, Lawrie, and Katharine Lawrence Balfour. *Democracy's Reconstruction: Thinking Politically with W. E. B. Du Bois.* New York: Oxford University Press, 2011.

Barboa, Adriann. "Eleven Women Were Found Murdered in the Desert in Albuquerque." *Reproductive Justice Blog.* February 2, 2011. www.reproductive justiceblog.org/2011/02/eleven-women-were-found-murdered-in.html.

Barger, Walter Kenneth, and Ernesto M. Reza. *The Farm Labor Movement in the Midwest: Social Change and Adaptation among Migrant Farmworkers.* Austin: University of Texas Press, 1994.

Bates, Beth Tompkins. *The Making of Black Detroit in the Age of Henry Ford.* Chapel Hill: University of North Carolina Press, 2012.

Beck, Elizabeth. "The National Domestic Workers Union and the War on Poverty." *Journal of Sociology and Social Welfare* 28 (2001): 195–211.

Beeching, Barbara J. "Paul Robeson and the Black Press: The 1950 Passport Controversy." *Journal of African American History* 87 (2002): 339–54. https://dx.doi.org/10.2307/1562482.

Bennett, Jessica. "What If Instead of Calling People Out, We Called Them In?" *New York Times.* November 19, 2020. www.nytimes.com/2020/11/19/style /loretta-ross-smith-college-cancel-culture.html?login=smartlock&auth =login-smartlock.

Bernasconi, Robert, and Tommy Lee Lott, eds. *The Idea of Race: Readings in Philosophy.* Indianapolis: Hackett, 2000.

Beveridge, Albert J. "U.S. Senator Albert J. Beveridge Speaks on the Philippine Question." US Senate. Washington, DC. January 9, 1900. UCLA Center for Chinese Studies. www.international.ucla.edu/ccs/article/18454.

Binelli, Mark. *Detroit City Is the Place to Be: The Afterlife of an American Metropolis.* New York: Macmillan, 2013.

Biswas, Shampa. "Patriotism in the US Peace Movement: The Limits of Nationalist Resistance to Global Imperialism." In *Interrogating Imperialism,* edited by Robin L. Riley and Naeem Inayatullah. New York: Springer, 2006, 63–69.

Bivens, Josh, and Heidi Shierholz. "Despite Some Good Provisions, the Cares Act Has Glaring Flaws and Falls Short of Fully Protecting Workers during the Coronavirus Crisis." *Working Economics Blog, Economic Policy Institute.* March 25, 2020. www.epi.org/blog/despite-some-good-provisions-the-cares -act-has-glaring-flaws-and-falls-short-of-fully-protecting-workers-during -the-coronavirus-crisis/.

Blackhawk, Maggie. "Federal Indian Law as Paradigm within Public Law." *Harvard Law Review* 132 (2019): 1791–1876.

Blackmon, Douglas A. *Slavery by Another Name: The Re-enslavement of Black Americans from the Civil War to World War II.* New York: Anchor, 2009.

"Black Workers Uprising." *Inner City Voice.* June 8, 1968. https://riseupdetroit .org/wp-content/uploads/2018/07/Inner-City-Voice-vol-1-no-8-June-1968 -v2.pdf.

Blakeley, Grace. *The Corona Crash: How the Pandemic Will Change Capitalism.* London: Verso, 2020.

Blumenbach, Johann Friedrich. "On the Natural Variety of Mankind." In *The Idea of Race,* edited by Robert Bernasconi and Tommy Lee Lott. Indianapolis: Hackett, 2000.

Boggs, Grace Lee. *Living for Change: An Autobiography.* Minneapolis: University of Minnesota Press, 2016.

Boggs, Grace Lee, and Scott Kurashige. *The Next American Revolution: Sustainable Activism for the Twenty-First Century.* Berkeley: University of California Press, 2012.

Boggs, James. *American Revolution.* New York: New York University Press, 1963.

———. *Racism and the Class Struggle: Further Pages from a Black Worker's Notebook:* New York: Monthly Review Press, 1970.

———. "Peace and War." In *Pages from a Black Radical's Notebook: A James Boggs Reader,* edited by Stephen M. Ward. Detroit: Wayne State University Press, 2011, 120–125.

Bolden, Dorothy. "Organizing Domestic Workers in Atlanta, Georgia." In *Black Women in White America: A Documentary History,* edited by Gerda Lerner. New York: Vintage, 1992, 234–39.

———. "Dorothy Bolden Oral History Interview." Interview by Chris Lutz. August 31, 1995. Dorothy Lee Bolden Thompson Collection. Auburn Avenue Research Library on African-American Culture and History, Georgia State University Library.

Boorstein, Michelle, and Hannah Natanson. "Mitt Romney, Marching with Evangelicals, Becomes First GOP Senator to Join George Floyd Protests in D.C." *Washington Post.* June 8, 2020. www.washingtonpost.com/dc-md-va/2020/06/07/romney-protest-black-lives-matter/.

Boris, Eileen. *Intimate Labors: Cultures, Technologies, and the Politics of Care.* Stanford: Stanford University Press, 2010.

Boris, Eileen, and Premilla Nadasen. "Domestic Workers Organize!," *WorkingUSA: The Journal of Labor and Society* 11, no. 4 (2008): 413–37.

———. "Introduction: Historicizing Domestic Workers' Resistance and Organizing." *International Labor and Working-Class History* 88 (2015): 4–10.

Burke, Anthony. *Uranium.* Malden, MA: Polity Press, 2017.

Byrd, Jodi, Alyosha Goldstein, Jodi Melamed, and Chandan Reddy. "Economies of Dispossession: Indigeneity, Race, Capitalism." *Social Text* 36, no. 2 (2018): 1–18.

Cacho, Lisa Marie. *Social Death: Racialized Rightlessness and the Criminalization of the Unprotected: Nation of Newcomers.* New York: New York University Press, 2012.

Camacho, Alicia Schmidt. *Migrant Imaginaries: Latino Cultural Politics in the US-Mexico Borderlands.* New York: New York University Press, 2008.

Camp, Jordan T., and Christina Heatherton. *Policing the Planet: Why the Policing Crisis Led to Black Lives Matter.* London: Verso, 2016.

The Care Collective. *The Care Manifesto: The Politics of Interdependence.* London: Verso, 2020.

Carmen, Andrea. "Native American Growing Fight against Sterilizations of Women." *Akwesasne* (Winter 1979): 6.

Carpio, Myla Vicenti. "The Lost Generation: American Indian Women and Sterilization Abuse." *Social Justice* 31, no. 4 (2004): 40–53.

Carson, Clayborne. *In Struggle: SNCC and the Black Awakening of the 1960s.* Cambridge: Harvard University Press, 1995.

Centers for Disease Control and Prevention. "Drug Overdose Mortality by State." National Center for Health Statistics. 2020. www.cdc.gov/nchs /pressroom/sosmap/drug_poisoning_mortality/drug_poisoning.htm.

Césaire, Aimé. *Discourse on Colonialism:* New York: New York University Press, 2001.

Chang, Grace. *Disposable Domestics: Immigrant Women Workers in the Global Economy.* Chicago: Haymarket Books, 2016.

Cho, Cindy. "In Koreatown, Los Angeles Workers Center Fights for Immigrant Worker Rights." *Labor Notes.* October 1, 2003. www.labornotes.org/2003/10 /koreatown-los-angeles-workers-center-fights-immigrant-worker-rights.

Clark, Daniel J. *Disruption in Detroit: Autoworkers and the Elusive Postwar Boom:* Champaign: University of Illinois Press, 2018.

Clark, E. Culpepper. *The Schoolhouse Door: Segregation's Last Stand at the University of Alabama.* New York: Oxford University Press, 1995.

Clements, Marie. *Burning Vision.* Vol. 9. Vancouver: Talonbooks, 2003.

Coates, Ta-Nehisi. *Between the World and Me.* New York: Spiegel and Grau, 2015.

Cobb, Daniel, ed. *Say We Are Nations: Documents of Politics and Protest in Indigenous America since 1887.* Chapel Hill: University of North Carolina Press, 2015.

Cohen, Felix S. *Handbook of Federal Indian Law: With Reference Tables and Index.* Washington, DC: US Government Printing Office, 1942.

Combahee River Collective. "Combahee River Collective Statement (1977)." In *Home Girls : A Black Feminist Anthology.* 1st ed., edited by Barbara Smith. New York: Kitchen Table—Women of Color Press, 1983, 264–74.

Committee to Stop Forced Sterilization. *Stop Forced Sterilization Now!* Los Angeles, 1975. www.freedomarchives.org/Documents/Finder/DOC46_scans /46.StopForcedSterilizationNow.pdf.

Cooper, Anna Julia. "Women's Cause Is One and Universal." In *The World's Congress of Representative Women.* Chicago: Rand McNally, 1894.

Cornum, Lou. "The Irradiated Individual." 2018. https://datasociety.net/wp -content/uploads/2018/06/ii-web.pdf.

Cowie, Jefferson. *The Great Exception: The New Deal and the Limits of American Politics.* Princeton: Princeton University Press, 2017.

Crenshaw, Kimberlé Williams. "Mapping the Margins: Intersectionality, Identity Politics, and Violence against Women of Color." *Stanford Law Review* 43, no. 6 (1991): 1241–99.

Crenshaw, Kimberlé Williams, and Andrea J. Ritchie. "Say Her Name: Resisting Police Brutality against Black Women. African American Policy Forum, July 2015.

Critical Resistance and Incite! Women of Color against Violence. "Gender Violence and the Prison-Industrial Complex." In *Color of Violence: The INCITE! Anthology,* edited by INCITE! Women of Color against Violence. Durham: Duke University Press, 2006, 223–26.

Crow, Barbara A. *Radical Feminism: A Documentary Reader.* New York: New York University Press, 2000.

Culverhouse College of Business. "Alabama's Income: Past and Present." 2019. https://cber.culverhouse.ua.edu/2019/08/07/alabamas-income-past-and -present/.

Davis, Angela. "Reflections on the Black Woman's Role in the Community of Slaves." *Massachusetts Review* 13, no. 1/2 (1972): 81–100.

———. "Joan Little: The Dialectics of Rape." *Ms. Magazine,* May 1975, 49.

———. *Abolition Democracy: Beyond Empire, Prisons, and Torture.* New York: Seven Stories Press, 2011.

Davis, Sasha. *The Empires' Edge: Militarization, Resistance, and Transcending Hegemony in the Pacific.* Athens: University of Georgia Press, 2015.

Debnam, Jewell Charmaine. "Black Women and the Charleston Hospital Workers' Strike of 1969." PhD diss., Michigan State University, 2016.

Deer, Sarah. *The Beginning and End of Rape: Confronting Sexual Violence in Native America.* Minneapolis: University of Minnesota Press, 2015.

deMaría, Jaelyn. "Lethal Intersections and 'Chicana Badgirls.'" In *De-Whitening Intersectionality: Race, Intercultural Communication, and Politics,* edited by Shinsuke Eguchi, Bernadette Marie Calafell, and Shadee Abdi. Lanham, MD: Lexington, 2020, 25–44.

Denning, Michael. "Wageless Life." *New Left Review* 66 (November/December 2010): 79–97.

Desis Rising Up and Moving. "Four Levels of Solidarity." DRUM. https://movementhub.org/resource/four-levels-of-solidarity/#:~:text=A%20 graphic%20from%20DRUM%20(Desis,embodied%20solidarity%2C%20 and%20transformative%20solidarity.

Diaz, Ella Maria. *Flying under the Radar with the Royal Chicano Air Force: Mapping a Chicano/a Art History.* Austin: University of Texas Press, 2017.

Dill, Bonnie Thornton. "Making Your Job Good Yourself: Domestic Service and the Construction of Personal Dignity." *Women and the Politics of Empower-*

ment, edited by Ann Bookman and Sandra Morgen. Philadelphia: Temple University Press, 1988, 33–52.

Douglass, Fredrick. "Peace! Peace! Peace!" *North Star.* March 17, 1848.

———. "The War with Mexico." *North Star,* January 21, 1848.

Du Bois, W. E. B. "The African Roots of War." *Atlantic Monthly,* 1915, 707–14. http://scua.library.umass.edu/digital/dubois/WarRoots.pdf.

———. *Black Reconstruction in America: An Essay toward a History of the Part Which Black Folk Played in an Attempt to Reconstruct Democracy in America, 1860–1880.* New York: Harcourt, Brace, 1935.

Dudziak, Mary L. *Cold War Civil Rights: Race and the Image of American Democracy.* Princeton: Princeton University Press, 2011.

Dunbar-Ortiz, Roxanne. *An Indigenous People's History of the United States.* Boston: Beacon Press, 2015.

———. *Loaded: A Disarming History of the Second Amendment.* San Francisco: City Lights Books, 2018.

Edwards, Erica Renee. *Charisma and the Fictions of Black Leadership.* Minneapolis: University of Minnesota Press, 2012.

Eidelson, Josh, and Sarah Jaffe. "Defending Public Education: An Interview with Karen Lewis of the Chicago Teachers Union." *Dissent* 60, no. 3 (2013): 77–80.

"ELRUM! We Will Win without a Doubt." *South End* 27, no. 121. May 14, 1969. https://riseupdetroit.org/the-south-end-v-27-no-121-may-14–1969/.

Espino, Virginia. "Women Sterilized as They Give Birth": Forced Sterilization and the Chicana Resistance in the 1970s." In *Las Obreras: Chicana Politics of Work and Family,* edited by Vicki L. Ruiz. Los Angeles: UCLA Chicano Studies Research Center Publications, 2000, 65–82.

Estes, Nick. *Our History Is the Future: Standing Rock versus the Dakota Access Pipeline, and the Long Tradition of Indigenous Resistance.* London: Verso, 2019.

———. "A Red Deal." *Jacobin Magazine.* August 6, 2019. www.jacobinmag .com/2019/08/red-deal-green-new-deal-ecosocialism-decolonization-indigenous-resistance-environment.

———. "Unplug Navajo Generating Station, Demand Diné Liberation." *The Red Nation* (blog). January 6, 2019. https://therednation.org/unplug-navajo -generating-station-demand-dine-liberation/.

Ewen, Stuart, and Elizabeth Ewen. *Typecasting : On the Arts and Sciences of Human Inequality : A History of Dominant Ideas.* New York: Seven Stories Press, 2006.

Fanon, Frantz. *The Wretched of the Earth.* Translated by Richard Philcox. New York: Grove Press, 2004.

Farmer, Ashley. "Free Joan Little: Anti-Rape Activism, Black Power, and the Black Feedom Movement." *Black Perspectives.* February 4, 2016. www.aaihs .org/free-joan-little/.

Favara, Jeremiah B. "Recruiting for Difference and Diversity in the US Military." PhD diss., University of Oregon, 2017.

Feinberg, Leslie. "Street Transvestite Action Revolutionaries: Lavender and Red, Part 73." *Workers World*. September 24, 2006. www.workers.org/2006/us/lavender-red-73/.

Ferguson, Kathy E. *Oh, Say, Can You See? The Semiotics of the Military in Hawai'i*. Minneapolis: University of Minnesota Press, 1999.

Ferguson, Roderick. *Aberrations in Black: Toward a Queer of Color Critique*. Minneapolis: University of Minnesota Press, 2004.

Ferris, Marc. *Star-Spangled Banner: The Unlikely Story of America's National Anthem*. Baltimore: Johns Hopkins University Press, 2014.

Fields, Barbara. "Slavery, Race, and Ideology in the United States of America." *New Left Review* (May/June 1990): 95–118.

Fields, Barbara, and Karen Fields. *Racecraft: The Soul of Inequality in American Life*. London: Verso, 2012.

Fine, Janice Ruth. *Worker Centers: Organizing Communities at the Edge of the Dream*. Ithaca: Cornell University Press, 2006.

Fink, Leon, and Brian Greenberg. *Upheaval in the Quiet Zone: A History of Hospital Workers' Union, Local 1199*. Champaign: University of Illinois Press, 1989.

Fischel, William. *The Homevoter Hypothesis: How Home Values Influence Local Government Taxation, School Finance, and Land-Use Policies*. Cambridge: Harvard University Press, 2001.

Florio, John, and Ouisie Shapiro. "The High Stakes of Singing 'The Star-Spangled Banner.'" *Atlantic*. July 4, 2015. www.theatlantic.com/entertainment/archive/2015/07/whats-the-right-way-to-sing-the-national-anthem/397526/.

Fregoso, Rosa Linda. *MeXicana Encounters: The Making of Social Identities on the Borderlands*. Berkeley: University of California Press, 2003.

Galster, George. *Driving Detroit: The Quest for Respect in the Motor City*. Philadelphia: University of Pennsylvania Press, 2012.

Gan, Jessi. "'Still at the Back of the Bus': Sylvia Rivera's Struggle." *Centro Journal* 19, no. 1 (2007): 124–39.

Gardner, Martha. *The Qualities of a Citizen: Women, Immigration, and Citizenship, 1870–1965*. Princeton: Princeton University Press, 2009.

Garrison, Rebekah. "Hawaiian Sovereignty and Island Knowledge: Interview with Dr. Haunani-Kay Trask." *Decolonial Gesture* 11, no. 1 (2014). https://hemisphericinstitute.org/en/emisferica-11-1-decolonial-gesture/11-1-dossier/hawaiian-sovereignty-and-island-knowledge.html.

———. "Settler Responsibility: Respatialising Dissent in 'America' Beyond Continental Borders." *Shima* 13, no. 2 (2019): 56–75.

Georgakas, Dan, and Marvin Surkin. *Detroit, I Do Mind Dying*. Vol. 2: Boston: South End Press, 1998.

Geschwender, James A. "The League of Revolutionary Black Workers: Problems Confronting Black Marxist-Leninist Organizations." *Journal of Ethnic Studies* 2, no. 3 (1974): 1–23.

Getachew, Adom. *Worldmaking after Empire: The Rise and Fall of Self -Determination*. Princeton: Princeton University Press, 2019.

Gilhooley, Simon J. *The Antebellum Origins of the Modern Constitution: Slavery and the Spirit of the American Founding*. Cambridge: Cambridge University Press, 2020.

Gilio-Whitaker, Dina. *As Long as Grass Grows: The Indigenous Fight for Environmental Justice, from Colonization to Standing Rock*. Boston: Beacon Press, 2019.

Gilmore, Ruth Wilson. "Fatal Couplings of Power and Difference: Notes on Racism and Geography." *Professional Geographer* 54, no. 1 (2002): 15–24.

———. "Race, Prisons and War: Scenes from the History of US Violence." In *We Have Not Been Moved: Resisting Racism and Militarism in 21st Century America*, edited by Elizabeth "Betita" Martínez, Mandy Carter, and Matt Meyer. Oakland: PM Press, 2012.

———. "Envisioning Abolition: Social Justice Organizing for Vulnerable Households, Communities, and Workers." Speech. DePaul University, 2019.

———. *Change Everything: Racial Capitalism and the Case for Abolition*. Edited by Naomi Murakawa. Chicago: Haymarket Books, 2021.

Glenn, Evelyn Nakano. "From Servitude to Service Work: Historical Continuities in the Racial Division of Paid Reproductive Labor." *Signs: Journal of Women in Culture and Society* 18, no. 1 (1992): 1–43.

———. "Creating a Caring Society." *Contemporary Sociology* 29, no. 1 (2000): 84–94.

———. *Forced to Care: Coercion and Caregiving in America*. Cambridge: Harvard University Press, 2010.

González, Daniel. "Illegal Migrants across U.S. Taking Protests to Defiant New Level." *Arizona Republic*. September 20, 2012. www.azcentral.com/news/art icles/2012/09/13/20120913illegal-migrants-us-protests-defiant-new-level .html#ixzz6d2oCrrUS.

Gordon, Linda, and Nancy Fraser. "A Genealogy of Dependency: Tracing a Keyword of the U.S. Welfare State." *Signs* 19, no. 2 (1994): 309–36.

Gordon, Michael R., Helene Cooper, and Michael D. Shear. "Dozens of U.S. Missiles Hit Air Base in Syria." *New York Times*. April 6, 2017. www .nytimes.com/2017/04/06/world/middleeast/us-said-to-weigh-military -responses-to-syrian-chemical-attack.html.

Grandin, Greg. "A Caucasian Democracy." In *The End of the Myth: From the Frontier to the Border Wall in the Mind of America*. New York: Metropolitan Books, 2019, 47–67.

Grandinetti, Tina. "In the Shadow of the Beast." *FLUX Hawaii* (2014): 35–40.

Greene, Christina. "She Ain't No Rosa Parks": The Joan Little Rape–Murder Case and Jim Crow Justice in the Post–Civil Rights South." *Journal of African American History* 100, no. 3 (2015): 428–47.

Grenier, John. *The First Way of War: American War Making on the Frontier, 1607–1814*. Cambridge: Cambridge University Press, 2005.

Grossman, Zoltn. *Unlikely Alliances: Native Nations and White Communities Join to Defend Rural Lands*. Seattle: University of Washington Press, 2017.

Gutiérrez, Elena R. *Fertile Matters : The Politics of Mexican-Origin Women's Reproduction*. Austin: University of Texas Press, 2008.

Hall, Stuart. "Race, Culture, and Communications: Looking Backward and Forward at Cultural Studies." *Rethinking Marxism* 5, no. 1 (1992): 10–18.

Hampshire College TV. "Loretta Ross Keynote Address—Hampshire College Commencement 2018." Recorded May 20, 2018. www.youtube.com/watch?v =RNT8K-XhJHM.

Harding, Rachel E., and Vincent Harding. "Biography, Democracy and Spirit: An Interview with Vincent Harding." *Callaloo* 20, no. 3 (1997): 682–98.

Harding, Vincent. *Martin Luther King: The Inconvenient Hero*. Maryknoll, NY: Orbis Books.

Harris, LaShawn. "Marvel Cooke: Investigative Journalist, Communist and Black Radical Subject." *Journal for the Study of Radicalism* 6, no. 2 (2012): 91–126.

Harrison, Christy. "They Led and a Community Followed: The Community Activism of Ella Mae Brayboy and Dorothy Bolden in Atlanta, Georgia, 1964–1994." MA thesis, Clark Atlanta University, 2007.

Hartman, Saidiya V. *Scenes of Subjection: Terror, Slavery, and Self-Making in Nineteenth-Century America*. New York: Oxford University Press, 1997.

Hastings, Deborah. "Uranium Mining Leaves a Bitter Scar on Navajo Reservation." *Los Angeles Times*. August 6, 2000. www.latimes.com/archives/la -xpm-2000-aug-06-me-65309-story.html.

Hennessy-Fiske, Molly, and Nabih Bulos. "Syrians Report 15 Dead in U.S. Airstrike." *Los Angeles Times*. April 6, 2017. www.latimes.com/world /middleeast/la-fg-syria-airstrike-20170406-story.html.

Herard, Tiffany Willoughby. "'The Whatever That Survived': Thinking Racialized Immigration through Blackness and the Afterlife of Slavery." In *Relational Formations of Race: Theory, Method, and Practice*, edited by Natalia Molina, Daniel Martinez HoSang, and Ramón A. Gutiérrez. Oakland: University of California Press, 2019.

Hernandez, Antonia. "Chicanas and the Issue of Involuntary Sterilization: Reforms Needed to Protect Informed Consent." *Chicana/o Latina/o Law Review* 3 (1976): 3–37.

Himes, Geoffrey. "Singer Ethel Ennis—'I Want to Do It My Way.'" *Washington Post.* May 20, 1979. www.washingtonpost.com/archive/lifestyle/1979/05 /20/singer-ethel-ennis-i-want-to-do-it-my-way/70b0253b-3aae-4111 -a312–1f9ca9a8b146/?noredirect=on&utm_term=.9a7867ecb85d.

Hinton, Elizabeth Kai. "The Black Bolsheviks: Detroit Revolutionary Union Movements and Shop-Floor Organizing." In *The New Black History: Revisiting the Second Reconstruction,* edited by Manning Marable and Elizabeth Kai Hinton. New York: Palgrave, 2011, 211–28.

Hobson, Emily K. *Lavender and Red: Liberation and Solidarity in the Gay and Lesbian Left.* Oakland: University of California Press, 2016.

Hodges, Kadi. "FLOC Pact in North Carolina 'Historic.'" *Toledo Blade.* September 17, 2004. www.toledoblade.com/business/2004/09/17/FLOC-pact-in -North-Carolina-historic.html.

Hondagneu-Sotelo, Pierrette. *Doméstica: Immigrant Workers Cleaning and Caring in the Shadows of Affluence.* Berkeley: University of California Press, 2007.

Honey, Michael K. *Going down Jericho Road: The Memphis Strike, Martin Luther King's Last Campaign.* New York: W. W. Norton, 2011.

HoSang, Daniel. "The Roots and Development of the Farm Labor Organizing Committee." BA thesis, Wesleyan University, 1993.

HoSang, Daniel Martinez. "The Ideological Alchemy of Contemporary Nativism: Revisiting the Origins of California's Proposition 187." *Kalfou* 1, no. 1 (2014). https://doi.org/10.15367/kf.v1i1.10.

Howell, Leon. "Boycotting Pickles: A Labor Strategy in North Carolina." *Christian Century.* January 21, 2001. http://main.nc.us/cnnews/ChristianCentury01 –19–01/.

Hunter, Tera W. *To'joy My Freedom: Southern Black Women's Lives and Labors after the Civil War.* Cambridge: Harvard University Press, 1997.

Hutchinson, Earl Ofari. "Where Are the Black Cindy Sheehan's?" *HuffPost* (blog). August 25, 2005. https://www.huffpost.com/entry/where-are-the-black -cindy_b_6183.

Ibe, Peniel. "Millions of Immigrants Are Being Left out of Coronavirus Relief." *News and Commentary, American Friends of Service Committee* (blog). July 21, 2020. www.afsc.org/blogs/news-and-commentary/millions-immigrants -are-being-left-out-coronavirus-relief.

"Ida Wells-Bartlett against Expansion," *Cleveland Gazette.* January 7, 1899.

Intondi, Vincent. "African American Leadership in the Fight for Nuclear Disarmament." *Arms Control Now* (blog). Arms Control Association. 2018.

www.armscontrol.org/blog/2018–02–22/african-american-leadership-fight
-for-nuclear-disarmament.

Jacobs, Margaret D. "Working on the Domestic Frontier: American Indian
Domestic Servants in White Women's Households in the San Francisco Bay
Area, 1920–1940." *Frontiers: A Journal of Women Studies* 28, no. 1/2
(2007): 165–99.

Jacobson, Matthew Frye. *Barbarian Virtues: The United States Encounters
Foreign Peoples at Home and Abroad, 1876–1917.* New York: Hill and Wang,
2000.

———. "Where We Stand: US Empire at Street Level and in the Archive."
American Quarterly 65, no. 2 (2013): 265–90.

Jaffe, Sarah. "The Chicago Teachers Strike Was a Lesson in 21st-Century
Organizing." *Nation,* November 16, 2019. www.thenation.com/article
/archive/chicago-ctu-strike-win/.

———. "How Chicago Teachers Built Power between Strikes." *Progressive.*
October 22, 2019. https://progressive.org/dispatches/chicago-teachers-
built-power-between-strikes-jaffe-191022/.

James, C. L. R. *Every Cook Can Govern: A Study of Democracy in Ancient
Greece: Its Meaning for Today.* Brooklyn: AGIT, 1956.

———. *A History of Pan-African Revolt.* Oakland: PM Press, 2012.

James, Joy. *Seeking the Beloved Community: A Feminist Race Reader.* Albany:
SUNY Press, 2013.

Jay, Mark, and Virginia Leavell. "Material Conditions of Detroit's Great
Rebellion." *Social Justice* 44, no. 4 (2017): 27–54.

Jefferson, Thomas. *Notes on the State of Virginia.* Philadelphia: Prichard and
Hall, 1785.

Johnson, B. E. "Reprise/Forced Sterilizations: Native Americans and the 'Last
Gasp of Eugenics.'" *Native Americans* (Winter 1998): 44–47.

Johnson, Gaye Theresa, and Alex Lubin, eds. *Futures of Black Radicalism.*
London: Verso, 2017.

Johnson, J. R. "The Revolution and the Negro." *New International* 5 (December
1939): 339–43.

Johnson, Lyndon B. "Remarks at the Signing of the Immigration Bill, Liberty
Island, New York." 1965. The American Presidency Project. www.presidency
.ucsb.edu/documents/remarks-the-signing-the-immigration-bill-liberty
-island-new-york.

Jones, Martha S. *Birthright Citizens: A History of Race and Rights in Antebellum America.* Cambridge: Cambridge University Press, 2018.

Jordan, June. "June Jordan Speaks Out against the 1991 Gulf War." History Is a
Weapon. 1991. www.historyisaweapon.com/defcon1/1991jordan.html.

Kaba, Mariame. "'Free Joan Little': Reflections on Prisoner Resistance and
Movement-Building." *Prison Culture.* January 4, 2011. www.usprisonculture

.com/blog/2011/01/04/free-joan-little-reflections-on-prisoner-resistance
-and-movement-building/.

Kang, Connie. "Activism Opens Generational Rift in Koreatown Workplaces."
Los Angeles Times. September 6, 1998.

Kelley, Robin D. G. *Freedom Dreams: The Black Radical Imagination.* Boston:
Beacon Press, 2003.

———. "Introduction." In *A History of Pan-African Revolt.* Oakland: PM Press,
2012.

Kennedy, John F. "Radio and Television Report to the American People on Civil
Rights, June 11, 1963." The White House, 1963.

King, Jamilah. "Mass Murders Still Unsolved in New Mexico." *Colorlines.*
February 4, 2011. www.colorlines.com/articles/mass-murders-still-unsolved
-new-mexico.

King, Martin Luther, Jr. "Beyond Vietnam." In *A Call to Conscience: The
Landmark Speeches of Dr. Martin Luther King, Jr.,* edited by Clayborne
Carson and Kris Shepard. New York: Grand Central Publishing, 1967,
133–64.

———. "Where Do We Go from Here?" Address Delivered at the Eleventh
Annual SCLC Convention." In *A Call to Conscience: The Landmark Speeches
of Dr. Martin Luther King, Jr.,* edited by Clayborne Carson, and Kris
Shepard. New York: Grand Central Publishing, 1967, 165–200.

———. "Why I Am Opposed to the War in Vietnam." Riverside Church, New
York. 1967.

King, Wayne. "Focus of Slaying Trial Had Humble Origins." *New York Times.*
July 29, 1975. www.nytimes.com/1975/07/29/archives/focus-of-slaying
-trial-had-humble-origins-joan-little.html.

Kirk, Gwyn, and Margo Okazawa-Rey. "Making Connections Building an East
Asia–US Women's Network against US Militarism." *Women and War
Reader,* edited by Lois Ann Lorentzen and Jennifer E. Turpin. New York:
New York University Press,1998, 308–22.

Kissinger, Henry A. "Transcript of Kissinger's News Conference on the Status of
the Cease-Fire Talks." *New York Times.* October 27, 1972.

KIWA. *Assi Market: Our Stories of Struggle.* Los Angeles: Korean Immigrant
Worker Advocates, 2002.

———. "KIWA 25th Anniversary Video." YouTube. 2019. https://youtu.be
/ZS1PIUZPNc4.

Korb, Lawrence J. "The Pentagon's Fiscal Year 2021 Budget More than Meets
U.S. National Security Needs." Center for American Progress. 2020. www
.americanprogress.org/issues/security/reports/2020/05/06/484620
/pentagons-fiscal-year-2021-budget-meets-u-s-national-security-needs/.

Kotsko, Adam. *Neoliberalism's Demons: On the Political Theology of Late
Capital.* Stanford: Stanford University Press, 2018.

Kramer, Paul. *The Blood of Government: Race, Empire, the United States, and the Philippines*. Chapel Hill: University of North Carolina Press, 2006.

———. "Race-Making and Colonial Violence in the U.S. Empire: The Philippine-American War as Race War." *Diplomatic History* 30, no. 2 (2006): 169–210.

Kurashige, Scott. *The Fifty-Year Rebellion: How the US Political Crisis Began in Detroit*. Vol. 2. Oakland: University of California Press, 2017.

Kwon, Jong Bum. "The Koreatown Immigrant Workers Alliance: Spatializing Justice in an Ethnic 'Enclave.'" In *Working for Justice: The LA Model of Organizing and Advocacy*, edited by Ruth Milkman, Joshua Bloom, and Victor Narro. Ithaca: Cornell University Press, 2010, 23–48.

LaDuke, Winona, with Sean Aaron Cruz. *The Militarization of Indian Country*. East Lansing: Michigan State University Press, 2013.

LeCavalier, Jesse. *The Rule of Logistics: Walmart and the Architecture of Fulfillment*. Minneapolis: University of Minnesota Press, 2016.

Lee, Hoon. "Displaced and Demanding Justice." *Third Force* (September /October 1994): 10–14.

Lewis, Helen M., Peter Reason, and Hilary Bradbury. "Participatory Research and Education for Social Change." In *Handbook of Action Research*. Thousand Oaks: Sage, 2005, 262–68

Linebaugh, Peter. *The London Hanged: Crime and Civil Society in the Eighteenth Century*. London: Verso, 2003.

Lipsitz, George. "Abolition Democracy and Global Justice." *Comparative American Studies: An International Journal* 2, no. 3 (2004): 271–86.

———. "Walleye Warriors and White Identities: Native Americans' Treaty Rights, Composite Identities and Social Movements." *Ethnic and Racial Studies* 31, no. 1 (2008): 101–22.

———. *How Racism Takes Place*. Philadelphia: Temple University Press, 2011.

———. "What Is This Black in the Black Radical Tradition?" *Futures of Black Radicalism*, edited by Gaye Theresa Johnson and Alex Lubin. London: Verso, 2017, 109.

London, Matt. "Black Conservative Warns Democratic Socialism Threatens to Gain Foothold in Black Community." *Fox News*. September 23, 2019. www .foxnews.com/media/black-conservative-democratic-socialism-lawrence -jones-sonnie-johnson.

Lopez, Ian Haney. *White by Law: The Legal Construction of Race*. New York: New York University Press, 1996.

Lorde, Audre. "Learning from the 60's." In *Sister Outsider: Essays and Speeches*. Berkeley: Crossings Press, 1982.

Lorentzen, Lois Ann, and Jennifer E. Turpin, eds. *The Women and War Reader*. New York: New York University Press, 1998.

Louie, Miriam Ching Yoon. "What Did KIWA and the Market Workers Justice Campaign Accomplish?" Miriam Ching Yoon Louie Papers. Sophia Smith Collection of Women's History, Smith College.

———. "'Each Day I Go Home with a New Wound in My Heart': Korean Immigrant Women Workers." In *Sweatshop Warriors: Immigrant Women Workers Take on the Global Factory*. Boston: South End Press, 2001, 123–78.

Lowe, Lisa. *The Intimacies of Four Continents*. Durham: Duke University Press, 2015.

Lowndes, Joseph E. *From the New Deal to the New Right: Race and the Southern Origins of Modern Conservatism*. New Haven: Yale University Press, 2008.

Loyd, Jenna M. "Race, Capitalist Crisis, and Abolitionist Organizing: An Interview with Ruth Wilson Gilmore, February 2010." In *Beyond Walls and Cages: Prisons, Borders, and Global Crisis: Prisons, Borders, and Global Crisis*, edited by Jenna M. Loyd, Matt Mitchelson, and Andrew Burridge. Athens: University of Georgia Press, 2012, 42–56.

Lubin, Alex. *Geographies of Liberation: The Making of an Afro-Arab Political Imaginary*. Chapel Hill: University of North Carolina Press, 2014.

Lucchesi, Annita, and Abigail Echo-Hawk. "Missing and Murdered Indigenous Women and Girls: A Snapshot of Data from 71 Urban Cities in the United States." Center for Victim Research. 2018. https://ncvc.dspacedirect.org /handle/20.500.11990/1000.

Maeda, Daryl J. *Chains of Babylon: The Rise of Asian America*. Minneapolis: University of Minnesota Press, 2009.

Major, Derek. "Amazon Founder Jeff Bezos Says He Supports Black Lives Matter but Activists Say Otherwise." *Black Enterprise*. June 10, 2020. www .blackenterprise.com/amazon-founder-jeff-bezos-says-he-supports-black -lives-matter-but-activists-say-otherwise/.

Man, Simeon. *Soldiering through Empire: Race and the Making of the Decolonizing Pacific*. Oakland: University of California Press, 2018.

Marable, Manning. *Black Liberation in Conservative America*. Boston: South End Press, 1997.

Marable, Manning, and Leith Mullings. *Let Nobody Turn Us Around: An African American Anthology: Voices of Resistance, Reform, and Renewal*. Lanham, MD: Rowman and Littlefield, 2009.

Mariscal, George. *Aztlán and Viet Nam: Chicano and Chicana Experiences of the War*. Vol. 4. Berkeley: University of California Press, 1999.

Marks, George P. *The Black Press Views American Imperialism, 1898–1900*. New York: Arno, 1971.

Martin, Isaac. *The Permanent Tax Revolt: How the Property Tax Transformed American Politics*. Stanford: Stanford University Press, 2008.

Martindale, Dayton. "9 Statistics That Show What a Miserable Failure the Cares Act Is." *In These Times.* June 15, 2020. https://inthesetimes.com /article/cares-act-bailout-business-loan-statistics-covid-19-pandemic.

Martínez, Elizabeth. "Looking for Color in the Anti-War Movement." In *We Have Not Been Moved: Resisting Racism and Militarism in 21st Century America,* edited by Elizabeth "Betita" Martínez, Matt Meyer, and Mandy Carter. Oakland: PM Press, 2012, 61–73.

Mattioli, Dana. " Big Tech Companies Reap Gains as Covid-19 Fuels Shift in Demand."*Wall Street Journal.* October 29, 2020. www.wsj.com/articles /amazon-sales-surge-amid-pandemic-driven-online-shopping -11604003107.

Maulik, Monami. "Our Movement Is for the Long Haul: Ten Years of DRUM's Community Organizing by Working-Class South Asian Migrants." *Race/ Ethnicity: Multidisciplinary Global Contexts* 4, no. 3 (2011): 455–67.

McAlevey, Jane. *No Shortcuts: Organizing for Power in the New Gilded Age.* New York: Oxford University Press, 2016.

———. "Chicago's Teachers Are Making History. Again." *Nation.* October 15, 2019. www.thenation.com/article/archive/union-strike-chicago-teachers/.

McGranahan, Carole. "Refusal and the Gift of Citizenship." *Cultural Anthropology* 31, no. 3 (2016): 334–41.

McGuire, Danielle. *At the Dark End of the Street.* New York: Knopf, 2010.

McNeil, Genna Rae. "The Body, Sexuality, and Self-Defense in State vs. Joan Little, 1974–1975." *Journal of African American History* 93, no. 2 (2008): 235–61.

Medovoi, Leerom. "Government." In *Keywords for American Cultural Studies,* edited by Bruce Burgett and Glenn Hendler. 3rd ed. New York: New York University Press, 2020, 129.

Melamed, Jodi. "Racial Capitalism. *Critical Ethnic Studies* 1, no. 1 (2015): 76–85.

Melamed, Jodi, and Chandan Reddy. "Using Liberal Rights to Enforce Racial Capitalism." Social Science Research Council. https://items.ssrc.org/race -capitalism/.

Mendel-Reyes, Meta, and Samantha Hamlin. "Racial Justice in Appalachia: Organizing White People for Change." Workshop presentation. Appalachian Studies Association. 2017.

Metres, Philip. "June Jordan's War against War." *Peace Review* 15, no. 2 (2003): 171–77.

Meyer, J. (C. L. R. James). "The Revolutionary Answer to the Negro Problem in US." *Fourth International* 9, no. 8 (1948): 242–51. www.marxists.org /archive/james-clr/works/1948/07/meyer.htm.

Meyer, Matt. "We Have Not Been Moved: How the Peace Movement Has Resisted Dealing with Racism in Our Ranks." In *We Have Not Been Moved:*

Resisting Racism and Militarism in 21st Century America, edited by Elizabeth "Betita" Martínez, Matt Meyer, and Mandy Carter. Oakland: PM Press, 2012, 403–20.

Mijente. *Defy, Defend, Expand Sanctuary: A Crowd-Sourced Document of Policy Solutions*. Phoenix: Mijente, 2017. https://mijente.net/2017/02 /sanctuary-policies/.

Milkman, Ruth, and Kim Voss. *Rebuilding Labor: Organizing and Organizers in the New Union Movement*. Ithaca: Cornell University Press, 2004.

Mingus, Mia. "Interdependency (Excerpts from Several Talks)." *Leaving Evidence*. 2010. https://leavingevidence.wordpress.com/2010/01/22 /interdependency-exerpts-from-several-talks/.

MMIWG2S. "4 out of 5 of Our Native Women Are Affected by Violence Today." Coalition to Stop Violence against Native Women. www.csvanw.org/mmiw/.

Molina, Natalia. *Fit to Be Citizens?: Public Health and Race in Los Angeles, 1879–1940*. Berkeley: University of California Press, 2006.

Molina, Natalia, Daniel Martinez HoSang, and Ramón A. Gutiérrez. *Relational Formations of Race: Theory, Method, and Practice*. Oakland: University of California Press, 2019.

Montgomery, Lucile. "Strike City." Montgomery—Mississippi, Tribbett and Brick Factory. Lucile Montgomery Papers, 1963–1967, Wisconsin Historical Society, 1965–1966.

Moraga, Cherríe. "La Güera." In *This Bridge Called My Back: Writings by Radical Women of Color*, edited by Cherríe Moraga and Gloria Anzaldúa. 4th ed. Albany: SUNY Press, 2015, 22–29.

Morey, Michael. *Fagen: An African American Renegade in the Philippine-American War*. Madison: University of Wisconsin Press, 2019.

Morrison, Toni. "A Humanist's View." Speech Given at Portland State University. 1975.

Muhammad, Khalil Gibran. *The Condemnation of Blackness: Race, Crime, and the Making of Modern Urban America*. Cambridge: Harvard University Press, 2019.

Myers, Josh. "A Validity of Its Own: C. L. R. James and Black Independence." *Black Scholar*. August 24, 2015. www.theblackscholar.org/a-validity-of-its -own-clr-james-and-black-independence/.

Nadasen, Premilla. "'Tell Dem Slavery Done': Domestic Workers United and Transnational Feminism." *Scholar and Feminist Online* 8, no. 1 (2009).

———. "Power, Intimacy and Contestation: Dorothy Bolden and Domestic Worker Organizing in Atlanta in the 1960s." *Intimate Labors: Care, Sex, and Domestic Work* (January 2010): 195–211.

———. "Citizenship Rights, Domestic Work, and the Fair Labor Standards Act." *Journal of Policy History* 24, no. 1 (2012): 74–94.

———. *Household Workers Unite: The Untold Story of African American Women Who Built a Movement.* Boston: Beacon Press, 2016.

Narro, Victor. "Sí Se Puede: Immigrant Workers and the Transformation of the Los Angeles Labor and Worker Center Movements." *Los Angeles Public Interest Law Journal* 1 (2008): 65–106.

National Institute on Drug Abuse. "Alabama: Opioid-Involved Deaths and Related Harms." 2020. www.drugabuse.gov/drug-topics/opioids/opioid -summaries-by-state/alabama-opioid-involved-deaths-related-harms.

National Visionary Leadership Project. "Ethel Ennis: Performing the National Anthem." Recorded March 17, 2010. www.youtube.com/watch?v =4Tg2iEhcGsY&ab_channel=visionaryproject.

Nelson, Jennifer. "'All This That Has Happened to Me Shouldn't Happen to Nobody Else': Loretta Ross and the Women of Color Reproductive Freedom Movement of the 1980s." *Journal of Women's History* 22, no. 3 (2010): 136–60.

Nguyen, Tram. "Detained or Disappeared." *ColorLines* 5, no. 2 (Summer 2002). www.colorlines.com/articles/detained-dissapeared.

Nielsen, Aldon Lynn. *C. L. R. James: A Critical Introduction.* Jackson: University Press of Mississippi, 2010.

No Más Bebés. Dir. Renee Tajima-Peña. PBS, 2016.

Nothing, Ehn. "Introduction: Queens against Society." *Street Transvestite Action Revolutionaries: Survival, Revolt, and Queer Antagonist Struggle.* N.p.: Untorelli Press, 2013.

O'Dell, Jack. "The July Rebellions and the Military State." *Freedomways* 7, no. 4 (1967): 288–301.

———. *Climbin' Jacob's Ladder: The Black Freedom Movement Writings of Jack O'Dell:* Univ of California Press, 2012.

Olaloku-Teriba, Annie. "Afro-Pessimism and the (Un) Logic of Anti-Blackness." *Historical Materialism* 26, no. 2 (2018): 96–122.

Olson, Joel. *The Abolition of White Democracy.* Minneapolis: University of Minnesota Press, 2004.

Omatsu, Glenn. "Immigrant Workers Take the Lead: A Militant Humility Transforms L.A. Koreatown." In *Immigrant Rights in the Shadows of Citizenship,* edited by Rachel Ida Buff. New York: New York University Press, 2008, 266–82.

O'Neill, Colleen. "Testing the Limits of Colonial Parenting: Navajo Domestic Workers, the Intermountain Indian School, and the Urban Relocation Program, 1950–1962." *Ethnohistory* 66, no. 3 (2019): 565–92.

O'Neill, Patrick. "A United Front: Activists Make a Unified Call for Workers' Rights." *Indy Week.* June 2001. https://indyweek.com/news/archives /united-front/.

Orth, Nikki. "Ella Baker." Address at the Hattiesburg Freedom Day Rally (21 January 1964)." *Voices of Democracy* 11 (2016): 25–43.

Ortiz, Paul. *An African American and Latinx History of the United States.* Boston: Beacon Press, 2018.

Paik, A. Naomi. *Bans, Walls, Raids, Sanctuary: Understanding US Immigration for the Twenty-First Century.* Oakland: University of California Press, 2020.

Painter, Nell Irvin. *The History of White People.* New York: W. W. Norton, 2011.

Parker, Kim, Juliana Menasce Horowitz, and Monica Anderson. "Amid Protests, Majorities across Racial and Ethnic Groups Express Support for the Black Lives Matter Movement." Social and Demographic Trends, Pew Research Center. 2020. www.pewsocialtrends.org/2020/06/12/amid -protests-majorities-across-racial-and-ethnic-groups-express-support-for -the-black-lives-matter-movement/.

Paskus, Laura. "Albuquerque Protesters Rally around a Suite of Issues, from Women's Rights and DACA to Economic Justice." *NM Political Report.* January 22, 2018. https://nmpoliticalreport.com/2018/01/22/albuquerque -protesters-rally-around-a-suite-of-issues-from-womens-rights-and-daca -to-economic-justice/.

Paul, Kari. "Amazon Says 'Black Lives Matter': But the Company Has Deep Ties to Policing." *Guardian.* June 9, 2020. www.theguardian.com/technology/2020 /jun/09/amazon-black-lives-matter-police-ring-jeff-bezos.

Payne, Charles. "Ella Baker and Models of Social Change." *Signs: Journal of Women in Culture and Society* 14, no. 4 (1989): 885–99.

Pennock, Pamela. "Third World Alliances : Arab-American Activists in American Universities, 1967–1973." *Mashriq and Mahjar: Journal of Middle East and North African Migration Studies* 2, no. 2 (2014): 55–78.

Pérez, Gail. "Through Our Blood: Historic Restoration of Chicano Park Murals Begins." *La Prensa San Diego.* July 8, 2011.

Pérez, Miriam Zoila. "Teen Moms Look for Support, but Find Only Shame." *Color Lines.* May 6, 2011. www.colorlines.com/articles/teen-moms-look -support-find-only-shame.

Pfaelzer, Jean. *Driven Out: The Forgotten War against Chinese Americans.* University of California Press, 2008.

Phillips, Kimberley L. *War! What Is It Good For?: Black Freedom Struggles and the US Military from World War II to Iraq.* Chapel Hill: University of North Carolina Press, 2012.

Phillips, Leigh, and Michal Rozworski. *The People's Republic of Wal-Mart: How the World's Biggest Corporations Are Laying the Foundation for Socialism.* London: Verso, 2019.

Powell, Dana E. *Landscapes of Power: Politics of Energy in the Navajo Nation.* Durham: Duke University Press, 2018.

Power, Christopher. "U.S. Companies Are Still Rushing to Juárez." *Bloomberg Businessweek*. 2010. www.bloomberg.com/news/articles/2010–06–10/u -dot-s-dot-companies-are-still-rushing-to-ju-rez.

Prashad, Vijay. *The Darker Nations: A People's History of the Third World*. New York: New Press, 2008.

———. "The Day Our Probation Ended." *Race/Ethnicity: Multidisciplinary Global Contexts* 4, no. 3 (2011): 361–71.

Press, Alex N. "Amazon Is No Ally in the Fight for Racial Justice: An Interview with John Hopkins." *Jacobin*. June 1, 2020. www.jacobinmag.com/2020/06 /amazon-racial-justice-worker-organizing-union.

Pulido, Laura. *Black, Brown, Yellow and Left: Radical Activism in Los Angeles*. Berkeley: University of California Press, 2006.

Rana, Aziz. *The Two Faces of American Freedom*. Cambridge: Harvard University Press, 2011.

Ransby, Barbara. *Ella Baker and the Black Freedom Movement: A Radical Vision*. Chapel Hill: University of North Carolina Press, 2003.

Raytheon Company. "Navajo Nation Honors Raytheon Diné Facility with Business of the Year Award." PR News Wire. 2016. www.prnewswire.com /news-releases/navajo-nation-honors-raytheon-dine-facility-with-business -of-the-year-award-300270898.html.

Reddy, Chandan. *Freedom with Violence: Race, Sexuality, and the US State*. Durham: Duke University Press, 2011.

Riehl, Dan. "Sonnie Johnson Announces 'Sonnie's Corner,' New SiriusXM Patriot Show at 1 pm on Saturdays." *Brietbart News*. January 4, 2018. www .breitbart.com/radio/2018/01/04/sonnie-johnson-announces-sonnies -corner-new-siriusxm-patriot-show-at-1-pm-on-saturdays/.

Robé, Chris. "Detroit Rising." *Film History* 28, no. 4 (2016): 125–58.

Roberts, Dorothy. *Killing the Black Body: Race, Reproduction, and the Meaning of Liberty*. New York: Vintage, 1998.

Robinson, Cedric. *Black Marxism: The Making of the Black Radical Tradition*. 2nd ed. Chapel Hill: University of North Carolina Press, 2000.

Roediger, David R., and Elizabeth D. Esch. *The Production of Difference: Race and the Management of Labor in US History*. New York: Oxford University Press, 2012.

Rosen, Martin D., and James Fisher. "Chicano Park and the Chicano Park Murals: Barrio Logan, City of San Diego, California." *Public Historian* 23, no. 4 (2001): 91–111.

Rosengarten, Frank. *Urbane Revolutionary: C. L. R. James and the Struggle for a New Society*. Jackson: University Press of Mississippi, 2007.

Ross, Loretta. *The Color of Choice: White Supremacy and Reproductive Justice*. Durham: Duke University Press, 2016.

———. "I'm a Black Feminist. I Think Call-out Culture Is Toxic." *New York Times.* August 17, 2019. www.nytimes.com/2019/08/17/opinion/sunday /cancel-culture-call-out.html.

Ross, Suzanne. "Cispes in the 1980s: Solidarity and Racism in the Belly of the Beast." In *We Have Not Been Moved: Resisting Racism and Militarism in 21st Century America,* edited by Elizabeth "Betita" Martínez, Matt Meyer, and Mandy Carter. Oakland: PM Press, 2012, 421–33.

Rubio, Elizabeth Hanna, and Xitlalli Alvarez Almendariz. "Refusing 'Undocumented': Imagining Survival beyond the Gift of Papers." Society for Cultural Anthropology. January 19, 2019. https://culanth.org/fieldsights/refusing -undocumented-imagining-survival-beyond-the-gift-of-papers.

Russell, Timothy D. "'I Feel Sorry for These People': African American Soldiers in the Philippine-American War, 1899–1902." *Journal of African American History* 99, no. 3 (2014): 197–222.

Sanchez, Jared, Mirabai Auer, Veronica Terriquez, and Mi Young Kim. "Koreatown: A Contested Community at a Crossroads." USC Program on Environmental and Regional Equity (PERE) in collaboration with the Koreatown Immigrant Workers Alliance (KIWA). Los Angeles.2012.

Sandoval, Gerardo Francisco. "Chicano Park's Urban Imaginary: Ethnic Ties Bonded to Place and Redistributive Urban Justice." In *The Routledge Companion to Urban Imaginaries,* edited by Christoph Lindner and Miriam Meissner. New York: Routledge, 2019, 304–17.

Sardana, Saloni. "US Billionaires' Wealth Grew by $845 Billion during the First Six Months of the Pandemic." *Business Insider.* September 17, 2020. https:// markets.businessinsider.com/news/stocks/us-billionaires-wealth-net-worth -pandemic-covid-billion-2020-9-1029599756.

Sawyer, Wendy, and Peter Wagner. "Mass Incarceration: The Whole Pie 2020." Press release. Prison Policy Initiative. March 24, 2020. www.prisonpolicy .org/reports/pie2020.html?c=pie&gclid=Cj0KCQiA0-6ABhDMARIsAFVdQv _QLuDg78vCW2Gy9ZklxqQcel1nucCge4t922WpvtxyPb0L5gGQWKwaAq _FEALw_wcB.

Sellers, Cleveland L., Jr. "Black Power and the Freedom Movement in Retrospect." In *Rebellion in Black and White: Southern Student Activism in the 1960s,* edited by Dan T. Carter: Baltimore: Johns Hopkins University Press, 2013, 280–306.

Sexton, Jared. "People-of-Color-Blindness: Notes on the Afterlife of Slavery." *Social Text* 28, no. 2 (103) (2010): 31–56.

Shepard, Benjamin. "Sylvia and Sylvia's Children: A Battle for a Queer Public Space." *That's Revolting: Queer Strategies for Resisting Assimilation,* edited by Mattilda Bernstein Sycamore. Berkeley: Soft Skull Press, 2008, 123–40.

Silko, Leslie Marmon. *Ceremony.* New York: Penguin, 2006.

Silliman, Jael, Marlene Gerber Fried, Loretta Ross, and Elena Gutiérrez. *Undivided Rights: Women of Color Organizing for Reproductive Justice.* Boston: South End Press, 2004.

Silva, Noenoe K. *Aloha Betrayed: Native Hawaiian Resistance to American Colonialism.* Durham: Duke University Press, 2004.

Simpson, Audra. *Mohawk Interruptus: Political Life across the Borders of Settler States.* Durham: Duke University Press, 2014.

Simpson, Leanne Betasamosake. *As We Have Always Done: Indigenous Freedom through Radical Resistance.* Minneapolis: University of Minnesota Press, 2017.

Singh, Nikhil. *Black Is a Country.* Cambridge: Harvard University Press, 2004.

———. "Racial Formation in an Age of Permanent War." *Racial Formation in the Twenty-First Century* (2012): 276–301.

Sirriyeh, Ala. "Felons Are Also Our Family": Citizenship and Solidarity in the Undocumented Youth Movement in the United States." *Journal of Ethnic and Migration Studies* 45, no. 1 (2019): 133–50.

Sloan, Allan. "The Cares Act Sent You a $1,200 Check but Gave Millionaires and Billionaires Far More." *Propublica.* June 8, 2020. www.propublica.org/article/the-cares-act-sent-you-a-1-200-check-but-gave-millionaires-and-billionaires-far-more.

Slotnik, Daniel E. "Overlooked No More: Dorothy Bolden, Who Started a Movement for Domestic Workers." *New York Time.* February 20, 2019. www.nytimes.com/2019/02/20/obituaries/dorothy-bolden-overlooked.html.

Smith, Andrea, and Luana Ross. "Introduction: Native Women and State Violence." *Social Justice* 31, no. 4 (2004): 1–7.

SNCC Affiliated Blacks against the Draft (BAD). Box 13, 72. James Haughton Papers. Schomburg Center for Research in Black Culture, New York Public Library.

Spade, Dean. *Normal Life: Administrative Violence, Critical Trans Politics, and the Limits of Law.* Durham: Duke University Press, 2015.

———. *Mutual Aid: Building Solidarity during This Crisis (and the Next).* London: Verso, 2020.

Spotted Eagle, Brook. "The Brave Heart Society: An Oral History of an Indigenous Women's Society." MA thesis, University of Montana, 2013.

Stanford, Karin L. *If We Must Die: African American Voices on War and Peace.* Lanham, MD: Rowman and Littlefield, 2008.

Steele, Sarah M. "Performing Utopia: Queer Counterpublics and Southerners on New Ground." In *A Critical Inquiry into Queer Utopias,* edited by Angela Jones. New York: Palgrave Macmillan, 2013, 131–47.

Stern, Alexandria Minna. *Eugenic Nation: Faults and Frontiers of Better Breeding in Modern America.* Berkeley: University of California Press, 2005.

———. "Sterilized in the Name of Public Health: Race, Immigration, and Reproductive Control in Modern California." *American Journal of Public Health* 95, no. 7 (2005): 1128–38.

Student Nonviolent Coordinating Committee Papers, 1959–1972. Pamphlet and Poster. Reel 21. University Microfilms International.

Sugrue, Thomas J. *Origins of the Urban Crisis: Race and Inequality in Postwar Detroit*. Princeton: Princeton University Press, 1996.

Syrian Observatory for Human Rights. "With ISIS Ends as a Dominant Force in the East of Euphrates, the 53rd Month of Coalition Bombing Witnesses the Killing of about 185 Civilians and Fighters." 2019. www.syriahr.com /en/118011/.

Tarr, Duncan. "50 Years since Detroit's Dodge Revolutionary Union Movement." *Black Perspectives*, African American Intellectual History Society. July 19, 2018. www.aaihs.org/50-years-since-detroits-dodge-revolutionary-union -movement/.

Terriquez, Veronica. "Intersectional Mobilization, Social Movement Spillover, and Queer Youth Leadership in the Immigrant Rights Movement." *Social Problems* 62, no. 3 (2015): 343–62.

Theoharis, Jeanne. *The Rebellious Life of Mrs. Rosa Parks*. New York: Penguin, 2015.

Thomas, Deja, and Juliana Menasce Horowitz. "Support for Black Lives Matter Has Decreased since June but Remains Strong among Black Americans." Fact Tank, Pew Research Center. 2020. https://pewrsr.ch/3hD9RYv.

Thompson, Chris. "Chris: Gay Prisoner in Bellevue." Interview by Sylvia Rivera Arthur Bell. *The Spirit Was . . . Gay Flames: A Bulletin of the Homofire Movement* 7. November 14, 1970. https://thespiritwas.tumblr.com/post /44308523726/sylvia-rivera-star-and-arthur-bell-gay-activist.

Thompson, Heather Ann, and John F. Lyons. "Whose Detroit? Politics, Labor, and Race in a Modern American City." *Labour* 51 (Spring 2003): 311–13.

Thuma, Emily. *All Our Trials: Prisons, Policing, and the Feminist Fight to End Violence*. Champaign: University of Illinois Press, 2019.

Trask, Haunani-Kay. "The Birth of the Modern Hawaiian Movement: Kalama Valley, O'ahu." *Hawaiian Journal of History* 21 (1987): 126–53.

Treat, John Whittier. *Writing Ground Zero: Japanese Literature and the Atomic Bomb*. Chicago: University of Chicago Press, 1996.

Tu, Thuy Linh, and Nikhil Pal Singh. "Morbid Capitalism and Its Racial Symptoms." *n+1* (Winter 2018). https://nplusonemag.com/issue-30/essays /morbid-capitalism/.

Twagirumukiza, Aimée-Josiane. "Unbossed: Black Domestic Worker Organizing Is Redefining the Future of Work." *Forge*. September 8, 2020. https:// forgeorganizing.org/article/unbossed-black-domestic-worker-organizing -redefining-future-work.

Uetricht, Micah. *Strike for America: Chicago Teachers against Austerity.* London: Verso, 2014.

US Army Materiel Command. *The 75th Anniversary of Redstone Arsenal, 1941–2016.* Redstone Arsenal, AL: US Army Materiel Command.

Valdez, Diana Washington. "Albuquerque Sex Workers Face Perils." *El Paso Times.* February 17, 2014. www.elpasotimes.com/story/news/local/blogs /border-cafe/2014/02/17/albuquerque-sex-workers-face-perils/30957173/.

Van den Berghe, Pierre L. *Race and Racism: A Comparative Perspective.* New York: Wiley, 1978.

Vine, David. *Base Nation: How US Military Bases Abroad Harm America and the World.* New York: Metropolitan Books, 2015.

Waldstreicher, David. *Slavery's Constitution: From Revolution to Ratification.* New York: Hill and Wang, 2010.

Ward, Stephen M. "'Ours Too Was a Struggle for a Better World': Activist Intellectuals and the Radical Promise of the Black Power Movement, 1962–1972." PhD diss., University of Texas at Austin, 2002.

———. "An Ending and a Beginning: James Boggs, C. L. R. James, and the American Revolution." *Souls* 13, no. 3 (2011): 279–302.

———. *In Love and Struggle: The Revolutionary Lives of James and Grace Lee Boggs.* Chapel Hill: University of North Carolina Press, 2016.

Washington, Booker T. Booker T. Washington to John Davis Long. March 15, 1898. In *Booker T. Washington Papers.* Vol. 4, 1895–98, edited by Louis R. Harlan. Champaign: University of Illinois Press, 1975, 389.

Watson, John. "To the Point of Production: An Interview with John Watson of the League of Revolutionary Black Workers." Interview by Fifth Estate. Booklet. July 1969.

Weiser, Sonia. "What Big Business Said in All Those Anti-Racism Statements: Not Much, Says Our Analysis." *Color Lines.* October 8, 2020. www.colorlines .com/articles/what-big-business-said-all-those-anti-racism-statements-not -much-says-our-analysis?utm_source=newsletter&utm_medium=email&utm _campaign=10_15_2020&utm_term=What%20Big%20Business%20Said %20in%20All%20Those%20Anti-Racism%20Statements%3A%20Not %20Much%2C%20Says%20Our%20Analysis&&utm_content=email&&.

Williams, Robert A., Jr. *Savage Anxieties: The Invention of Western Civilization.* New York: Macmillan, 2012.

Wilson, Bobby M. *America's Johannesburg: Industrialization and Racial Transformation in Birmingham.* Athens: University of Georgia Press, 2019.

Wilson, John S. "It's a Banner Year for Ethel Ennis." *New York Times.* January 26, 1973. www.nytimes.com/1973/01/26/archives/its-a-banner-year-for -ethel-ennis-other-zooming-times.html.

Windham, Lane. *Knocking on Labor's Door: Union Organizing in the 1970s and the Roots of a New Economic Divide.* Chapel Hill: University of North Carolina Press, 2017.

WISE Uranium Project. "Impacts of Uranium Mining at Port Radium, NWT, Canada." September 7, 2005. www.wise-uranium.org/uippra.html.

Wood, Nick. "Mt. Olive: Blood on the Cucumbers." *Against the Current* 102 (January/February 2003). https://againstthecurrent.org/atc102/p681/.

Worcester, Kent. *C. L. R. James: A Political Biography.* Albany: SUNY Press, 1995.

Wright, Melissa W. "A Manifesto against Femicide." *Antipode* 33, no. 3 (2001): 550–66.

Yamin, Priscilla. *American Marriage: A Political Institution.* Philadelphia: University of Pennsylvania Press, 2012.

Yassin, Jaime Omar. "The Shortest Distance between Palestine and Ferguson." *CounterPunch.* August 15, 2014. www.counterpunch.org/2014/08/15/the -shortest-distance-between-palestine-and-ferguson/.

Zavella, Patricia. "Intersectional Praxis in the Movement for Reproductive Justice: The Respect Abq Women Campaign." *Signs: Journal of Women in Culture and Society* 42, no. 2 (2017): 509–33.

Zinn, Howard. *SNCC: The New Abolitionists.* Vol. 1. Boston: South End Press, 2002.

Zinn, Howard, and Anthony Arnove. *Voices of a People's History of the United States.* New York: Seven Stories Press, 2004.

Index

Page numbers in *italics* indicate an illustation.

Founded in 1893,
UNIVERSITY OF CALIFORNIA PRESS
publishes bold, progressive books and journals
on topics in the arts, humanities, social sciences,
and natural sciences—with a focus on social
justice issues—that inspire thought and action
among readers worldwide.

The UC PRESS FOUNDATION
raises funds to uphold the press's vital role
as an independent, nonprofit publisher, and
receives philanthropic support from a wide
range of individuals and institutions—and from
committed readers like you. To learn more, visit
ucpress.edu/supportus.